Papers on Playmaking

Papers on Playmaking

Edited by

BRANDER MATTHEWS

With a Preface by Henry W. Wells

Essay Index Reprint Series

 BOOKS FOR LIBRARIES PRESS
FREEPORT, NEW YORK

INTERNATIONAL STANDARD BOOK NUMBER:

0-8369-1890-8

LIBRARY OF CONGRESS CATALOG CARD NUMBER:

75-111852

PRINTED IN THE UNITED STATES OF AMERICA

CONTENTS

PREFACE

Between 1914 and 1926 a series of twenty-one small books were published by The Brander Matthews Dramatic Museum, at Columbia University, under the general direction of the distinguished founder of the Museum, whose name it bears. By the first decade of the present century Brander Matthews had established himself as a prominent figure in drama and the stage. Born in New Orleans, in 1852, he shortly became a resident of New York City, his home until his death in 1929. He commenced teaching at Columbia College in 1891. In 1900 he was assigned to the first chair of drama established in any university. This distinction has been kept in mind by the subsequent designation of his academic position as the Brander Matthews Chair of Dramatic Literature, occupied in turn by G. C. D. Odell, Joseph Wood Krutch, and Eric Bentley.

At approximately the time of his fortunate shift from the teaching of English literature in general to the history and theory of the stage, a visit to the small theatre museum in the Paris Opera House suggested to him the establishment of an institution of similar purpose in New York. The nucleus was his own large collection of books, pamphlets, programs, pictures, stage models, puppets, and memorabilia of the theatre. After an informal existence, during which the collection was divided between his home and the University, the Museum was officially organized in 1911 and housed on the Columbia campus. It was the first of its kind in this country. Important materials were acquired from Europe and the Orient, often as gifts from Brander Matthews' wide circle of acquaintance. With the help of an endowment, the general work of the Museum continues to the present.

Although the editorial labor for several further publications by the Museum was largely completed before Brander Matthews' death in 1929, the series of volumes, like so many other projects associated with the theatre and the arts, terminated with the beginning of the economic depression. The collection is best understood as a record of one of America's most stimulating minds in theatrical research. Among Matthews' many eminent friends were several of the authors of the papers themselves. He was a playwright, critic, scholar, reviewer, and author of some twoscore books, a man of surprisingly wide interests and activities, an enthusiastic advocate of language reform, one of the founders of The Authors Club, The Players Club, and similar institutions, a prolific contributor to newspapers and periodicals, and widely known for his "Sunday Evening Salon." At his death he left to Columbia University a wide correspondence received from his friends in this country and abroad. Indeed, he was almost as familiar a figure in London and Paris as in New York. Among his chief books are *The Development of Drama, Studies of the Stage, Molière, Shakespeare as a Playwright, Principles of Playwriting,* and *Essays on English.*

Brander Matthews was essentially a collector—of books, works of art, friends, anecdotes, ideas. Possessed of an extraordinarily acquisitive and eclectic mind, he neglected nothing, forgot nothing. His roving wit, though often dry, was even more ingratiating than caustic. None of his multitudinous labors remains today more typical or valuable than this compilation of papers comprising the two companion volumes* that now bring to the public the fruit of a career at its height nearly half a century ago. It was for several years the pleasure of the present writer to be Brander Matthews' assistant in his University classes and a youthful participant in the activities of his literary circle; it is an equal pleasure to introduce to a new group of readers essays whose selection confirms the good judgment of one of America's most searching scholars of the stage.

HENRY W. WELLS

Curator of the Brander Matthews Dramatic Museum

The New Art of Writing Plays

An Address to the Academy at Madrid

by

LOPE DE VEGA

Translated by William T. Brewster
With an Introduction by Brander Matthews

Introduction

By a significant coincidence the marvelous outflowering of the drama is simultaneous in Spanish literature and in English. Spain almost exhausted her immense resources in fitting out the Invincible Armada; and England strained every nerve to compass the defeat of the dread fleet. Lope de Vega, the foremost of the Iberian playwrights, actually sailed as a soldier on the fatal voyage to the English Channel; and it is dimly possible that Shakespeare also saw service on blue water; the year of the running sea fight is one of those in his biography about which we have no information, and his use of sea terms has been declared by an expert to be scientifically accurate. In this simultaneous development of the drama in England and in Spain at the moment when the energy of the two peoples was aroused to the utmost, we have a confirmation of Brunetière's theory that the foundation of our pleasure in the playhouse is the assertion of the human will.

Shakespeare came forward after the English drama had already developed a variety of forms; and he found the road broken for him by Marlowe and Kyd, by Lyly and Greene. At first he followed in their footsteps, however far beyond them he was to advance in the end. Lope de Vega, on the other hand, was a pioneer; he it was who blazed the new trails in which all the succeeding playwrights of Spain gladly trod. Shakespeare seems to have cared little for invention, borrowing his plots anywhere and everywhere, and reserving his imagination for the interpretation of tales first told by others. Lope, on the other hand again, abounded rather in invention than in the interpreting imagination; he was won-

2

derfully fecund and prolific, unsurpassed in production even by Defoe or Dumas. It was he who made the pattern that Calderón and all the rest were to employ. It was he who worked out the formula of the Spanish *comedia,* often not a comedy at all in our English understanding of the term, but rather a play of intrigue, peopled with hot-blooded heroes who wore their hearts on their sleeves and who carried their hands on the hilts of their swords.

Where Lope de Vega and Shakespeare are again alike is that they both wrote all their plays for the popular theatre, apparently composing these pieces solely with a view to performance and caring nothing for any praise which might be derived from publication. Martinenche, in his study of the *Comedia Espagnole* (p. 243, note), dwells on Lope's carelessness for the literary renown to be won by the printing of his dramatic poems; in his nondramatic poems he took pride, just as Shakespeare seems to have read carefully the proofs of his lyrical narratives although he did not himself choose to publish a single one of his plays. And Molière, it may be noted, tells us frankly that he was completely satisfied with the success of his earlier pieces on the stage, and that he had been content to leave them unprinted until his hand was forced by a pirate publisher.

Shakespeare is abundant in his allusions to the art of acting and reticent in his allusions to the art of playmaking. In fact, there is no single recorded expression of his opinion in regard to the principles or the practice of dramaturgy; and here he is in marked contrast with Ben Jonson, who had a body of doctrine about the drama, which he set forth in his *Discoveries* and in his prologues, as well as in his conversations with Drummond of Hawthornden. In general Lope's attitude toward dramaturgic theory is the same as Shakespeare's; but on one occasion he was induced to discuss the principles of the art he adorned, and to express his opinions upon its methods. This single occasion was when he was persuaded to deliver a poetic address upon the "New Art of Making Plays in This Age."

This "Arte neuvo de hazer comedias en este tiempo" was originally published in the *Rimas* of Lope de Vega, Madrid, 1609. A facsimile reprint was issued by Mr. Archer M. Huntington in New York in 1903. A critical edition with an introduction and notes by A. Morel-Fatio appeared in the *Bulletin Hispanique* for October–December 1904 and also in a separate pamphlet. The French editor accepts the year of publication as probably the year of delivery; and he believes the Academy of Madrid, before whom the poem was read, to be "no doubt one of those literary assemblies, imitated from those flourishing in Italy and holding their meetings at the house of some cultivated gentleman."

Lope's metrical address is plainly a remote imitation of Horace's epistle to the Pisos, the model of countless critical codes cast into verse. It is the chief Spanish example of this type, as Boileau's *Art Poétique* is the chief French example and Pope's *Essay on Criticism* the chief English example. While most of these Horatian imitations have for their main topic poetry and more especially dramatic poetry, attempts were not lacking to borrow the familiar form for nonliterary themes; and as a result there are a host of poems in all the modern tongues on the Art of War and the Art of Painting, on the Art of Bookbinding and on the Art of Cookery. Even so late as the first half of the nineteenth century Samson (of the Comédie-Française) condensed his histrionic advice into riming couplets on the Art of Acting.

Most of those imitations of Horace's didactic poem which deal with poetry and the drama borrow from the Latin lyrist not only their method but also much of their material. The supersubtle Italian theorists of the theatre were relying on Horace even when they supposed that they were interpreting Aristotle; and these expounders of Horace had elaborated legislative enactments for the theatre which were readily accepted by all who desired the purification of the drama. This Classicist code of rules for playwrights was mainly negative; it was made up largely of restrictions upon the poet's freedom; it ordered him to do a few things, but it forbade him to do many things. It prescribed the total separation of tragedy and comedy, admitting nothing humorous into the former and excluding everything serious from the latter. It insisted severely upon the austere dignity of tragedy. It told the dramatist to avoid all scenes of violence; and it advised him to use messengers to narrate all events which might not be exhibited with propriety. Above all, it laid stress upon the strict observance of the Three Unities, demanding that the playwright should have but one story to set on the stage; that he should show this single action in one place only; and that this single action, shown in a single place, should be begun and completed in a single day.

Lope's "New Art of Making Plays" is not a familiar epistle like Horace's *Ars Poetica;* rather is it a familiar discourse having the playful ease of an after-dinner speech. It consists of a series of paragraphs of irregular length, varying from four to forty lines each. It is written in blank verse, hendecasyllabics, except that the last two lines of every paragraph are in rime. These terminal couplets recall the riming exit speeches common in contemporary Elizabethan drama; and in both cases apparently the rimes serve to heighten the emphasis at the end of the rhetorical period. At the conclusion of his address, Lope drops into Latin and inserts ten lines in that tongue—ten lines of unidentified origin. These Latin verses may be his own composition or they may yet be traced to some overlooked poem. They are brought into harmony with the rest of the work by the ingenious device of riming the last Latin line with a line in Spanish, thus making a couplet half in the learned language and half in the vernacular. These two hybrid lines are immediately followed by the usual terminal couplet, so that there are only three lines in Spanish after the ten lines of Latin. In the translation which follows the Latin verse has been rendered into English rime by Professor Edward Delavan Perry.

Professor Rennert in his authoritative biography of Lope (p. 179) declares that Lope's address "is written in a bantering spirit, and a vein of good humor pervades the whole poem. Lope evidently did not take the matter very seriously, nor reflect deeply on what he was about to say. It probably did not take him much longer to write the 'New Art of Making Plays' than it took him to write as many lines of a comedia. The versification, strangely enough, lacks Lope's habitual ease and fluency; it is careless and sometimes halting, while the sense is not always clear,—an additional sign that this treatise was hastily composed."

Morel-Fatio notes that the "Arte Nuevo" was reprinted only three times during Lope's lifetime, at Madrid in 1613 and 1621 and at Hueva in 1623; and he finds in the poem itself ample explanation for its lack of popularity. Lope was the superb leader of an astounding development of the Spanish drama; and he himself tells us that when he delivered this address he had already written nearly five hundred plays. Yet he utters no paean of triumph; he blows no bugle blast of defiance to the defenders of other standards than those under which he himself was fighting; he does not anticipate the ardor and the fervor which were to animate Victor Hugo's preface to *Cromwell;* he does not stand to his guns and point to what he has accomplished on the stage as his own justification and as a sufficient answer to the caviling of criticasters. His attitude seems to be humble and apologetic; he admits the validity of the Classicist code of rules; and in his own defense he proffers only what the lawyers call a plea of confession and avoidance, declaring that he would have obeyed the behest of the learned theorists if only he had been permitted by the public. He acknowledges the faultiness of all his dramatic works and throws the blame on the depravity of public taste, since

We who live to please, must please to live.

He supports his acceptance of the Classicist doctrine with a brave show of erudition and with mention of Cicero, Donatus, Robortello, Julius Pollux, Manetti, Plutarch, Athenaeus, Xenophon, Valerius, Maximus, Pietro Crinito, and Vitruvius; and Morel-Fatio declares that this pedantic parade has no solid foundation of scholarship, being derived entirely from two writers, Donatus, the commentator on Terence, and Robortello, the commentator on Aristotle and on Horace. In this second-hand echoing of the codifiers of critical theory the great Spanish playwright reveals no independence of interpretation, accepting without question whatever he has found in the commentaries and never asking himself whether the commentators had any valid reason for the rules they laid down so authoritatively. In other words, the "Arte Nuevo" does not disclose Lope's possession of any critical curiosity or of any critical acumen, or even of any real interest in the discussion of critical theories.

We have no right to expect that those as richly endowed with the creative faculty as Lope indisputably was, should also have an equal share of the critical faculty. The analysis of the principles of their own special art by the poets and painters and playwrights who venture into the critical arena is always interesting but it is rarely philosophic and it is generally technical. And it is to technique that Lope devotes the most of his discourse. He trips lightly down the history of the new Spanish drama; and then he proceeds to bestow practical advice on aspiring young playwrights. He tells these novices that they must give the public what it wants, and he counsels them as to the best methods of tickling the taste of the uncritical playgoer. He descends to minute practical details; and, in short, his suggestions are those of a veteran of the craft supplying lessons in playwriting for a correspondence school.

In so far as Lope lays down any critical principles at all, these are but the codification of his own instinctive practice. His address is like "the speech of a carpenter standing on the peak of a building he has just erected"—to borrow Richter's sarcastic phrase. Lope had himself succeeded as a practical playwright; and his plays had certain characteristics and were put together in a certain fashion. As these plays had pleased the public, beginners would do well to consider these characteristics and to follow this fashion. He utters his shrewd recommendations most unpretentiously, with no hint of arrogance and with a friendly geniality of tone. Behind his modest precepts stand his own plays, in which his ideal is more sharply made manifest. Lope's ideal is that of all his contemporaries, including Calderón (who followed in his footsteps and often borrowed his plots). It is that the stage is intended primarily for storytelling, for presenting in action a serial tale which shall excite the constant interest of curiosity.

He bids the beginner to put together his story with the utmost care, laying the foundations in the first act, contriving unexpected complications for the second and concealing the solution of the action until the very last moment possible, as otherwise the spectators may get up and go out, when once they can foresee the end. He lays all his stress upon adroitness and ingenuity of plot building; and such casual remarks as he makes upon character delineation seem perfunctory. In this emphasizing the primary importance of the action Lope is only echoing Aristotle—although he probably was not aware of this. And the practice of the Spanish playwrights under the lead of Lope was closely akin to that of their contemporaries, the English playwrights under the lead of Kyd, and again later under the lead of Beaumont and Fletcher. Like Lope, Kyd in his way and Beaumont and Fletcher in theirs were storytellers on the stage. Poets they were all of them, but as playwrights they depended on plot, on suspense and especially on surprise—often achieved only by contradiction of character.

The abiding interest of the "Arte Nuevo" is twofold. It resides partly in the suggestiveness of the elementary lessons in the art of playmaking which Lope here proffers to apprentices in the art, and which are invaluable as an aid for properly appreciating the methods of the Spanish playwrights of the Age of Gold. It resides partly in the curiously deprecating attitude taken by Lope toward his own works, although he was approaching the pinnacle of his fame when he penned this didactic poem. Is the great Spanish playwright sincere in his humility before the code of the Classicists? Is his self-abasement genuine—or is it ironic? Morel-Fatio follows Menéndez y Pelayo in accepting it at its face value. Guillaume Huszar, in his useful book on Corneille and the Spanish theatre, thinks that when Lope pretends to disparage his own plays he is not to be taken seriously. I confess that I should like to agree with this latter view; and there is some little internal evidence in support of it. But the balance is rather in favor of the former opinion. Yet however honest may be Lope's willingness to do penance to the Classicist code, which he admits to have outraged, his is a proud humility after all. He is not really as abased and as plaintive as some of his critics have asserted. Modest as he may be, he takes care to make his own position plain. For all his easy attitude and his tolerant geniality, for all his lightness of touch on the one side and his pedantic citation on the other, he does not fail to insist on his authorship of nearly half a thousand plays and to remind his auditors that he has continuously succeeded in pleasing the public, even though he had to violate the rules in order to win this success.

Lope assumes a detached attitude and his tone is bantering, as Professor Rennert has suggested. He does not here display the intense personal interest in the analysis of his own work which glows and burns through all Corneille's *Examens*, in spite of the French dramatic poet's occasional confession of a lapse from the strict letter of the law. Lope has none of the prophetic fire of Hugo's famous preface in anticipatory defense of the plays he was going to write. In fact, it is difficult to deny that this poem is a pretty careless piece of work, tossed off in an idle hour, evoked by a special occasion when it behooved the speaker to assume a self-deprecatory attitude. But it is not the "lamentable palinode" that Menéndez y Pelayo called it; nor is it exactly what Mr. Ormsby termed it (in the *Quarterly Review* for January 1894), "virtually the manifesto of a triumphant dictator, a dramatic Napoleon who, while professing the profoundest respect for the sovereign will of the public, scarcely cared to

hide his contempt for its intelligence or its taste, which foreign critics, he says, justly called barbarous; or to disguise
the fact that he owed his power to his knowledge and adroit
manipulation of its weaknesses." That scholars so well
equipped for the consideration of Spanish literature and so
well fitted for the interpretation of the Spanish character as
Ormsby and Rennert, Morel-Fatio and Menéndez y Pelayo
can take views as conflicting as those severally expressed by
them—this is proof positive that Lope has not taken the
pains necessary to make his position clear.

While Lope was willing at least to render lip service to the
code of the Classicists, one of his followers in the theatre,
Tirso de Molina (best known as the author of the earliest
dramatization of the Don Juan legend), in his *Cigarrales de
Toledo,* published in 1624, fifteen years after Lope's address,
is bold in denying the validity of any rule limiting the duration of time or forbidding a change of scene. (See Breitinger's
Unités d' Aristote, pp. 29 seq.) But Cervantes in the first part
of *Don Quixote,* published in 1605, four years before the delivery of the "Arte Nuevo," had revealed a plentiful lack of
sympathy for the so-called Aristotelian rules. There is no dis-
puting the irony in his portrait of the Canon of Toledo who
demanded the appointment of "some intelligent and sensible
person at the capital to examine all plays before they were
acted, not only those produced in the capital itself, but all
that were intended to be acted in Spain; without whose approval, seal and signature, no local magistracy should allow
any play to be acted." (Ormsby's translation, ii, 387, chapter
xlviii.) Earlier remarks of the Canon show us that he was
familiar with the whole Classicist code; indeed, Ormsby (in
a footnote to his translation of this chapter) calls attention
to the substantial identity of the canon's opinions with those
expressed by Sir Philip Sidney in the *Apologie for Poesie.* In
another work of fiction written more than two centuries later,
in the *Nicholas Nickleby* of Dickens, we are introduced to
a Mr. Murdle whose knowledge is obviously vaguer than the
Canon's but who is quite as strenuous in his insistence upon
"the preservation of the unities."

Into the vexed question of the personal relations of Cervantes and Lope, it is not needful to enter here. It would be
pleasant to believe that each really appreciated the genius of
the other; but however pleasant this is not quite possible.
Cervantes seems not to have suspected the greatness of his

own masterpiece; and it is plain that he had a special fondness for his plays, which had not succeeded. Lope must have been conscious of his own position at the head of all Spanish poets; he might assume a humble attitude when he was the author of fewer than five hundred plays, but by the time that he had more than a thousand pieces to his credit the garment of humility is no longer becoming. Martinenche in his *Comedia Espagnole* (pp. 113–14) follows Morel-Fatio in pointing out Lope's later satisfaction with what he had accomplished, even to the extent of claiming for himself the invention of the new type of play which had established itself on the Spanish stage.

When we consider the extraordinary vogue of Lope as a playwright in the Golden Age of Spanish literature and the swift diffusion of his fame throughout Europe, when we recall his unparalleled productivity, and when we remember his supreme importance as a representative of a superb development of the modern drama, we cannot fail to be surprised to discover that no adequate attempt has ever been made to present him to the English reading public. In French there are two translations of selections from his dramatic works; and there are also varied renderings into German. But in English there is little or nothing. Lord Holland in 1787 analyzed *The Star of Seville* and turned the more striking episodes into English; and it was on this summary and on these fragments that Mrs. Kemble founded her five-act *Star of Seville*, published in 1837. Holcroft had utilized Lope's *Padre Engañado* in the plot of his *Father Outwitted*, published in 1805. A perversion of Lope's play on the Romeo and Juliet story had been issued in English in 1770; and this moved F. W. Cosens to print (for private distribution) in 1869 a careful translation of *Castelvines y Montreses*. In the sixth volume of *The Drama*, edited by Alfred Bates and published in 1903, there is a translation of the *Perro del Hortelano (The Gardener's Dog)* by W. H. H. Chambers. These scattered versions and perversions apparently represent all of Lope's dramatic work which has found its way into our language. It is greatly to be desired that at least one volume might be issued in English to contain *The Star of Seville*, *The Gardener's Dog*, the *Romeo and Juliet* and the *Duchess of Malfi* plays, and also *The Physician of his own Honor* and *The Alcalde of Zalamea*, of which Calderón's rehandlings are already accessible in Fitzgerald's free rendering.

A few scattered passages from the "Arte Nuevo" were turned into English couplets by Lord Holland; and some of those were borrowed (without credit) in G. H. Lewes's stimulating study of the Spanish Drama, issued in 1846. An inadequate and incomplete version, derived mainly from the French translation of Dumas-Hinard, was included in an essay on Lope published in the *Catholic World* for September 1878. There is a careful abstract in Professor Rennert's standard biography of Lope (1904). But Professor Brewster's translation is the first attempt to render into English the whole of Lope's advice to the aspiring playwrights of his own time and country.

BRANDER MATTHEWS

June 1914

The New Art of Writing Plays

An Address to the Academy at Madrid

1.   You command me, noble spirits, flower of Spain—who
in this congress and renowned academy will in short space
of time surpass not only the assemblies of Italy which Cicero,
envious of Greece, made famous with his own name, hard
by the Lake of Avernus, but also Athens where in the Lyceum of Plato was seen high conclave of philosophers—to
write you an art of the play which is today acceptable to the
taste of the crowd.

2.   Easy seems this subject, and easy it would be for anyone of you who had written very few comedies, and who
knows more about the art of writing them and of all these
things; for what condemns me in this task is that I have
written them without art.

3.   Not because I was ignorant of the precepts; thank
God, even while I was a tyro in grammar, I went through
the books which treated the subject, before I had seen the
sun run its course ten times from the Ram to the Fishes;

4.   But because, in fine, I found that comedies were not
at that time, in Spain, as their first devisers in the world
thought that they should be written; but rather as many rude
fellows managed them, who confirmed the crowd in its own
crudeness; and so they were introduced in such wise that he
who now writes them artistically dies without fame and
guerdon; for custom can do more among those who lack light
of art than reason and force.

5.   True it is that I have sometimes written in accordance
with the art which few know; but, no sooner do I see com-

ing from some other source the monstrosities full of painted scenes where the crowd congregates and the women who canonize this sad business, than I return to that same barbarous habit, and when I have to write a comedy I lock in the precepts with six keys, I banish Terence and Plautus from my study that they may not cry out at me; for truth, even in dumb books, is wont to call aloud; and I write in accordance with that art which they devised who aspired to the applause of the crowd; for, since the crowd pays for the comedies, it is fitting to talk foolishly to it to satisfy its taste.

6. Yet true comedy has its end established like every kind of poem or poetic art, and that has always been to imitate the actions of men and to paint the customs of their age. Furthermore, all poetic imitation whatsoever is composed of three things, which are discourse, agreeable verse, harmony, that is to say music, which so far was common also to tragedy; comedy being different from tragedy in that it treats of lowly and plebeian actions, and tragedy of royal and great ones. Look whether there be in our comedies few failings.

7. *Auto* was the name given to them, for they imitate the actions and the doings of the crowd. Lope de Rueda was an example in Spain of these principles, and today are to be seen in print prose comedies of his so lowly that he introduces into them the doings of mechanics and the love of the daughter of a smith; whence there has remained the custom of calling the old comedies *entremeses,* where the art persists in all its force, there being one action and that between plebeian people; for an *entremés* with a king has never been seen. And thus it is shown how the art, for very lowness of style, came to be held in great disrepute, and the king in the comedy to be introduced for the ignorant.

8. Aristotle depicts in his *Poetics*—although obscurely— the beginning of comedy; the strife between Athens and Megara as to which of them was the first inventor; they of Megara say that it was Epicarmus, while Athens would have it that Magnetes was the man. Elias Donatus says it had its origin in ancient sacrifices. He names Thespis as the author of tragedy—following Horace, who affirms the same—as of comedies, Aristophanes. Homer composed the *Odyssey* in imitation of comedy, but the *Iliad* was a famous example of tragedy, in imitation of which I called my *Jerusalem* an epic, and added the term *tragic;* and in the same manner all people

commonly term the *Inferno,* the *Purgatorio,* and the *Paradiso* of the celebrated poet Dante Alighieri a comedy, and this Manetti recognizes in his prologue.

9. Now everybody knows that comedy, as if under suspicion, was silenced for a certain time, and that hence also satire was born, which, being more cruel, more quickly came to an end, and gave place to the New Comedy. The choruses were the first things; then the fixed number of the characters was introduced; but Menander, whom Terence followed, held the choruses in despite, as offensive. Terence was more circumspect as to the principles; since he never elevated the style of comedy to the greatness of tragedy, which many have condemned as vicious in Plautus; for in this respect Terence was more wary.

10. Tragedy has as its argument history, and comedy fiction; for this reason it was called flat-footed, of humble argument, since the actor performed without buskin or stage. There were comedies with the *pallium,* mimes, comedies with the toga, *fabulae atellanae,* and comedies of the tavern, which were also, as now, of various sorts.

11. With Attic elegance the men of Athens chided vice and evil custom in their comedies, and they gave their prizes both to the writers of verse and to the devisers of action. For this Tully called comedies "the mirror of custom and a living image of the truth"—a very high tribute, in that comedy ran even with history. Look whether it be worthy of this crown and glory!

12. But now I perceive that you are saying that this is merely translating books and wearying you with painting this mixed-up affair. Believe me, there has been a reason why you should be reminded of some of these things; for you see that you ask me to describe the art of writing plays in Spain, where whatever is written is in defiance of art; and to tell how they are now written contrary to the ancient rule and to what is founded on reason, is to ask me to draw on my experience, not on art, for art speaks truth which the ignorant crowd gainsays.

13. If, then, you desire art, I beseech you, men of genius, to read the very learned Robortello of Udine and you will see in what he says concerning Aristotle, and especially in what he writes about comedy, as much as is scattered among many books; for everything of today is in a state of confusion.

14. If you wish to have my opinion of the comedies which now have the upper hand and to know why it is necessary that the crowd with its laws should maintain the vile chimera of this comic monster, I will tell you what I hold, and do you pardon me, since I must obey whoever has power to command me—that, gilding the error of the crowd, I desire to tell you of what sort I would have them; for there is no recourse but to follow art observing a mean between the two extremes.

15. Let the subject be chosen and do not be amused—may you excuse these precepts!—if it happens to deal with kings; though, for that matter, I understand that Philip the Prudent, King of Spain and our lord, was offended at seeing a king in them; either because the matter was hostile to art or because the royal authority ought not to be represented among the lowly and the vulgar.

16. This is merely turning back to the Old Comedy, where we see that Plautus introduced gods, as in his *Amphitryon* he represents Jupiter. God knows that I have difficulty in giving this my approbation, since Plutarch, speaking of Menander, does not highly esteem Old Comedy. But since we are so far away from art and in Spain do it a thousand wrongs, let the learned this once close their lips.

17. Tragedy mixed with comedy and Terence with Seneca, though it be like another minotaur of Pasiphaë, will render one part grave, the other ridiculous; for this variety causes much delight. Nature gives us good example, for through such variety it is beautiful.

18. Bear in mind that this subject should contain one action only, seeing to it that the story in no manner be episodic; I mean the introduction of other things which are beside the main purpose; nor that any member be omitted which might ruin the whole of the context. There is no use in advising that it should take place in the period of one sun, though this is the view of Aristotle; but we lose our respect for him when we mingle tragic style with the humbleness of mean comedy. Let it take place in as little time as possible, except when the poet is writing history in which some years have to pass; these he can relegate to the space between the acts, wherein, if necessary, he can have a character go on some journey; a thing that greatly offends whoever perceives it. But let not him who is offended go to see them.

19. Oh! how lost in admiration are many at this very time at seeing that years are passed in an affair to which an artificial day sets a limit; though for this they would not allow the mathematical day! But, considering that the wrath of a seated Spaniard is immoderate, when in two hours there is not presented to him everything from Genesis to the Last Judgment, I deem it most fitting, if it be for us here to please him, for us to adjust everything so that it succeeds.

20. The subject once chosen, write in prose, and divide the matter into three acts of time, seeing to it, if possible, that in each one the space of the day be not broken. Captain Verués, a worthy wit, divided comedy into three acts, which before had gone on all fours, as on baby's feet, for comedies were then infants. I wrote them myself, when eleven or twelve years of age, of four acts and of four sheets of paper, for a sheet contained each act; and then it was the fashion that for the three intermissions were made three little *entremeses*, but today scarce one, and then a dance, for the dancing is so important in comedy that Aristotle approves of it, and Athenaeus, Plato, and Xenophon treat of it, though this last disapproves of indecorous dancing; and for this reason he is vexed at Callipides, wherein he pretends to ape the ancient chorus. The matter divided into two parts, see to the connection from the beginning until the action runs down; but do not permit the untying of the plot until reaching the last scene; for the crowd, knowing what the end is, will turn its face to the door and its shoulder to what it has awaited three hours face to face; for in what appears nothing more is to be known.

21. Very seldom should the stage remain without someone speaking, because the crowd becomes restless in these intervals and the story spins itself out at great length; for, besides its being a great defect, the avoidance of it increases grace and artifice.

22. Begin then, and, with simple language, do not spend sententious thoughts and witty sayings on family trifles, which is all that the familiar talk of two or three people is representing. But when the character who is introduced persuades, counsels, or dissuades, then there should be gravity and wit; for then doubtless is truth observed, since a man speaks in a different style from what is common when he gives counsel, or persuades, or argues against anything. Aristides, the rhetorician, gave us warrant for this; for he wishes the language

of comedy to be pure, clear, and flexible, and he adds also that it should be taken from the usage of the people, this being different from that of polite society; for in the latter case the diction will be elegant, sonorous, and adorned. Do not drag in quotations, nor let your language offend because of exquisite words; for, if one is to imitate those who speak, it should not be by the language of Panchaia, of the Metaurus, of hippogriffs, demigods, and centaurs.

23. If the king should speak, imitate as much as possible the gravity of a king; if the sage speak, observe a sententious modesty; describe lovers with those passions which greatly move whoever listens to them; manage soliloquies in such a manner that the recitant is quite transformed, and in changing himself, changes the listener. Let him ask questions and reply to himself, and if he shall make plaints, let him observe the respect due to women. Let not ladies disregard their character, and if they change costumes, let it be in such wise that it may be excused; for male disguise usually is very pleasing. Let him be on his guard against impossible things, for it is of the chiefest importance that only the likeness of truth should be represented. The lackey should not discourse of lofty affairs, nor express the conceits which we have seen in certain foreign plays; and in no wise let the character contradict himself in what he has said; I mean to say, forget—as in Sophocles one blames Oedipus for not remembering that he has killed Laius with his own hand. Let the scenes end with epigram, with wit, and with elegant verse, in such wise that, at his exit, he who spouts leave not the audience disgusted. In the first act set forth the case. In the second weave together the events, in such wise that until the middle of the third act one may hardly guess the outcome. Always trick expectancy; and hence it may come to pass that something quite far from what is promised may be left to the understanding. Tactfully suit your verse to the subjects being treated. *Décimas* are good for complainings; the sonnet is good for those who are waiting in expectation; recitals of events ask for *romances*, though they shine brilliantly in *octavas*. *Tercets* are for grave affairs and *redondillas* for affairs of love. Let rhetorical figures be brought in, as repetition or anadiplosis, and in the beginning of these same verses the various forms of anaphora; and also irony, questions, apostrophes, and exclamations.

24. To deceive the audience with the truth is a thing that

has seemed well, as Miguel Sánchez, worthy of this memorial for the invention, was wont to do in all his comedies. Equivoque and the uncertainty arising from ambiguity have always held a large place among the crowd, for it thinks that it alone understands what the other one is saying. Better still are the subjects in which honor has a part, since they deeply stir everybody; along with them go virtuous deeds, for virtue is everywhere loved; hence we see, if an actor chance to represent a traitor, he is so hateful to everyone that what he wishes to buy is not sold him, and the crowd flees when it meets him; but if he is loyal, they lend to him and invite him, and even the chief men honor him, love him, seek him out, entertain him, and acclaim him.

25. Let each act have but four sheets, for twelve are well suited to the time and the patience of him who is listening. In satirical parts, be not clear or open, since it is known that for this very reason comedies were forbidden by law in Greece and Italy; wound without hate, for if, perchance, slander be done, expect not applause, nor aspire to fame.

26. These things you may regard as aphorisms which you get not from the ancient art, which the present occasion allows no further space for treating; since whatever has to do with the three kinds of stage properties which Vitruvius speaks of concerns the impresario; just as Valerius Maximus, Petrus Crinitus, Horace in his epistles, and others describe these properties, with their drops, trees, cabins, houses, and simulated marbles.

27. Of costume Julius Pollux would tell us if it were necessary, for in Spain it is the case that the comedy of today is replete with barbarous things: a Turk wearing the neck-gear of a Christian and a Roman in tight breeches.

28. But of all, nobody can I call more barbarous than myself, since in defiance of art I dare to lay down precepts, and I allow myself to be borne along in the vulgar current, wherefore Italy and France call me ignorant. But what can I do if I have written four hundred and eighty-three comedies, along with one which I finished this week? For all of these, except six, gravely sin against art. Yet, in fine, I defend what I have written, and I know that, though they might have been better in another manner, they would not have had the vogue which they have had; for sometimes that which is contrary to what is just, for that very reason, pleases the taste.

How Comedy reflects this life of man,
　　How true her portraiture of young and old;
How subtle wit, polished in narrow span,
　　And purest speech, and more too you behold;
What grave consideration mixed with smiles,
　　What seriousness, along with pleasant jest;
Deceit of slaves; how woman oft beguiles
　　How full of slyness is her treacherous breast;
How silly, awkward swains to sadness run,
　　How rare success, though all seems well begun,

Let one hear with attention, and dispute not of the art; for in comedy everything will be found of such a sort that in listening to it everything becomes evident.

The Autobiography of a Play

As read before the Shakspere Club of Harvard University

by

BRONSON HOWARD

With an Introduction by Augustus Thomas

Introduction

The qualities that made Bronson Howard a dramatist, and then made him the first American dramatist of his day, were his human sympathy, his perception, his sense of proportion, and his construction. With his perception, his proportion, and his construction, respectively, he could have succeeded as a detective, as an artist, or as a general. It was his human sympathy, his wish and his ability to put himself in the other man's place, that made playwriting definitely attractive to him. As a soldier he would have shown the courage of the dogged defender in the trench or the calmly supervising general at headquarters, rather than the mad bravery that carried the flag at the front of a forlorn hope. His gifts were intellectual. His writing was more disciplined than inspired. If we shall claim for him genius, it must be preferably the genius of infinite pains.

He saw intimately and clearly. His proportion made him write with discretion and a proper sense of cumulative emphasis, and his construction enabled him so to combine his materials as to secure this effect. He was intensely self-critical; and while almost without conceit concerning his own work, he had an accuracy of detached estimation that enabled him to stand by his own opinion with a proper inflexibility when his judgment convinced him that the opinion was correct.

He worked slowly. At one time, in his active period, it was his custom to go from New York, where he lived, to New Rochelle, where he had formerly lived. There, upon the rear end of a suburban lot, he had a plain board cabin not more than ten feet square. In it were a deal table, a hard chair, and a small stove. He would go to this cabin in the morning when the tide of suburban travel was setting the other way, and spend his entire day there with his manuscript and his cigars. He carried a small lunch from his home. He once told me he was satisfied with his day's work if it provided him with ten good lines that would not have to be abandoned. I did not take that statement to imply that there were not in his experience the more profitable days that are in the work of every writer—days when the subject seems to command the pen and when the hand cannot keep pace with the vision. He was often too saturated with his story, too much the prisoner of his people, for it to have been otherwise; but his training had verified for him the truth that easy writing is hard reading.

Then, too, while Bronson Howard arranged his characters for the eye and built his story for the judgment, he wrote his speeches for the ear. This attention to the cadence of a line was so essential to him that when writing as he sometimes did for a magazine he studied the sound of his phrase as if the print were to be read aloud. This same care for the dialogue would retard its production; and critical revision would enforce still further delay.

William Gillette once said to an interviewer that "plays were not written, but were rewritten." The experience of many playwrights would support that statement. In the case of Bronson Howard, the autobiography of his *Banker's Daughter* certainly does so. His most profitable play, perhaps, and the one which also brought him the greatest popular recognition, was *Shenandoah*. That play was produced by a manager who, after its first performance, believed that it would not succeed. A younger and more hopeful one saw in it its great elements of popularity, and encouraged him to rewrite it.

Mr. William H. Crane, in a recent felicitous talk to the Society of American Dramatists, said that the *Henrietta* was played exactly as its author had delivered it to the actors, without the change or the need of change in a single word, and with only the repetition late in the play of a line that had been spoken in an early act. That fact does not exclude the possibility of rewritings before the manuscript came to the company, but rather, in view of Bronson Howard's thoroughness as a workman and his masterly sense of proportion, makes such rewritings the more probable. The effect, however, of his rewriting, wherever it may have been, and the slow additions of his daily contributions, was that of spontaneity.

Some philosopher tells us that a factor of greatness in any field is the power to generalize, the ability to discover the principle underlying apparently discordant facts. Bronson Howard's plays are notable for their evidence of this power. He saw causes, tendencies, results. His plays are expositions of this chemistry. *Shenandoah* dealt broadly with the forces and feelings behind the Civil War; the *Henrietta* with the American passion for speculation—the money-madness that was dividing families. *Aristocracy* was a very accurate, although satirical, seizure of the disposition, then in its strongest manifestation, of a newly-rich and Western family of native force to break into the exclusive social set of New York and to do so through a preparatory European alliance.

He has a human story in every instance. There is always dramatic conflict between interesting characters, of course, but behind them is always the background of some considerable social tendency—some comprehensive generalization—that includes and explains them all. The commander from his eminence saw all the combatants: he knew what the fight was about, and it always was about something worth while. Bronson Howard never dramatized piffle.

He was an observer of human nature and events, a traveler, a thinker, a student of the drama of all ages. He had been a reporter and an editorial writer. His plays were written by a watchful, sympathetic, and artistic military general turned philosopher.

AUGUSTUS THOMAS

June 1914

The Autobiography of a Play

I have not come to Newcastle with a load of coals; and I shall not try to tell the faculty and students of Harvard University anything about the Greek drama or the classical unities. I will remind you of only one thing in that direction; and say even this merely because it has a direct bearing upon some of the practical questions connected with play-writing which I purpose to discuss. Aeschylus, Sophocles, and Euripides—perhaps we should give the entire credit, as some authorities do, to Aeschylus—taught the future world the art of writing a play. But they did not create the laws of dramatic construction. Those laws exist in the passions and sympathies of the human race. They existed thousands of years before the Father of the Drama was born: waiting, like the other laws of nature, to be discovered and utilized by man.

A lecturer on "Animal Magnetism" failed to make his appearance one night, many years ago, in the public hall of a little town in Michigan, and a gentleman from Detroit consented to fill the vacant place. His lecture began and ended as follows: "Animal magnetism is a great subject, and the less said about it the better; we will proceed to experiments."

I will take that wise man as my own exemplar today, and I will begin by echoing his words: The drama in general is a great subject, and the less I say about it the better; we will proceed to experiments.

It happens that one of my own plays has had a very curious history. It has appeared before the American public in two forms, so radically different that a description of the changes made, and of the reasons for making them, will involve the consideration of some very interesting laws of dramatic construction. I shall ask you to listen very carefully to the story, or plot, of the piece as it was first produced in Chicago in 1873. Then I shall trace the changes that were made in this story before the play was produced in New York five years later. And after that, to follow the very odd adventures of the same play still further, I shall point out briefly the changes which were made necessary by adapting it to English life with English characters, for its production at the Court Theatre, London, in 1879. All the changes which I shall describe to you were forced upon me (as soon as I had decided to make the general alterations in the play) by the laws of dramatic construction; and it is to the experimental application of these laws to a particular play that I ask your attention. The learned professors of Harvard University know much more about them than I do, so far as a study of dramatic literature, from the outside, can give them that knowledge; and the great modern authorities on the subject—Hallam, Lessing, Schlegel, and many others—are open to the students of Harvard in her library; or, rather, shall I say, they lie closed on its shelves. But I invite you today to step into a little dramatic workshop, instead of a scientific library; and to see an humble workman in the craft, trying, with repeated experiments—not to elucidate the laws of dramatic construction, but to obey them, exactly as an inventor (deficient, it may be, in all scientific knowledge) tries to apply the general laws of mechanics to the immediate necessities of the machine he is working out in his mind. The moment a professor of chemistry has expressed a scientific truth, he must illustrate it at once by an experiment, or the truth will evaporate. An immense amount of scientific truth is constantly evaporating, for want of practical application; the air above every university in the world is charged with it. But what are the laws of dramatic construction? No one man knows much about them. As I have already reminded you, they bear about the same relation to human character and human sympathies as the laws of nature bear to the material universe. When all the mysteries of humanity have been solved, the laws of dramatic construction can be codified and clearly explained; not until then. But every scientific man can tell you a little about nature, and every dramatist can tell you a little about dramatic truth. A few general principles have been discovered by experiment and discussion. These few principles can be brought to your attention. But after you have learned all that has yet been learned by others, the field of humanity will still lie before you, as the field of nature lies before the scientist, with millions of times more to be discovered, by you or by someone else, than has ever yet been known. All I purpose tonight is to show you how certain laws of dramatic construction asserted themselves from time to time as we were making the changes in this play; how they thrust themselves upon our notice; how we could not possibly ignore them. And you will see how a man comes to understand any particular law, after he has been forced to obey it, although, perhaps, he has never heard of it or dreamed of it before.

And let me say here, to the students of Harvard—I do not presume to address words of advice to the faculty—it is to you and to others who enjoy the high privileges of liberal education that the American stage ought to look for honest and good dramatic work in the future. Let me say to you, then: Submit yourselves truly and unconditionally to the laws of dramatic truth, so far as you can discover them by honest mental exertion and observation. Do not mistake any mere defiance of these laws for originality. You might as well show your originality by defying the law of gravitation. Keep in mind the historical case of Stephenson. When a member of the British Parliament asked him, concerning his newfangled invention, the railroad, whether it would not be very awkward if a cow were on the track when a train came along, he answered: "Very ark'ard, indeed—for the cow." When you find yourself standing in the way of dramatic truth, my young friends—clear the track! If you don't, the truth can stand it; you can't. Even if you feel sometimes that your genius—that's always the word in the secret vocabulary of our own minds—even if your genius seems to be hampered by these dramatic laws, resign yourself to them at once, with that simple form of Christian resignation so beautifully illustrated by the poor German woman on her deathbed. Her husband being asked, afterward, if she were resigned to her death, responded with that touching and earnest recognition of eternal law: "Mein Gott, she had to be!"

The story of the play, as first produced in Chicago, may be told as follows:

Act first—Scene, New York. A young girl and a young man are in love, and engaged to be married. The striking original-

ity of this idea will startle any one who has never heard of
such a thing before. Lilian Westbrook and Harold Routledge
have a lovers' quarrel. Never mind what the cause of it. To
quote a passage from the play itself: "A woman never quarrels
with a man she doesn't love"—that is one of the minor laws
of dramatic construction—"and she is never tired of quarrel-
ing with a man she does love." I dare not announce this as
another law of female human nature; it is merely the opinion
of one of my characters—a married man. Of course, there
are women who do not quarrel with anyone; and there are
angels; but, as a rule, the women we feel at liberty to fall in
love with do quarrel now and then; and they almost invariably quarrel with their husbands or lovers first, their other
acquaintances must often be content with their smiles. But,
when Lilian announces to Harold Routledge that their engagement is broken forever, he thinks she means to imply
that she doesn't intend to marry him.

Women are often misunderstood by our more grossly practical sex; we are too apt to judge of what they mean by
what they say. The relations, if there are any, between a
woman's tongue and her thoughts form the least understood
section, perhaps, of dramatic law. You will get some idea of
the intricacies of this subject, if one of your literary professors will draw you a diagram of what a woman doesn't mean
when she uses the English language. Harold Routledge, almost
broken-hearted, bids Lilian farewell, and leaves her presence.
Lilian herself, proud and angry, allows him to go; waits petu-
lantly a moment for him to return; then, forlorn and
wretched, she bursts into the flood of tears which she intended to shed upon his breast. Under ordinary circumstances,
those precious drops would not have been wasted. Young
girls, when they quarrel with their lovers, are not extravagant
with their tears; they put them carefully to the best possible
use; and, I dare say, some of Lilian's tears would have fallen
on a sheet of notepaper; and the stained lines of a letter
would have reached Harold by the next post, begging him to
come back, and to let her forgive him for all the spiteful
things she had said to him. Unfortunately, however, just at
this critical juncture in the affairs of love—while Cupid was
waiting, hat in hand, to accompany the letter to its destina-
tion and keep an eye on the postman—Lilian's father enters.
He is on the verge of financial ruin, and he has just received
a letter from Mr. John Strebelow, a man of great wealth,

asking him for his daughter's hand in marriage. Mr. Westbrook urges her to accept him, not from any selfish motives,
but because he dreads to leave, in his old age, a helpless girl,
trained only to luxury and extravagance, to a merciless world.
Lilian, on her part, shudders at the thought of her father
renewing the struggle of life when years have exhausted his
strength. She knows that she will be the greatest burden that
will fall upon him; she remembers her dead mother's love for
them both; and she sacrifices her own heart. Mr. Strebelow
is a man of about forty years, of unquestioned honor, of
noble personal character in every way. Lilian had loved him,
indeed, when she was a little child, and she feels that she can
at least respect and reverence him as her husband. Mr.
Strebelow marries her without knowing that she does not
love him; much less, that she loves another.

Act second—Paris. Lilian has been married five years, and
is residing with her husband in the French capital. As the
curtain rises, Lilian is teaching her little child, Natalie, her
alphabet. All the warm affection of a woman's nature, suppressed and thrown back upon her own heart, has concen-
trated itself upon this child. Lilian has been a good wife, and
she does reverence her husband as she expected to do. He is
a kind, generous, and noble man. But she does not love him
as a wife. Mr. Strebelow now enters, and, after a little
domestic scene, the French nurse is instructed to dress the
child for a walk with its mother. Strebelow then tells Lilian
that he has just met an old friend of hers and of himself—
the American artist, Mr. Harold Routledge, passing through
Paris on his way from his studio in Rome. He has insisted
on a visit from Mr. Routledge, and the two parted lovers
are brought face to face by the husband. They are afterwards
left alone together. Routledge has lived a solitary life, nurs-
ing his feelings toward a woman who had heartlessly cast
him off, as he thinks, to marry a man merely for his wealth.
He is bitter and cruel. But the cruelty to a woman which is
born of love for her has a wonderful, an almost irresistible
fascination for the female heart. Under the spell of this fascination, Lilian's old love reasserts its authority against that
of his will. She forgets everything except the moment when
her lover last parted from her. She is again the wayward girl
that waited for his return; he has returned!—and she does
what she would have done five years before; she turns, passionately, to throw herself into his arms. At this moment, her

little child, Natalie, runs in. Lilian is a mother again, and a wife. She falls to her knees and embraces her child at the very feet of her former lover. Harold Routledge bows his head reverently, and leaves them together.

Act third. The art of breaking the tenth commandment—thou shalt not covet thy neighbor's wife—has reached its highest perfection in France. One of the most important laws of dramatic construction might be formulated in this way: If you want a particular thing done, choose a character to do it that an audience will naturally expect to do it. I wanted a man to fall in love with my heroine after she was a married woman, and I chose a French count for that purpose. I knew that an American audience would not only expect him to fall in love with another man's wife, but it would be very much surprised if he didn't. This saved much explanation and unnecessary dialogue. Harold Routledge overhears the Count de Carojac, a hardened roué and a duellist, speaking of Lilian in such terms as no honorable man should speak of a modest woman. Routledge, with a studio in Rome, and having been educated at a German university, is familiar with the use of the rapier. A duel is arranged. Lilian hears of it through a female friend, and Strebelow, also, through the American second of Mr. Routledge. The parties meet at the Château Chateaubriand, in the suburbs of Paris, at midnight, by the light of the moon, in winter. A scream from Lilian, as she reaches the scene in breathless haste, throws Routledge off his guard; he is wounded and falls. Strebelow, too, has come on the field, not knowing the cause of the quarrel, but anxious to prevent a meeting between two of his own personal friends. Lilian is ignorant of her husband's presence, and she sees only the bleeding form of the man she loves lying upon the snow. She falls at his side, and words of burning passion, checked a few hours before by the innocent presence of her child, spring to her lips. The last of these words are as follows: "I have loved you—and you only—Harold, from the first."

These words, clear, unmistakable, carrying their terrible truth straight to his heart, come to John Strebelow as the very first intimation that his wife did not love him when she married him. Crushed by this sudden blow, an expression of agony on his face, he stands for a moment speechless. When his voice returns, he has become another man. He is hard and cold, still generous, so far as those things a generous man cares least for are concerned. He will share all his wealth with her; but, in the awful bitterness of a great heart, at that moment, he feels that the woman who has deceived him so wickedly has no natural right to be the guardian of their child. "Return to our home, madam; it will be yours, not mine, hereafter; but our child will not be there." Ungenerous words! But if we are looking in our own hearts, where we must find nearly all the laws of dramatic construction, how many of us would be more generous, with such words as John Strebelow had just heard ringing in our ears? As the act closes, the startled love of a mother has again and finally asserted itself in Lilian's heart, its one overmastering passion of her nature. With the man she has loved lying near her, wounded, and, for aught she knows, dying, she is thinking only of her lost child. Maternal love, throughout the history of the world, has had triumphs over all the other passions; triumphs over destitution and trials and tortures; over all the temptations incident to life; triumphs to which no other impulse of the human heart—not even the love of man for woman—has ever risen. One of the most brilliant men I had ever known once said in court: "Woman, alone, shares with the Creator the privilege of communing with an unborn human being"; and, with this privilege, the Creator seems to have shared with woman a part of His own great love. All other love in our race is merely human. The play, from this time on, becomes the story of a mother's love.

Acts fourth and fifth. Two years later Lilian is at the home of her father in New York. Her husband has disappeared. His name was on the passenger list of a wrecked steamer; and no other word of him or of the child has been heard. If he had left the little girl in the care of others, it is unknown to whom or where. So Lilian is a widow and childless. She is fading, day by day, and is hardly expected to live. Her mind, tortured by a suspense worse than certainty, is gradually yielding to hallucinations which keep her little one ever present to her fancy. Harold Routledge was wounded seriously in the duel, but not killed; he is near Lilian; seeing her every day; but he is her friend, rather than her lover, now; she talks with him of her child, and he feels how utterly hopeless his own passion is in the presence of an all-absorbing mother's love. It is discovered that the child is living peacefully among kind guardians in a French convent; and Routledge determines to cross the ocean with the necessary evidence and bring the little one back to its mother. He breaks the news to Lilian tenderly and gently. A gleam of joy illuminates her face for the first time since the terrible night, two years before, and Routledge feels that the only barrier to his own happiness has been removed. But the sudden return and reappearance of the husband falls like a stroke of fate upon both. As the curtain descends on the fourth act, Lilian lies fainting on the floor, with Natalie at her side, while the two men stand face to face above the unconscious woman whom they both love. Three lives ruined—because Lilian's father, having lost his wealth, in his old age, dared not, as he himself expressed it, leave a tenderly nurtured daughter to a merciless world. The world is merciless, perhaps, but it is not so utterly and hopelessly merciless to any man or woman as one's heart may be.

Lilian comes back to consciousness on her deathbed. Her child had returned to her only as a messenger from heaven, summoning her home. But the message had been whispered in unconscious ears; for she had not seen the little girl, who was removed before the mother had recovered from her swoon. They dare not tell her now that Natalie is on this side of the ocean and asleep in the next room. Mr. Strebelow had heard in a distant land, traveling to distract his mind from the great sorrow of his own life, of Lilian's condition, and he hastened back to undo the wrong he felt that he had committed. She asks to see him; she kisses his hand with tenderness and gratitude, when he tells her that Natalie shall be her own hereafter; his manly tears are tears of repentance, mingled with a now generous love. The stroke of death comes suddenly; they have only a moment's time to arouse the little one from its sleep; but they are not too late, and Lilian dies at last, a smile of perfect happiness on her face, with her child in her arms.

The Mississippi darky, in Mark Twain's story, being told that his heroic death on the field of battle would have made but little difference to the nation at large, remarked, with deep philosophy; "It would have made a great deal of difference to me, sah." The radical change made in the story I have just related to you, before the production of the play in New York, was this: Lilian lives, instead of dying, in the last act. It would have made very little difference to the American nation what she did; but it made a great deal of difference to her, as you will see, and to the play also in nearly every part. My reasons for making the change were

based upon one of the most important principles of the
dramatic art, namely: A dramatist should deal, so far as possible, with subjects of universal interest, instead of with such
as appeal strongly to a part of the public only. I do not mean
that he may not appeal to certain classes of people, and depend upon those classes for success; but, just so far as he does
this, he limits the possibilities of that success. I have said
that the love of offspring in woman has shown itself the
strongest of all human passions; and it is the most nearly
allied to the boundless love of Deity. But the one absolutely
universal passion of the race—which underlies all other passions—on which, indeed, the very existence of the race depends—the very fountain of maternal love itself, is the love
of the sexes. The dramatist must remember that his work
cannot, like that of the novelist or the poet, pick out the
hearts, here and there, that happen to be in sympathy with
its subject. He appeals to a thousand hearts at the same
moment; he has no choice in the matter; he must do this.
And it is only when he deals with the love of the sexes that
his work is most interesting to that aggregation of human
hearts we call the audience. This very play was successful
in Chicago; but, as soon as that part of the public had been
exhausted which could weep with pleasure, if I may use the
expression, over the tenderness of a mother's love, its success
would have been at an end. Furthermore—and here comes in
another law of dramatic construction—a play must be, in one
way or another, "satisfactory" to the audience. This word has
a meaning which varies in different countries, and even in
different parts of the same country; but, whatever audience
you are writing for, your work must be "satisfactory" to it.
In England and America, the death of a pure woman on the
stage is not "satisfactory," except when the play rises to the
dignity of tragedy. The death, in an ordinary play, of a woman
who is not pure, as in *Frou-Frou*, is perfectly satisfactory, for
the reason that it is inevitable. Human nature always bows
gracefully to the inevitable. The only griefs in our own lives
to which we could never reconcile ourselves are those which
might have been averted. The wife who has once taken the
step from purity to impurity can never reinstate herself in
the world of art on this side of the grave; and so an audience
looks with complacent tears on the death of an erring woman.
But Lilian had not taken the one fatal step which would have
reconciled an audience to her death. She was still pure, and

every one left the theatre wishing she had lived. I yielded, therefore, to the sound logic, based on sound dramatic principle, of my New York manager, Mr. A. M. Palmer, and the piece was altered.

I have called the play, as produced in New York and afterward in London, the "same play" as the one produced in Chicago. That one doubt, which age does not conquer—which comes down to us from the remotest antiquity of our own youth, which will still exist in our minds as we listen to the music of the spheres, through countless ages, when all other doubts are at rest; that never-to-be answered doubt: Whether it was the same jackknife, or another one, after all its blades and handle had been changed—must ever linger in my own mind as to the identity of this play. But a dramatic author stops worrying himself about doubts of this kind very early in his career. The play which finally takes its place on the stage usually bears very little resemblance to the play which first suggested itself to his mind. In some cases the public has abundant reason to congratulate itself on this fact, and especially on the way plays are often built up, so to speak, by the authors, with advice and assistance from other intelligent people interested in their success. The most magnificent figure in the English drama of this century was a mere faint outline, merely a fatherly old man, until the suggestive mind of Macready stimulated the genius of Bulwer-Lytton, and the great author, eagerly acknowledging the assistance rendered him, made Cardinal Richelieu the colossal central figure of a play that was written as a pretty love story. Bulwer-Lytton had an eye single, as every dramatist ought to have—as every successful dramatist must have—to the final artistic result; he kept before him the one object of making the play of *Richelieu* as good a play as he possibly could make it. The first duty of a dramatist is to put upon the stage the very best work he can, in the light of whatever advice and assistance may come to him. Fair acknowledgment afterward is a matter of mere ordinary personal honesty. It is not a question of dramatic art.

So Lilian is to live, and not die, in the last act. The first question for us to decide—I say "us"—the New York manager, the literary attaché of the theatre, and myself—the first practical question before us was: As Lilian is to live, which of the two men who love her is to die? There are axioms among the laws of dramatic construction, as in mathematics. One of them is this: three hearts cannot beat as one. The world is not large enough, from an artistic point of view, for three good human hearts to continue to exist, if two of them love the third. If one of the two hearts is a bad one, art assigns it to the hell on earth of disappointed love; but if it is good and tender and gentle, art is merciful to it, and puts it out of its misery by death. Routledge was wounded in a duel. Strebelow was supposed to be lost in the wreck of a steamer. It was easy enough to kill either of them, but which? We argued this question for three weeks. Mere romance was on the side of the young artist. But to have had him live would have robbed the play of all its meaning. Its moral, in the original form, is this: It is a dangerous thing to marry, for any reason, without the safeguard of love, even when the person one marries is worthy of one's love in every possible way. If we had decided in favor of Routledge, the play would have had no moral at all, or rather a very bad one. If a girl marries the wrong man, she need only wait for him to die; and if her lover waits, too, it'll be all right. If, on the other hand, we so reconstruct the whole play that the husband and wife may at last come together with true affection, we shall have the moral: Even if a young girl makes the worst of all mistakes, and accepts the hand of one man when her heart belongs to another, fidelity to the duty of a wife on her side, and a manly, generous confidence on the part of her husband, may, in the end, correct even such a mistake. The dignity of this moral saved John Strebelow's life, and Harold Routledge was killed in the duel with the Count de Carojac.

All that was needed to effect this first change in the play was to instruct the actor who played Routledge to lie still when the curtain fell at the end of the third act, and to go home afterward. But there are a number of problems under the laws of dramatic construction which we must solve before the play can now be made to reach the hearts of an audience as it did before. Let us see what they are.

The love of Lilian for Harold Routledge cannot now be the one grand passion of her life. It must be the love of a young girl, however sincere and intense, which yields, afterward, to the stronger and deeper love of a woman for her husband. The next great change, therefore, which the laws of dramatic construction forced upon us was this: Lilian must now control her own passion, and when she meets her lover in the second act she must not depend for her moral safety on the awakening of a mother's love by the appearance of her child. Her love for Harold is no longer such an all-controlling force as will justify a woman—justify her dramatically, I mean—yielding to it. For her to depend on an outside influence would be to show a weakness of character that would make her uninteresting. Instead, therefore, of receiving her former lover with dangerous pent-up fires, Lilian now feels pity for him. She hardly yet knows her own feelings toward her husband; but his manhood and kindness are gradually forcing their way to her heart. Routledge, in his own passion, forgets himself, and she now repels him. She even threatens to strike the bell, when the Count de Carojac appears, and warns his rival to desist. This is now the end of the second act, a very different end, you see, from the other version, where the little girl runs in, and, in her innocence, saves the mother from herself.

Here let me tell you a curious experience, which illustrates how stubbornly persistent the dramatic laws are, in having their own way. We were all three of us—manager, literary attaché, and author—so pleased with the original ending of the second act, the picture of the little girl in her mother's arms, and the lover bowing his head in its presence of innocence, that we retained it. The little girl ran on the stage at every rehearsal at the usual place. But no one knew what to do with her. The actress who played the part of Lilian caught her in her arms, in various attitudes; but none of them seemed right. The actor who played Routledge tried to drop his head, according to instructions, but he looked uncomfortable, not reverential. The next day we had the little girl run on from another entrance. She stopped in the center of the stage. Lilian stared at her a moment and then exclaimed: "Mr. Howard, what shall I do with this child?" Routledge, who had put his hands in his pocket, called out: "What's the girl doing here, anyway, Howard?" I could only answer: "She used to be all right; I don't know what's the matter with her now." And I remember seeing an anxious look on the face of the child's mother, standing at the side of the stage. She feared there was something wrong about her own little darling who played the part of Natalie. I reassured her on this point; for the fact that I was in error was forcing itself on my mind, in spite of my desire to retain the scene. You will hardly believe that I am speaking literally, when I tell you that it was not until the nineteenth rehearsal that we yielded to the inevitable, and decided not to have the child come on, at all at that point. The truth was this: now that Lilian saved herself in her own strength, the child had no dramatic function to fulfill. So strongly did we all feel the force of a dramatic law which we could not, and would not, see. Our own natural human instinct—the instinct which the humblest member of an audience feels, without knowing anything of dramatic law—got the better of three men, trained in dramatic work, only by sheer force, and against our own determined opposition. We were three of Stephenson's cows—or shall I say three calves?—standing on the track, and we could not succeed where Jumbo failed.

The third step, in the changes forced upon us by the laws of dramatic construction, was a very great one; and it was made necessary by the fact, just mentioned, that the child, Natalie, had no dramatic function to fulfill in the protection of her mother's virtue. In other words, there is no point in the play, now, where sexual love is, or can be, replaced by maternal love, as the controlling passion of the play. Consequently, the last two acts in their entirety, so far as the serious parts are concerned, disappear; one new scene and a new act taking their place. The sad mother, playing with a little shoe or toy, passes out of our view. The dying woman, kissing the hand of the man she has wronged; the husband, awe-stricken in the presence of a mother's child; the child clasped in Lilian's arms; her last look on earth, a smile, and her last breath, the final expression of maternal tenderness—these scenes belong only to the original version of the play, as it lies in its author's desk. With an author's sensitive interest in his own work, I wasted many hours in trying to save these scenes. But I was working directly against the laws of dramatic truth, and I gave up the impossible task.

The fourth great change—forced on us, as the others were —concerns the character of John Strebelow. As he is now to become the object of a wife's mature affection, he must not merely be a noble and generous man; he must do something worthy of the love which is to be bestowed on him. He must command a woman's love. When, therefore, he hears his wife, kneeling over her wounded lover, use words which tell him of their former relations, he does not what most of us would do, but what an occasional hero among us would do. Of course, the words of Lilian cannot be such, now, as to close the gates to all hopes of love, as they were before. She still utters a wild cry, but her words merely show the awakened tenderness and pity of a woman for a man she had once loved. They are uttered, however, in the presence of others, and they compromise her husband's honor. At that moment he takes her gently in his arms, and becomes her protector, warning the French roué and duellist that he will call him to account for the insults which the arm of the dead man had failed to avenge. He afterward does this, killing the count— not in the action of the play; this is only told. John Strebe-low thus becomes the hero of the play, and it is only necessary to follow the workings of Lilian's heart and his a little further, until they come together at last, loving each other truly, the early love of the wife for another man being only a sad memory in her mind. There is a tender scene of explanation and a parting, until Lilian's heart shall recall her husband. This scene, in my opinion, is one of the most beautiful scenes ever written for the stage. At the risk of breaking the tenth commandment myself, I do not hesitate to say, I wish I had written it. As I did not, however, I can express the hope that the name of Mr. A. R. Cazauran, who did write it, will never be forgotten in connection with this play as long as the play itself may be remembered. I wrote the scene myself first; but when he wrote it according to his own ideas, it was so much more beautiful than my own that I would have broken a law of dramatic art if I had not accepted it. I should not have been giving the public the best play I could, under the circumstances. Imbued, as my own mind was, with all the original motives of the piece, it would have been impossible for me to have made changes within a few weeks without the assistance Mr. Cazauran could give me; this assistance was invaluable to me in all parts of the revised piece. In the fifth act the husband and wife come together again, the little child acting as the immediate cause of their reconciliation; the real cause lies in their own true hearts.

Before we leave the subject, another change which I was obliged to make will interest you, because it shows very curiously what queer turns these laws of dramatic construction may take. As soon as it was decided to have Lilian live, in the fifth act, and love John Strebelow, I was compelled to cut out the quarrel scene between Lilian and Harold Routledge in the first act. This is a little practical matter, very much like taking out a certain wheel at one end of a machine because you have decided to get a different mechanical result at the other end. I was very fond of this quarrel scene, but I lost no time in trying to save it, for I saw at once that Harold Routledge must not appear in the first act at all. He could only be talked about as Lilian's lover. John Strebelow must be present alone in the eyes and sympathy of the audience. If Routledge did not appear until the second act, the audience would regard him as an interloper; it would rather resent his presence than otherwise, and would be easily reconciled to his death in the next act. It was taking an unfair advantage of a young lover; but there was no help for it. Even if Harold had appeared in the first act, the quarrel scene would have been impossible. He might have made love to Lilian, perhaps, or even kissed her, and the audience would have forgiven me reluctantly for having her love another man afterward. But if the two young people had a lovers' quarrel in the presence of the audience, no power on earth could have convinced any man or woman in the house that they were not intended for each other by the eternal decrees of divine Providence.

I have now given you the revised story of this play as it was produced at the Union Square Theatre in New York, under the name of *The Banker's Daughter*. I have said nothing about the comic scenes or characters, because the various changes did not affect them in any way that concerns the principles of dramatic art. They are almost identically the same in both versions. Now, if you please, we will cross the ocean. I have had many long discussions with English managers on the practice in London of adapting foreign plays, not merely to the English stage, but to English life, with English characters. The Frenchmen of a French play become, as a rule, Englishmen; so do Italians and Spaniards and Swedes. They usually, however, continue to express foreign ideas and to act like foreigners. In speaking of such a transplanted character, I may be permitted to trifle with a sacred text:

> The manager has said it,
> But it's hardly to his credit,
>   That he is an Englishman!
> For he ought to have been a Roosian,
> A French, or Turk, or Proosian,
>   Or perhaps I-tali-an!
> But in spite of Art's temptations,

To belong to other nations,
He becomes an Englishman!

Luckily, the American characters of *The Banker's Daugh-ter,* with one exception, could be twisted into very fair Eng-lishmen, with only a faint suspicion of our Yankee accent. Mr. James Albery, one of the most brilliant men in England, author of *The Two Roses,* was engaged to make them as nearly English as he could. The friendship, cemented as Al-berry and I were discussing for some weeks the international social questions involved, is among the dearest and tenderest friendships I have ever made; and I learned more about the various minor differences of social life in England and Amer-ica while we were thus at work together than I could have learned in a residence there of five years. I have time to give you only a few of the points. Take the engagement of Lilian, broken in act first. An engagement in England is necessarily a family matter, and it could neither be made nor broken by the mere fiat of a young girl, without consultation with others, leaving the way open for the immediate acceptance of an-other man's hand. In the English version, therefore, there is no engagement with Harold Routledge. It is only an under-standing between them that they love each other. Not even the most rigid customs of Europe can prevent such an un-derstanding between two young people, if they can once look into each other's eyes. They could fall in love through a pair of telescopes. Then the duel—it is next to impossible to per-suade an English audience that a duel is justifiable or natural with an Englishman as one of the principals. So we played a rather sharp artistic trick on our English audience. In the American version, I assume that, if a plucky young American in France insults a Frenchman purposely, he will abide by the local customs, and give him satisfaction, if called upon to do so. So would a young Englishman, between you and me; but the laws of dramatic construction deal with the sympathies of the audience as well as with the natural mo-tives and actions of the characters in a play; and an English audience would think the French count ought to be perfectly satisfied if Routledge knocked him down. How did we get over the difficulty? First, we made Routledge a British officer re-turning from India, instead of an artist on his way from Rome —a fighting man by profession; and then we made the Count de Carojac pile so many sneers and insults on this British officer, and on the whole British nation, that I verily believe a London audience would have mobbed him if he hadn't tried to kill him. The English public walked straight into the trap, although they abhor nothing on earth more than the dueling system. I said that the comic characters were not affected by the changes made in America; the change of nationality did affect them to a certain extent. A young girl, Florence St. Vincent, afterward Mrs. Browne, represents, here, with dramatic exaggeration, of course, a type of young girl more or less familiar to all of us. In England she is not a type, but an eccentric personality, with which the audience must be made acquainted by easy stages. It was necessary, therefore, to introduce a number of preliminary speeches for her, before she came to the lines of the original version. After that, she ran on without any further change, except a few excisions. Mrs. Browne is married to a very old man, who afterward dies, and in the last act she illustrates the various grades of affliction endured by every young widow, from the darkness of despair to the becoming twilight of sentimental sadness. This was delicate ground in England. They have not that utter horror of marriage between a very old man and a very young woman which, in this country, justifies all the satire which a dramatist can heap upon the man who commits this crime, even after he is in the grave. And the English people do not share with us—I say it to their credit—our universal irreverence for what is solemn and sacred. One must not, either in social life or on the stage, speak too lightly there of any serious subject; of course, they can laugh, however, at an old man that makes a fool of himself. So we merely toned down the levity by leaving old Mr. Browne out of the cast entirely. There is a great difference, as in the case of Routledge left out of the first act, between what the audience sees and what it only hears talked about; and none of the laws of dramatic construction are more important than those which concern the questions whether you shall appeal to the ear of an audience, to its eye, or both. Old Mr. Browne was only talked about, then, and as long as the English audience did not know him personally, it was perfectly willing to laugh at him after Mrs. Browne was a widow. Another change made for the London version will interest American business men. In our own version, Lilian's father and his partner close up their affairs in the last act and retire from their business as private bankers. "That will never do in England," said Mr.

Albery. "An old established business like that might be worth £100,000. We must sell it to some one, not close it." So we sold it to Mr. George Washington Phipps. This last character illustrates, again, the stubbornness of dramatic law. Mr. Albery and I tried to make him an Irishman, or a Scotchman, or some kind of Englishman. But we could not. He remains an American in England in 1886, as he was in Chicago in 1873. He declined to change either his citizenship or his name; "G. Washington—Father of his Country— Phipps."

The peculiar history of the play is my only justification for giving you all these details of its otherwise unimportant career. I only trust that I have shown you how very practical the laws of dramatic construction are in the way they influence a dramatist. The art of obeying them is merely the art of using your common sense in the study of your own and other people's emotions. All I now add is, if you want to write a play, be honest and sincere in using your common sense. A prominent lawyer once assured me that there was only one man he trembled before in the presence of a jury— not the learned man, nor the eloquent man; it was the sincere man. The public will be your jury. That public often condescends to be trifled with by mere tricksters, but, believe me, it is only a condescension and very contemptuous. In the long run, the public will judge you, and respect you, according to your artistic sincerity.

Robert Louis Stevenson as a Dramatist

A Lecture delivered to the Members of the Philosophical Institution of Edinburgh at the Music Hall in Edinburgh, Tuesday, February 24, 1903

by

Arthur Wing Pinero

With an Introduction by Clayton Hamilton

Introduction

I

In the preface to his *Life of Robert Louis Stevenson*, Mr. Graham Balfour has reminded us of the traditional opinion that "All Biography would be Autobiography if it could." On similar grounds, it might be stated that all dramatic criticism should be written by dramatists. No one but a dramatist can fully appreciate the difficulty of achieving "that *compression* of life which the stage undoubtedly demands *without* falsification"; and no one else is fitted to understand so well the infinitude of technical devices that must be employed strategically to overcome this difficulty.

It is unfortunate for criticism that most dramatists are kept so busy putting plays together that they are left no leisure for pulling plays apart, in order to explain the method of their making, for the benefit of students of the craft. Aristotle is rightly considered one of the greatest of dramatic critics; but how much more instructive than even the *Poetics* might have been an analysis of *Œdipus the King* from the pen, say, of Euripides, or best of all, from that of Sophocles himself.

There are, of course, exceptions to the rule that great dramatists have rarely written criticisms. The most notable instance is that of Lessing, who attained an equal eminence in literary history as a dramatist and as a critic. In our own day, Mr. Bernard Shaw has written a great deal of spirited dramatic criticism, and Mr. Henry Arthur Jones has labored earnestly in many lectures to increase the public understanding of the fundamental principles of the modern drama. The

44

critical utterances of professional playmakers such as these are especially to be commended to the attention of students of stagecraft.

Sir Arthur Pinero has appeared before the public only once as a dramatic critic. This was on the twenty-fourth of February 1903, when he delivered his lecture on "Robert Louis Stevenson: The Dramatist" to the members of the Philosophical Institution of Edinburgh at the Music Hall in Stevenson's native city. This lecture has been printed only privately, because Sir Arthur has an ineradicable habit of reserving the limelight for his plays and keeping out of it himself; but it is greatly to be regretted that so sound a piece of criticism has not been made accessible to all who are interested in the technique of the drama.

There are four points in this lecture that are especially pertinent to the study of the drama at large. The first of these is that "One of the great rules—perhaps the only universal rule—of the drama is that you cannot pour new wine into old skins." . . . "The art of drama is not stationary but progressive." . . . "Its conditions are always changing, and . . . every dramatist whose ambition it is to produce live plays is absolutely bound to study carefully, and I may even add respectfully—at any rate not contemptuously—the conditions that hold good for his own age and generation." The tendency of most men of letters who remain out of touch with the theatre of their time is to write plays in imitation of outworn models. Thus, in the nineteenth century, most of the great English poets wrote plays in imitation of the Elizabethan dramatists, and instead of "showing the age and body of the time his form and pressure," produced mere curiosities of literature that were essentially anachronistic. Stevenson himself, instead of imitating Shakespeare, imitated the transpontine melodramatists of the early nineteenth century. The model, indeed, was different; but the faulty principle of deliberate anachronism remained the same. If this simple point could only become more generally understood, we should hear less talk, among half cultured people who habitually absent themselves from the contemporary theatre, in favor of what they call the "literary" or the "closet" drama.

The second important point is Sir Arthur's statement that "*dramatic* talent" is of service in the theatre only as "the raw material of *theatrical* talent." . . . "Dramatic, like poetic, talent is born, not made; if it is to achieve success on the stage, it must be developed into theatrical talent by hard study, and generally by long practice." In many circles the heresy is still assumed that any novelist or poet who is gifted with dramatic talent can write a play—as he would write a novel or a poem—by sitting down before a pile of copy paper and taking his pen in hand. The essence of this heresy is the failure to perceive that the task of making a play, under the conditions of the contemporary theatre, is less a task of writing than a task of building. The modern drama is necessarily more an architectonic than a literary art; and a fine innate dramatic talent will be wasted in the modern theatre unless it is expressed in terms of a theatrical talent that must be developed "by hard study, and generally by long practice," of the conditions of the contemporary stage.

Also equally suggestive is Sir Arthur's distinction between what he calls the "strategy" and the "tactics" of playmaking. He defines *strategy* as "the general laying out of a play" and *tactics* as "the art of getting the characters on and off the stage, or conveying information to the audience and so forth." The tactics of the theatre are still spoken of with scorn by critics who persist in ignoring the extraliterary elements of the dramatic art. Such critics are fond of quoting a disgruntled ejaculation of Gustave Flaubert's, which was written in a letter to George Sand: "One of the most comical things of our time is this new-fangled theatrical mystery. They tell us that the art of the theatre is beyond the limits of human intelligence, and that it is a mystery reserved for men who write like cab-drivers." The implied negation that there is any technical difference between the task of building *The Demi-Monde* and the task of writing *Madame Bovary* proves conclusively that there must be a "theatrical mystery" that is sufficiently elusive to escape the apprehension of even a great novelist. It would be better to construct a play with architectonic genius and to write it like a cab driver, than to write a play with literary genius and to build it like a cab driver. A critic less familiar than Flaubert with the literary style of cab drivers might be willing to admit, for the sake of argument, that *The Two Orphans* is written in that style; yet it is a far better play than Tennyson's *Queen Mary*, which is written in a style that sometimes emulates the eloquence of angels.

And this brings us to the consideration of the fourth important point in the lecture now before us. This is the point that fine speeches, and fine speeches alone, will not carry a drama to success—either to actual success in the theatre, or even to that more dubious and illusory success in the library on which believers in the "closet" drama seem to set such store. Sir Arthur's clear distinction between "the absolute beauty of words, such beauty as Ruskin or Pater or Newman might achieve in an eloquent passage," and "the beauty of dramatic fitness to the character and the situation" is of the very utmost importance to all readers who desire to appreciate the modern drama and to judge its element of dialogue from a proper point of view.

In the light of these four principles, Sir Arthur has examined the plays that were written by Robert Louis Stevenson in collaboration with William Ernest Henley; and, at each of the four points, he has found the plays defective. Stevenson's work in the drama was anachronistic; and the models that he imitated not only were outworn but also were unworthy. Stevenson never took the trouble to develop into theatrical talent the keen dramatic talent he was born with. He never taught himself the tactics of modern playmaking, and did not even appreciate the good points in the strategy of the transpontine melodramatists he was imitating. Finally, Stevenson never managed to unlearn the heresy that fine speeches, and fine speeches alone, will carry a drama to success.

Sir Arthur is an ardent Stevensonian, and his criticism is delivered in a sympathetic spirit. It is, however, utterly destructive of any effort that might be made to claim an important place for Stevenson in the records of our literary drama. Mr. Francis Watt, in a recent book entitled *R. L. S.*, has stated his opinion that "the Plays were too good to win a popular success." Whenever a great writer has failed in the theatre, this plea has always been advanced by his admirers. It is as if, when a hammer thrower had been beaten in a hundred yard dash, his backers should explain that sprinting is an inferior sport to hammer throwing. Plays do not fail because they are too good: they fail because they are not good enough in the right way.

Sir Arthur's explanation of "Stevenson's—I will not say failure, but inadequate success—as a playwright" is equally acute. He finds that Stevenson failed to take the drama seriously, that he worked at it "in a smiling, sportive, half-contemptuous spirit," that he "played at being a playwright" and "was fundamentally in error in regarding the drama as a matter of child's play." And, in a very interesting parallel, Sir Arthur has pointed out the close resemblance between Stevenson's own plays and those typical examples of Skelt's Juvenile Drama that are celebrated with such a gusto of memorial eloquence in that delightful essay in *Memories and Portraits* called "A Penny Plain and Twopence Coloured." "Even to his dying day," Sir Arthur adds, "he continued to regard the actual theatre as only an enlarged form of the toy theatres which had fascinated his childhood. . . . he considered his function as a dramatist very little more serious than that child's-play with paint-box and pasteboard on which his memory dwelt so fondly."

This criticism must be regarded as final; for it would not be possible to make out a good brief for the other side. Stevenson must have felt this himself; for, though Henley always regarded their joint plays very highly and continued to believe in them, not merely as literature but also as practicable pieces for the theatre, Stevenson soon lost belief and interest in them, and in the end considered them as nothing. In July 1884 Stevenson wrote to Sir Sidney Colvin, apropos of a public performance of *Deacon Brodie* that Henley was arranging for, "and anyhow the *Deacon* is damn bad"; and in March 1885 he remonstrated with Henley, in the following terms, for sending copies of their joint plays to their literary friends: "Do you think you are right to send *Macaire* and the *Admiral* about? Not a copy have I sent, nor (speaking for myself personally) do I want sent. The reperusal of the *Admiral*, by the way, was a sore blow; eh, God, man, it is a low, black, dirty, blackguard, ragged piece; vomitable in many parts—simply vomitable. Pew is in places a reproach to both art and man. But of all that afterwards. What I mean is that I believe in playing dark with second- and third-rate work. *Macaire* is a piece of job-work, hurriedly bockled; might have been worse, might have been better; happy-go-lucky; act-it-or-let-it-rot piece of business. Not a thing, I think, to send in presentations."

"The Plays were too good to win a popular success." . . . Were they, indeed! Not so thought Robert Louis Stevenson himself, in his most candid correspondence with his collaborator.

What remains to be added to Sir Arthur Pinero's masterly and final criticism of Stevenson as dramatist? Only some account of the causes of Stevenson's comparative lack of preparation for the task of making plays. We must delve into Stevenson's biography, must test his relations with the theatre wherever such relations show themselves, and must endeavor to determine what he actually knew, and what he could not know, about an art which was undergoing an exceedingly significant renascence at the very time when his own career as a novelist and essayist was at its culmination.

II

In reviewing any phase of Stevenson's work, we must always bear in mind that his art was prevailingly memorial. That is to say, the substance of his utterances—whether the medium of expression, for the time being, happened to be a story or an essay or a poem—was always an emotion; and this emotion was invariably induced from the recollection of some keen sensation which he had personally experienced in the past. This point, which is the key to Stevenson's art, cannot be expounded and illustrated adequately in the brief space which is available for the present discussion. Suffice it to say that the muse of Stevenson was essentially a muse of memory; and that everything he ever wrote was an artistic record of some emotion recollected from his individual experience.

If, now, we delve into his personal experience of the theatre, we are amazed to find it almost utterly blank. All the great plays of the world have been written by men who have been familiar with the theatre from their childhood; but, when Stevenson tried his hand at writing plays, he had no fund of memory to draw upon, except his memory of the pasteboard and paint-box plays that have immortalized, through him, the name of Skelt.

In Mr. Balfour's biography of his cousin and friend (Volume I, page 161) there is a very significant passage which most Stevensonians have merely darted through in passing. It reads as follows: "Although he had read (and written) plays from his early years, had revelled in the melodramas of the toy-theatre, and had acted with the Jenkins and in other private theatricals, I find no reference to his having visited a theatre before December, 1874, when he found Irving's Hamlet 'interesting (for it is really studied) but not good'; and there is no sign of his having been really impressed until he saw Salvini as Macbeth in Edinburgh in the spring of 1876. Of this performance he wrote a criticism for the *Academy,* which he afterwards condemned as dealing with a subject that was still beyond the resources of his art. He himself, I am told, was never a tolerable actor, and certainly was never allotted a part of any great importance. But his enthusiasm for the drama was great, and during these years" (viz., 1873–76) "was heightened and instructed by the two chief friends who shared his taste—Professor Fleeming Jenkin and Mr. Henley."

The end of our entire investigation is compressed within that paragraph; and all that will be necessary for our present purpose is to expand and annotate it. First of all, let us consider the astounding statement of Stevenson's own cousin that he could "find no reference to his having visited a theatre before December, 1874"—when Stevenson was twenty-four years old!

In considering this statement, we must remember that Stevenson was born into a family that never went to the theatre. To this day it seems to be a tenet of the Scottish religion that all forms of public entertainment are pitfalls of the devil; and this opinion must have been held still more emphatically when Stevenson was a boy. For religious reasons, the drama is still frowned upon in Edinburgh, which remains —in the slang phrase of the stage folk—the "poorest theatre town" among the great cities of the English-speaking world. We know from Stevenson's own essay on his father that the eminent lighthouse engineer and exemplary citizen of Edinburgh held fast to the old ways of thinking on matters of religion. Thomas Stevenson was one of the officers of the congregation of St. Stephen's Church; and no man in that position, in the middle of the nineteenth century, could have countenanced the playhouse. As a result of this curious coincidence of birth, it seems more than probable—as Mr. Balfour has suggested—that Stevenson never entered a theatre till he was twenty-four years old.

For this reason the only impressions of the drama that Stevenson could possibly receive in his childhood and his youth were those received from the toy theatre—which made, in consequence, a disproportionate effect upon his memory— and those received from a casual and unguided reading of printed plays. Of this latter experience, a record is afforded in a passage of his essay on "A College Magazine," wherein he catalogues a number of his earliest attempts at writing: "In *Monmouth,* a tragedy, I reclined on the bosom of Mr.

Swinburne; . . . in the first draft of *The King's Pardon*, a tragedy, I was on the trail of no lesser man than John Webster; in the second draft of the same piece, with staggering versatility, I had shifted my allegiance to Congreve, and of course conceived my fable in a less serious vein—for it was not Congreve's verse, it was his exquisite prose, that I admired and sought to copy." Here we find the young apprentice "playing the sedulous ape" to many dramatists whose strategy and tactics had long been outworn as matters of technical convention, and remaining utterly unaware of this anachronism because he had had as yet no actual experience of the contemporary theatre.

Of the drama as a living reality, he received his first inkling from his friend Professor Fleeming Jenkin. In Chapter VI, Section II, of his *Memoir of Fleeming Jenkin*, Stevenson has recorded in detail the passionate fondness of Jenkin for the drama in general and for private theatricals in particular. It was Jenkin who inspired Stevenson to undertake his only effort in dramatic criticism, the notice in the *Academy*, dated April 15, 1876, of Salvini's first performance of Macbeth. Apropos of the appearance of this criticism, Stevenson remarks: "Fleeming opened the paper, read so far, and flung it on the floor. 'No,' he cried, 'that won't do. You were thinking of yourself, not of Salvini!' The criticism was shrewd as usual, but it was unfair through ignorance; it was not of myself that I was thinking, but of the difficulties of my trade which I had not well mastered." In this characteristically modest addendum to the anecdote, we perceive a clear realization, on the part of Stevenson, of his lack of a sufficient background of experience to warrant his undertaking a major task in histrionic criticism. In truth, the paper on Salvini's Macbeth, though keenly perceptive of several details, is lacking in scholarly completeness and finality.

The most important part with which Stevenson was ever intrusted in Jenkin's private theatricals was that of Orsino in *Twelfth Night*, which was undertaken in April 1875. A humorous account of his rehearsals in this part is conveyed in a letter that was written, at the time, to Mrs. Sitwell (*Letters*, new edition, Volume I, pages 213–14). In the summer of 1910 it was my privilege to converse with Mrs. Fleeming Jenkin (who was the Viola of that performance set forth thirty-five years before) concerning Stevenson's qualities as an actor. She told me that he had a fine voice, and read well (though somewhat artificially); that he was too self-conscious on the stage to sink his own personality into that of any character he might be playing; and that his work was marred by the fact that he never took the rehearsals seriously but regarded them merely as an occasion for antic sport and gaiety. This personal reminiscence of Stevenson's acting affirms Mr. Balfour's information that he "was never a tolerable actor" and also supports Sir Arthur Pinero's contention that Stevenson was temperamentally inclined to "regard the drama as a matter of child's-play."

Stevenson was rarely in London, and seems never to have formed a habit of going to the theatre on the occasions of his fleeting visits to the capital. It is certain, at least, that he never received an adequate impression of what was being attempted and accomplished in the English theatre of "his own age and generation." He went to the theatre more frequently in Paris, and received his most vivid impressions of the art of acting from the performances of the Comédie-Française. From first to last, however, these impressions were those of an outsider, instead of those of an initiate and an apprentice to the craft.

On one of his visits to Paris, in the middle of his twenties, Stevenson attended a performance of *The Demi-Monde* of Dumas *fils;* and, on this occasion, the incident occurred which he narrated, several years later, in a letter to Mr. William Archer (dated Saranac Lake, February 1888): "It happened thus. I came forth from that performance in a breathing heat of indignation. . . . On my way down the Française stairs, I trod on an old gentleman's toes, whereupon with that suavity which so well becomes me, I turned to apólogize, and on the instant, repenting me of that intention, stopped the apology midway, but added something in French to this effect: 'No, you are one of the *laches* who have been applauding that piece. I retract my apology.' Said the old Frenchman, laying his hand on my arm, and with a smile that was truly heavenly in temperance, irony, good-nature, and knowledge of the world, *'Ah, monsieur, vous êtes bien jeune!'* " This anecdote is delightful from many points of view; but, for our present purpose, it is most necessary to observe that in the presence of what is now generally regarded as one of the greatest masterpieces of the technique of the drama in the nineteenth century, Stevenson remained unmoved by any admiration of its artistic excellence and merely exhibited his Scottish temperament in revolting against its subject matter. Here, indeed, we observe the attitude of a congenital outsider, instead of that of an admitted apprentice to the craft of dramaturgy.

On one occasion (as we learn from the new edition of the *Letters*) Stevenson made a careful study of the plays of Dumas *père* and set down several cogently appreciative comments on the craft of this rude but mighty giant of the theatre; but this is the only recorded instance of his having made a systematic analysis of the work of any dramatist. In the third paragraph of his essay on "Victor Hugo's Romances," Stevenson set forth a theory of the respective limitations of the drama and the novel; but this theory, though acute in many ways, was easily exploded by Sir Leslie Stephen in a letter (accepting Stevenson's essay for publication in the *Cornhill Magazine*) which is printed in full in the new edition of the Stevenson *Letters* (Volume I, pages 155–57). Again, in the second paragraph of his essay entitled "A Gossip on Romance," Stevenson draws a distinction between drama as "the poetry of conduct" and romance as "the poetry of circumstance." But such utterances as these belong obviously to the realm of abstract theory and afford no evidence of any practical consideration of the drama as a craft.

With the exception of *Deacon Brodie*, which was merely a revision of an early work, the plays of Stevenson and Henley were composed during the period of Stevenson's residence at Bournemouth, from 1884 to 1887. He was, at that time, from thirty-four to thirty-seven years of age. His health was at its lowest ebb; most of his time was spent perforce in bed; and his main motive in embarking on the collaboration was merely to enliven the intervals of his lingering in "the land of counterpane" by a playful exercise of spirits in the company of a spirited and eager friend. Henley took the task more seriously; but Stevenson never came to consider it with that intentness through which alone a sure success might possibly have been attained in an endeavor that, according to Sir Arthur Pinero, can be accomplished "only in the sweat of the brain, with every mental nerve and sinew strained to its uttermost."

It remains also to be added that, though *Deacon Brodie*, *Admiral Guinea,* and *Beau Austin* have all been acted in the theatre, Stevenson never witnessed a performance of any of his plays. He was never even privileged to see a scene of his enacted in rehearsal. This simple fact affords emphatic evidence of that unfortunate aloofness from the actual theatre which Sir Arthur Pinero had adduced in explanation of our inability to "acclaim him among the masters of the modern stage."

CLAYTON HAMILTON

July 1914

Robert Louis Stevenson as a Dramatist

Ladies and Gentlemen: Some of you, perhaps—and some, too, who would call themselves ardent Stevensonians—are scarcely aware that Robert Louis Stevenson was a dramatist at all, that he ever essayed the dramatic form. If I were to ask those among my audience who have read his three plays to hold up a hand, I fear the demonstration would not be a very considerable one; and that demonstration would be still less imposing, I think, if my question were to take this shape —"How many of you have seen one or other of these works upon the stage?" Yet it is a fact that Stevenson wrote, or at any rate actively collaborated in, three plays. Three plays? More—four, five. But two of the five I propose to disregard entirely. One, *The Hanging Judge*, written in collaboration with Mrs. Stevenson, has never been published and may therefore be regarded as exempt from criticism. The other, *Macaire*, does not profess to be an original work except in details of dialogue. We will, therefore, with your permission, put that, also, aside and concentrate our attention on the three original plays—*Deacon Brodie, Beau Austin*, and *Admiral Guinea*—which Stevenson produced in collaboration with Mr. William Ernest Henley. Now, I wish to enquire why it is that these two men, both, in their different ways, of distinguished talent, combining, with great gusto and hopefulness, to produce acting dramas, should have made such small mark with them, either on or off the stage. *Deacon Brodie* was acted a good many times in America, but only once, I believe, in Great Britain. *Beau Austin* has been publicly presented some score of times; *Admiral Guinea* has enjoyed but a single performance. Nor have these pieces pro-

55

duced a much greater effect in the study, as the phrase goes. They have their admirers, of whom, in many respects, I am one. I hope to draw your attention, before we part this evening—if you will allow me to do so—to some of the sterling beauties they contain. But no one, I think, gives even *Beau Austin* a very high place among Stevenson's works as a whole; and many people who have probably read every other line that Stevenson wrote, have, as I say, scarcely realized the existence of his drama. Why should Stevenson the dramatist take such a back seat, if you will pardon the expression, in comparison with Stevenson the novelist, the essayist, the poet?

This question seems to me all the more worth asking because Stevenson's case is by no means a singular one. There is hardly a novelist or poet of the whole nineteenth century who does not stand in exactly the same position. They have one and all attempted to write for the stage, and it is scarcely too much to say that they have one and all failed, not only to achieve theatrical success but even, in any appreciable degree, to enrich our dramatic literature. Some people, perhaps, will claim Shelley and Browning as exceptions. Well, I won't attempt to argue the point—I will content myself with asking you what rank Shelley would have held among our poets had he written nothing but *The Cenci*, or Browning if his fame rested solely on *Strafford* and *A Blot in the 'Scutcheon*. For the rest, Scott, Coleridge, Wordsworth, Keats, all produced dramas of a more or less abortive kind. Some of Byron's plays, which he justly declared unsuited for the stage, were forced by fine acting and elaborate scenic embellishment into a sort of success; but how dead they are to-day! and how low a place they hold among the poet's works! Dickens and Thackeray both loved the theatre, and both wrote for it without the smallest success. Of Lord Tennyson's plays, two, *The Cup* and *Becket*, in the second of which Sir Henry Irving has given us one of his noblest performances, were so admirably mounted and rendered by that great actor that they enjoyed considerable prosperity in the theatre; but no critic ever dreamt of assigning either to them or to any other of Tennyson's dramas a place co-equal with his non-dramatic poems. Mr. Swinburne has written many plays—has any one of them the smallest chance of being remembered along with *Poems and Ballads* and *Songs before Sunrise?* There is only one exception to the rule that during the nineteenth century

no poet or novelist of the slightest eminence made any success upon the stage, and even that solitary exception is a
dubious one. I refer, as you may surmise, to Bulwer-Lytton.
There is no doubt as to his success; but what does the twentieth century think of his eminence?

If we can lay our finger on the reason of Stevenson's—I
will not say failure—but inadequate success as a playwright,
perhaps it may help us to understand the still more inadequate success of greater men.

And let me here follow the example of that agreeable essayist, Euclid, and formulate my theorem in advance—or in
other words indicate the point towards which I hope to lead
you. We shall find, I think, that Stevenson, with all his genius, failed to realize that the art of drama is not stationary,
but progressive. By this I do not mean that it is always im-
proving; but what I do mean is that its conditions are always
changing, and that every dramatist whose ambition it is to
produce live plays is absolutely bound to study carefully, and
I may even add respectfully—at any rate not contemptuously
—the conditions that hold good for his own age and generation. This Stevenson did not—would not—do. We shall find,
I think, that in all his plays he was deliberately imitating
outworn models, and doing it, too. in a sportive, half-disdain-
ful spirit, as who should say, "The stage is a realm of absurdities—come, let us be cleverly absurd!" In that spirit,
ladies and gentlemen, success never was and never will be
attained. I do not mean to imply, of course, that this was the
spirit in which the other great writers I have mentioned—
Shelley, Browning, Tennyson, and the rest—approached their
work as dramatists. But I do suggest that they one and all,
like Stevenson, set themselves to imitate outworn models, instead of discovering for themselves, and if necessary ennobling, the style of drama really adapted to the dramatist's
one great end—that of showing the age and body of the time
his form and pressure. The difference is that while Stevenson imitated the transpontine plays of the early nineteenth
century, most of the other writers I have named imitated
the Elizabethan dramatists. The difference is not essential to
my point—the error lies in the mere fact of imitation. One
of the great rules—perhaps the only universal rule—of the
drama is that you cannot pour new wine into old skins.

Some of the great men I have mentioned were debarred
from success for a reason which is still more simple and ob-

vious—namely, that they had no dramatic talent. But this was not Stevenson's case. No one can doubt that he had in him the ingredients of a dramatist. What is dramatic talent? Is it not the power to project characters, and to cause them to tell an interesting story through the medium of dialogue? This is *dramatic* talent; and dramatic talent, if I may so express it, is the raw material of theatrical talent. Dramatic, like poetic, talent is born, not made; if it is to achieve success on the stage it must be developed into theatrical talent by hard study, and generally by long practice. For theatrical talent consists in the power of making your characters, not only tell a story by means of dialogue, but tell it in such skilfully-devised form and order as shall, within the limits of an ordinary theatrical representation, give rise to the greatest possible amount of that peculiar kind of emotional effect, the production of which is the one great function of the theatre. Now, dramatic talent Stevenson undoubtedly possessed in abundance; and I am convinced that theatrical talent was well within his reach, if only he had put himself to the pains of evolving it.

Need I prove the dramatic talent of the author of *Prince Otto, The Master of Ballantrae, The Ebb-Tide,* and *The Weir of Hermiston?* If I once began reading scenes to demonstrate it, I should not know where to leave off. I prefer, then, to read you, not any single scene, but a whole drama which, as Stevenson assures us in his "Chapter on Dreams," came to him in the visions of the night. He is showing how his Little People—his Brownies as he calls them; the Brownies of the brain—go on working in sleep, independently of the dreamer's volition, and how in his case they would sometimes hit upon strange felicities. "This dreamer," he says—and by "this dreamer" he means himself—"this dreamer has encountered some trifling vicissitudes of fortune. When the bank begins to send letters and the butcher to linger at the back gate, he sets to belabouring his brains after a story, for that is his readiest money-winner; and behold! at once the Little People begin to bestir themselves in the same quest, and labouring all night long, and all night long set before him truncheons of tales upon their lighted theatre. . . . How often have these sleepless Brownies done him honest service, and given him, as he sat idly taking his pleasure in the boxes, better tales than he could fashion for himself. Here is one, exactly as it came to him. It seemed he was the son of a

very rich and wicked man, the owner of broad acres and a
most damnable temper. The dreamer (and that was the son)
had lived much abroad, on purpose to avoid his parent; and
when at length he returned to England, it was to find him
married again to a young wife, who was supposed to suffer
cruelly and to loathe her yoke. Because of this marriage (as
the dreamer indistinctly understood) it was desirable for
father and son to have a meeting; and yet both being proud
and both angry, neither would condescend upon a visit. Meet
they did accordingly, in a desolate, sandy country by the sea;
and there they quarrelled; and the son, stung by some intolerable insult, struck down the father dead. No suspicion was
aroused; the dead man was found and buried, and the
dreamer succeeded to the broad estates, and found himself
installed under the same roof with his father's widow, for whom
no provision had been made. These two lived very much alone,
as people may after a bereavement, sat down to table together, shared the long evenings, and grew daily better
friends; until it seemed to him of a sudden that she was
prying about dangerous matters, that she had conceived a
notion of his guilt, that she watched him and tried him with
questions. He drew back from her company as men draw back
from a precipice suddenly discovered; and yet so strong was
the attraction that he would drift again and again into the
old intimacy, and again and again be startled back by some
suggestive question or some inexplicable meaning in her eye.
So they lived at cross-purposes, a life full of broken dialogue, challenging glances, and suppressed passion; until, one
day, he saw the woman slipping from the house in a veil, followed her to the station, followed her in the train to the sea-
side country, and out over the sand-hills to the very place
where the murder was done. There she began to grope among
the bents, he watching her, flat upon his face; and presently
she had something in her hand—I cannot remember what it
was, but it was deadly evidence against the dreamer—and as
she held it up to look at it, perhaps from the shock of the discovery, her foot slipped, and she hung at some peril on the
brink of the tall sandwreaths. He had no thought but to
spring up and rescue her; and there they stood face to face,
she with that deadly matter openly in her hand—his very
presence on the spot another link of proof. It was plain she
was about to speak, but this was more than he could bear—
he could bear to be lost, but not to talk of it with his de-

stroyer; and he cut her short with trivial conversation. Arm
in arm, they returned together to the train, talking he knew
not what, made the journey in the same carriage, sat down
to dinner, and passed the evening in the drawing-room as in
the past. But suspense and fear drummed in the dreamer's
bosom. 'She has not denounced me yet'—so his thoughts ran;
'when will she denounce me? Will it be to-morrow?' And it
was not to-morrow, nor the next day, nor the next; and their
life settled back on the old terms, only that she seemed kinder
than before, and that, as for him, the burden of his suspense
and wonder grew daily more unbearable, so that he wasted
away like a man with a disease. Once indeed, he broke all
bounds of decency, seized an occasion when she was abroad,
ransacked her room, and at last, hidden away among her
jewels, found the damning evidence. There he stood, holding
this thing, which was his life, in the hollow of his hand, and
marvelling at her inconsequent behaviour, that she should
seek, and keep, and yet not use it; and then the door opened,
and behold herself. So, once more, they stood, eye to eye,
with the evidence between them; and once more she raised to
him a face brimming with some communication; and once
more he shied away from speech and cut her off. But before
he left the room, which he had turned upside down, he laid
back his death-warrant where he had found it; and at that,
her face lighted up. The next thing he heard, she was explaining to her maid, with some ingenious falsehood, the disorder
of her things. Flesh and blood could bear the strain no longer;
and I think it was the next morning (though chronology is
always hazy in the theatre of the mind) that he burst from
his reserve. They had been breakfasting together in one corner
of a great, parqueted, sparsely-furnished room of many win-
dows; all the time of the meal she had tortured him with sly
allusions; and no sooner were the servants gone, and these
two protagonists alone together, than he leapt to his feet. She
too sprang up, with a pale face; with a pale face she heard
him as he raved out his complaint: Why did she torture him
so? she knew all, she knew he was no enemy to her; why
did she not denounce him at once? what signified her whole
behaviour? why did she torture him? and yet again, why did
she torture him? And when he had done, she fell upon her
knees, and with outstretched hands: 'Do you not understand?' she cried. 'I love you!' "
An intensely dramatic tale, I venture to think, ladies and

gentlemen! one perhaps calculated to shock those who deny
to dramatic art the right—in the words of Browning—"to
paint man man, whatever the issue"; nevertheless, an intensely dramatic tale. Now, we will not enquire whether we
are bound to believe that this highly dramatic story actually
came to Stevenson in a dream. No doubt he believed that it
did; but perhaps, like ordinary mortals, he unconsciously
touched up the dream in the telling, and touched it up with
the vivacity of genius. But that is nothing to our purpose. It
is certain that in one way or another, whether in his sleeping
or his waking moments, the drama I have just recounted to
you came into, and came out of, Stevenson's brain; and I
fancy you will agree with me that a finer dramatic conception has seldom come out of any brain. Now mark what is
his own comment upon it. Having finished the tale, he proceeds: "Hereupon, with a pang of wonder and mercantile
delight, the dreamer awoke. His mercantile delight was not
of long endurance; for it soon became plain that in this
spirited tale there were unmarketable elements; which is
just the reason why you have it here so briefly told." I will
ask you, ladies and gentlemen, to bear in mind this "mercantile delight," this abandonment of the theme because of its
"unmarketable elements." To these points we will return
later on. Meanwhile, the extract I have so lamely recited has,
I hope, served its purpose in enabling you to realize beyond
all question that Stevenson had in him a large measure of
dramatic talent—what I have called the ingredients, the mak-
ings, of a dramatist.

Now let me revive in your memory another of Stevenson's
essays which throws a curious light upon his mental attitude
towards the theatre. I refer to that delightful essay in *Memories and Portraits* called "A Penny Plain and Twopence Coloured." It describes, as many of you will remember, his juvenile delight in those sheets of toy-theatre characters, which,
even when he wrote, had "become, for the most part, a memory" and are now, I believe, almost extinct. "I have at different times," he says, "possessed *Aladdin, The Red Rover,
The Blind Boy, The Old Oak Chest, The Wood Demon, Jack
Shepard, The Miller and His Men, The Smuggler, The Forest
of Bondy, Robin Hood,* and *Three-Fingered Jack, The Terror
of Jamaica*; and I have assisted others in the illumination of
The Maid of the Inn and *The Battle of Waterloo*." Then he
tells how, in a window in Leith Walk, all the year round,

"there stood displayed a theatre in working order, with a 'forest set,' a 'combat,' and a few 'robbers carousing' in the slides; and below and about, tenfold dearer to me! the plays themselves, those budgets of romance, lay tumbled one upon another. Long and often have I lingered there with empty pockets. One figure, we shall say, was visible in the first plate of characters, bearded, pistol in hand, or drawing to his ear the clothyard arrow; I would spell the name; was it Macaire" —one of the subjects, you see, which he afterwards chose for stage treatment—"or Long Tom Coffin, or Grindoff, 2d dress? Oh, how I would long to see the rest! how—if the name by chance were hidden—I would wonder in what play he figured, and what immortal legend justified his attitude and strange apparel!" He then goes on to describe the joy that attended the colouring of the "penny plain" plates—"nor can I quite forgive," he says, "that child who, wilfully foregoing pleasure, stoops to 'twopence coloured.' With crimson lake (hark to the sound of it—crimson lake!—the horns of elf-land are not richer on the ear)—with crimson lake and Prussian blue, a certain purple is to be commended which, for cloaks especially, Titian could not equal. The latter colour with gamboge, a hated name, though an exquisite pigment, supplied a green of such savoury greenness that to-day my heart regrets it. Nor can I recall without a tender weakness the very aspect of the water where I dipped my brush." All this is delightful—is it not?—deliciously and admirably Stevensonian. The unfortunate thing is that even to his dying day he continued to regard the actual theatre as only an enlarged form of the toy theatres which had fascinated his childhood —he continued to use in his dramatic colouring the crimson lake and Prussian blue of transpontine romance—he considered his function as a dramatist very little more serious than that child's-play with paint-box and pasteboard on which his memory dwelt so fondly. He played at being a playwright; and, ladies and gentlemen, he was fundamentally in error in regarding the drama as a matter of child's-play.

Observe, too, that these dramas of the toy theatre were, before they reached the toy theatre, designed for almost the lowest class of theatrical audiences. They were stark and staring melodramas. Most of them were transpontine in the literal sense of the word—that is to say, they had originally seen the light at the humbler theatres beyond the bridges— the Surrey and the Coburg. Many of them were unacknowledged adaptations from the French—for in the early years of the nineteenth century the English dramatist had not acquired that nice conscientiousness which he has since displayed. Yet a drama which was sufficiently popular to be transferred to the toy theatres was almost certain to have a sort of rude merit in its construction. The characterization would be hopelessly conventional, the dialogue bald and despicable—but the situations would be artfully arranged, the story told adroitly and with spirit. Unfortunately these merits did not come within Stevenson's ken. I don't know whether any one could have discovered them in the text-books issued with the sheets of characters; he, at any rate, did not, for he tells us so. "The fable," he says, "as set forth in the play-book, proved to be not worthy of the scenes and characters. . . . Indeed, as literature, these dramas did not much appeal to me. I forget the very outline of the plots." In other words, what little merit there was in the plays escaped him. What he remembered and delighted in was simply their absurdities —the crude inconsistencies of their characters, the puerilities of their technique. But here we must distinguish. There are two parts of technique, which I may perhaps call its strategy and its tactics. In strategy—in the general laying out of a play—these transpontine dramatists were often, as I have said, more than tolerably skilful; but in tactics, in the art of getting their characters on and off the stage, of conveying information to the audience and so forth, they were almost incredibly careless and conventional. They would make a man, as in the Chinese theatre, tell the whole story of his life in a soliloquy; or they would expound their plot to the audience in pages of conversation between characters who acquaint each other with nothing that is not already perfectly well known to both. Well, his childish studies accustomed Stevenson to the miserable tactics of these plays. Keenly as he afterwards realized their absurdities, he had nevertheless in a measure become inured to them. For the merits of their strategy, on the other hand, he had naturally, as a mere child, no eye whatever. And one main reason of his inadequate success as a dramatist was that he never either unlearned their tactics or learned their strategy. Had he ever thoroughly understood what was good in them, I have no doubt that, on the basis of this rough-and-ready melodramatic technique, he would have developed a technique of his own as admirable as that which he ultimately achieved in fiction.

When he first attempts drama, what is the theme he chooses? A story of crime, a story of housebreaking, of dark lanterns, jimmies, center-bits, masks, detectives, boozing-kens—in short a melodrama of the deepest dye, exactly after the Surrey, the Coburg, the toy-theatre type. It evidently pleased him to think that he could put fresh life into this old and puerile form, as he had put, or was soon to put, fresh life into the boy's tale of adventure. And he did, indeed, write a good deal of vivacious dialogue—the literary quality of the play, though poor in comparison with Stevenson's best work, is of course incomparably better than that of the models on which he was founding. But unfortunately it shows no glimmer of their stagecraft. The drama is entitled, you remember, *Deacon Brodie or the Double Life*. Its hero is a historical character who held a position of high respectability in eighteenth-century Edinburgh while he devoted his leisure moments to the science and art of burglary. Here was a theme in which Fitzball, or any of the Coburg melodramatists, would indeed have revelled, a theme almost as fertile of melodramatic possibilities as that of *Sweeny Todd, the Barber of Fleet Street*. And one would have thought that the future author of *Dr. Jekyll and Mr. Hyde* was precisely the man to get its full effect out of the "double life" of his burglar hero. But not a bit of it. From sheer lack of stagecraft, the effect of the "double life" is wholly lost. Brodie is a patent, almost undisguised scoundrel throughout. There is no contrast between the respectable and the criminal sides to his life, no gradual unmasking of his depravity, no piling up, atom by atom, of evidence against him. Our wonder from the first is that anyone should ever have regarded him as anything else than the poor, blustering, blundering villain he is. From the total ineffectiveness of the character, one cannot but imagine that Stevenson was hampered by the idea of representing strictly the historical personage. In this, for aught I know, he may have succeeded; but he has certainly not succeeded in making his protagonist interesting in the theatre, or in telling the story so as to extract one tithe of its possibilities of dramatic effect. As for his technique, let one specimen suffice. I will read you one of the many soliloquies—the faulty method of conducting action and revealing character by soliloquy was one from which Stevenson could never emancipate himself. It is a speech delivered by Deacon Brodie

while he is making preparations for a midnight gambling ex-
cursion.

"(*Brodie closes, locks, and double-locks the doors of his
bedroom.*)
"Now for one of the Deacon's headaches! Rogues all,
rogues all! (*He goes to the clothes-press and proceeds to
change his coat.*) On with the new coat, and into the new
life! Down with the Deacon and up with the robber! Eh
God! how still the house is! There's something in hypocrisy
after all. If we were as good as we seem, what would the
world be? The city has its vizard on, and we—at night we
are our naked selves. Trysts are keeping, bottles cracking,
knives are stripping; and here is Deacon Brodie flaming forth
the man of men he is! How still it is. . . . My father and
Mary— Well! the day for them, the night for me; the grimy
cynical night that makes all cats grey, and all honesties of
one complexion. Shall a man not have *half* a life of his own?
not eight hours out of twenty-four? Eight shall he have,
should he dare the pit of Tophet. Where is the blunt? I must
be cool tonight, or . . . steady, Deacon, you must win; damn
you, you must! You must win back the dowry that you've
stolen, and marry your sister, and pay your debts, and gull
the world a little longer! The Deacon's going to bed—the
poor sick Deacon! *Allons!* Only the stars to see me! I'm a
man once more till morning."

But it is needless to dwell long on *Deacon Brodie*—ripe-
ness of stagecraft is not to be looked for in a first attempt,
a prentice piece. The play is chiefly interesting as exemplify-
ing the boyish spirit of gleeful bravado in which Stevenson
approached the stage. Again I say his instinct was to play
with it, as he had played, when a boy, with his pasteboard
theatre.

In *Admiral Guinea*—a much better drama—the influence
of his penny-plain-twopence-coloured studies is, if possible,
still more apparent. *Deacon Brodie* was the melodrama of
crime; this was to be the nautical melodrama. As the one
belonged to the school of *Sweeny Todd*, so the other was to
follow in the wake of *Black-Ey'd Susan, The Red Rover, Ben
Backstay,* and those other romances of the briny deep in
which that celebrated impersonator of seafaring types, T. P.

Cooke, had made his fame. If you require a proof of the intimate relation between *Admiral Guinea* and *Skelt's Juvenile Drama,* as the toy-theatre plays are called, let me draw your attention to this little coincidence. In his essay on the Juvenile Drama, Stevenson enlarges not only on the sheets of characters, but also on the scenery which accompanied them. "Here is the cottage interior," he writes, "the usual first flat, with the cloak upon the nail, the rosaries of onions, the gun and powder-horn and corner cupboard; here is the inn —(this drama must be nautical: I foresee Captain Luff and Bold Bob Bowsprit)—here is the inn with the red curtains, pipes, spittoons, and eight-day clock." Well now, the two scenes of *Admiral Guinea* reproduce, with a little elaboration, exactly the two scenes here sketched. The first is the cottage interior with the corner cupboard; the second is thus described: "The stage represents the parlor of the Admiral Benbow inn. Fire-place right, with high-backed settles on each side. . . . Tables left, with glasses, pipes, etc. . . . window with red half curtains; spittoons; candles on both the front tables." Here, you see, he draws in every detail upon his memories of the toy-theatre. And in writing this play his effort was constantly, and one may almost say confessedly, to reproduce the atmosphere of conventional nautical melodrama—to re-handle its material while replacing its bald language with dialogue of high literary merit. And of course he succeeded in writing many speeches of great beauty. Take this for instance. It is the scene in the first act between John Gaunt—called *Admiral Guinea*—Kit French, a privateersman, and Gaunt's daughter Arethusa. Arethusa, you will remember, is the pretty virtuous maiden of nautical melodrama; Kit the careless, harem-scarem young sea-dog in love with the virtuous maiden and desirous, in his weak way, of casting his reckless habits behind him and of becoming a respectable and respected coasting skipper. Gaunt, a vigorously-drawn character, was once, I may remind you, captain of a slaver but is now an altered man, harsh, pious, repentant. Gaunt, entering his room, surprises Kit French and his daughter together.

Kit standing beside Arethusa, her hand in his, says to the father, "Captain Gaunt, I have come to ask you for your daughter." The old man sinks into his chair with a growl. "I love her," says Kit, "and she loves me, sir. I've left the privateering. I've enough to set me up and buy a tidy sloop—

Jack Lee's, you know the boat, Captain; clinker built, not four years old, eighty tons burden, steers like a child. I've put my mother's ring on Arethusa's finger; and if you'll give us your blessing, I'll engage to turn over a new leaf and make her a good husband."

GAUNT. In whose strength, Christopher French?

KIT. In the strength of my good, honest love for her; as you did for her mother, and my father for mine. And you know, Captain, a man can't command the wind; but (excuse me, sir) he can always lie the best course possible, and that's what I'll do, so God help me.

GAUNT. Arethusa, you at least are the child of many prayers; your eyes have been unsealed; and to you the world stands naked, a morning watch for duration, a thing spun of cobwebs for solidity. In the presence of an angry God, I ask you: have you heard this man?

ARETHUSA. Father, I know Kit, and I love him.

GAUNT. I say it solemnly, this is no Christian union. To you, Christopher French, I will speak nothing of eternal truths; I will speak to you the language of this world. You have been trained among sinners who glorified in their sin; in your whole life you never saved one farthing; and now, when your pockets are full, you think you can begin, poor dupe, in your own strength. You are a roysterer, a jovial companion; you mean no harm—you are nobody's enemy but your own. No doubt you tell this girl of mine, and no doubt you tell yourself, that you can change. Christopher, speaking under correction, I defy you! You ask me for this child of many supplications, for this brand plucked from the burning: I look at you: I read you through and through; and I tell you—no!

KIT. Captain Gaunt, if you mean that I am not worthy of her, I'm the first to say so. But, if you'll excuse me, sir, I'm a young man, and young men are no better'n they ought to be; it's known, they're all like that; and what's their chance? To be married to a girl like this! And would you refuse it to me? Why, sir, you yourself, when you came courting, you were young and rough; and yet I'll make bold to say that Mrs. Gaunt was a happy woman, and the saving of yourself into the bargain. Well, now, Captain Gaunt, will you deny another man, and that man a sailor, the very salvation that you had yourself?

GAUNT. Salvation, Christopher French, is from above.

KIT. Well, sir, that is so; but there's means, too; and what means so strong as the wife a man has to strive and toil for, and that bears the punishment whenever he goes wrong? Now, sir, I've spoke with your old shipmates in the Guinea trade. Hard as nails, they said, and true as the compass; as rough as a slaver but as just as a judge. Well, sir, you hear me plead: I ask you for my chance; don't you deny it to me.

GAUNT. You speak of me? In the true balance we both weigh nothing. But two things I know; the death of iniquity, how foul it is; and the agony with which a man repents. Not until seven devils were cast out of me did I awake; each rent me as it passed. Ay, that was repentance. Christopher, Christopher, you have sailed before the wind since first you weighed your anchor, and now you think to sail upon a bowline? You do not know your ship, young man: you will go to leeward like a sheet of paper; I tell you so that know— I tell you so that have tried, and failed, and wrestled in the sweat of prayer, and at last, at last, have tasted grace. But, meanwhile, no flesh and blood of mine shall lie at the mercy of such a wretch as I was then, or as you are this day. I could not own the deed before the face of heaven, if I sanctioned this unequal yoke. Arethusa, pluck off that ring from off your finger. Christopher French, take it, and go hence.

KIT. Arethusa, what do you say?

ARETHUSA. O Kit, you know my heart. But he is alone, and I am his only comfort; and I owe all to him; and shall I not obey my father? But, Kit, if you will let me, I will keep your ring. Go, Kit; go, and prove to my father that he was mistaken; go and win me. And O, Kit, if ever you should weary, come to me—no, do not come! but send me a word— and I shall know all, and you shall have your ring.

KIT. Don't say that, don't say such things to me; I sink or swim with you. Old man, you've struck me hard; give me a good word to go with. Name your time; I'll stand the test. Give me a spark of hope, and I'll fight through for it. Say just this—"Prove I was mistaken"—and by George, I'll prove it.

GAUNT. (*Looking up.*) I make no such compacts. Go, and swear not at all.

Again, take the scene between Gaunt and Pew, the ruffianly blind beggar, once boatswain of the *Arethusa*, who, armed with the knowledge of Gaunt's past, comes to his old captain to extort money from him. They stand face to face. "Well?" says Gaunt. "Well, Cap'n?" says Pew. "What do you want?" asks Gaunt.

PEW. Well, Admiral, in a general way, what I want in a manner of speaking is money and rum.

GAUNT. David Pew, I have known you a long time.

PEW. And so you have; aboard the old *Arethusa*; and you don't seem that cheered up as I'd looked for, with an old shipmate dropping in, one as has been seeking you two years and more—and blind at that. What a swaller you had for a pannikin of rum, and what a fist for the shiners! Ah, Cap'n, they didn't call you Admiral Guinea for nothing. I can see that old sea-chest of yours—her with the brass bands, where you kept your gold dust and doubloons; you know?—I can see her as well this minute as though you and me was still at it playing put on the lid of her. . . . You don't say nothing, Cap'n? . . . Well, here it is: I want money and I want rum. You don't know what it is to want rum, you don't: it gets to that p'int, that you would kill a 'ole ship's company for just one guttle of it. What, Admiral Guinea, my old Commander, go back on poor old Pew? and him high and dry?

GAUNT. David Pew, it were better for you that you were sunk in fifty fathom. I know your life; and first and last, it is one broadside of wickedness. You were a porter in a school, and beat a boy to death; you ran for it, turned slaver, and shipped with me, a green hand. Ay, that was the craft for you; that was the right craft, and I was the right captain; there was none worse that sailed to Guinea. Well, what came of that? In five years' time you made yourself the terror and abhorrence of your messmates. The worst hands detested you; your captain—that was me, John Gaunt, the chief of sinners—cast you out for a Jonah. Ay, you were a scandal to the Guinea coast from Lagos down to Calabar; and when at last I sent you ashore, a marooned man—your shipmates, devils as they were, cheering and rejoicing to be quit of you —by heaven, it was a ton's weight off the brig.

PEW. Cap'n Gaunt, Cap'n Gaunt, these are ugly words.

GAUNT. What next? You shipped with Flint the Pirate. What you did then I know not; the deep seas have kept the secret; kept it, ay, and will keep it against the Great Day. God smote you with blindness, but you heeded not the sign.

That was His last mercy; look for no more. To your knees, man, and repent. Pray for a new heart; flush out your sins with tears; flee while you may from the terrors of the wrath to come.

PEW. Now, I want this clear: Do I understand that you're going back on me, and you'll see me damned first?

GAUNT. Of me you shall have neither money nor strong drink; not a guinea to spend in riot; not a drop to fire your heart with deviltry.

PEW. Cap'n, do you think it wise to quarrel with me? I put it to you now, Cap'n, fairly as between man and man—do you think it wise?

GAUNT. I fear nothing. My feet are on the Rock, Begone!

The play is full of speeches as beautiful as these I have just read you of Gaunt's; and if beautiful speeches, and even beautiful passages, of dialogue, made a good drama, *Admiral Guinea* would indeed be a great success. But what chiefly strikes one after seeing or reading the play is that Stevenson's idea of dramatic writing was that fine speeches, and fine speeches alone, would carry everything before them. I can picture the collaborators sitting together and discussing the composition of their work, and saying to each other, "This position, or that, will furnish a capital opportunity for a good speech"; I can imagine Stevenson subsequently telling his friend what a splendid "speech" he had just written. In short, *Admiral Guinea* is mainly rhetoric, beautifully done but with no blood in it. The second act—the inn scene—is a monument of long-windedness; while the situation of Gaunt's walking in his sleep—by which Stevenson's friends and admirers, on the occasion of the production of the play in London, set such store—could be cut out of the drama bodily for any bearing it has upon the development of the story or the bringing about of the dénouement. I was a witness of the single performance of this piece in London and can testify to the ineffectiveness of its representation.

In *Beau Austin* we have certainly Stevenson's nearest approach to an effective drama. In spite of its inacceptable theme, it is a charming play and really interesting on the stage. A little more careful handling of the last act might have rendered it wholly successful. But still we see traces of the old crudity of technique of the toy-theatre, and still the author evidently conceived that the essence of the drama resides in rhetoric, in fine speeches. How artless, for instance, is the scene of exposition, between the heroine's aunt, Miss Foster, and the maid, Barbara, in which half the time Miss Foster is telling Barbara things she knows perfectly well already, and the other half saying things she would never have said to a maid. Then, when it comes to revealing to us the recesses of Dorothy's heart, what do the authors do? They make her speak a solid page and a half of soliloquy—exquisitely composed, but again how rhetorical, how undramatic. So elegant is this soliloquy that I cannot refrain from murdering it for your benefit. You remember the position—Dorothy Musgrave is hugging a terrible secret to her breast, her betrayal by George Frederick Austin, the Beau Austin of the play. She has just received a letter from John Fenwick, an old and faithful lover, and her aunt has been upbraiding the girl on account of her declared determination never to marry. Dorothy, left alone, says:

"How she tortures me, poor aunt, my poor blind aunt; and I—I could break her heart with a word. That she should see nothing, know nothing—there's where it kills. Oh, it is more than I can bear. . . . and yet how much less than I deserve! Mad girl, of what do I complain? that this dear innocent woman still believes me good, still pierces me to the soul with trustfulness. Alas, and were it otherwise, were her dear eyes opened to the truth, what were left me but death? He, too—she must still be praising him, and every word is a lash upon my conscience. If I could die of my secret; if I could cease—but one moment cease—this living lie; if I could sleep and forget and be at rest! (*She reads John Fenwick's letter.*) Poor John! He at least is guiltless; and yet for my fault he too must suffer, he too must bear part in my shame. Poor John Fenwick! Has he come back with the old story; with what might have been perhaps, had we stayed by Edenside? Eden? yes, my Eden, from which I fell. O my old north country, my old river—the river of my innocence, the old country of my hopes—how could I endure to look on you now? And how to meet John?—John, with the old love on his lips, the old, honest, innocent, faithful heart? There was a Dorothy once who was not unfit to ride with him, her heart as light as his, her life as clear as the bright rivers we forded; he called her his Diana, he crowned her so with rowan. Where is that Dorothy now? that Diana? she that was everything to John? For, oh, I did him good; I know I did him good; I will still believe I did him good; I made him honest and kind and a true man; alas, and could not guide myself! And now, how will he despise me! For he shall know; if I die, he shall know all; I could not live, and not be true with him."

She produces a necklace which she has discovered in the possession of the maid, a necklace with which the woman has been bribed by Beau Austin as an inducement to keep her out of the way upon a certain occasion. Dorothy contemplates the trinket and says:

"That he should have bought me from my maid! George, George, that you should have stooped to this! Basely as you have used me, this is the basest. Perish the witness. (*She throws the thing to the ground and treads upon it.*) Break, break, like my heart, break like my hopes, perish like my good name!"

Poorly as I render this soliloquy, you cannot, I think, fail to perceive its extreme gracefulness. Even finer, because it is more naturally introduced, and therefore more dramatic, is an earlier speech of Dorothy's wherein she turns almost fiercely upon her aunt, who has, in ignorance, been praising Beau Austin for his gallantries. "Stop," cries the girl, "Aunt Evelina, stop; I cannot endure to hear you. What is he after all but just Beau Austin? What has he done—with half a century of good health, what has he done that is either memorable or worthy? Diced and danced and set fashions; vanquished in a drawing-room, fought for a word; what else? As if these were the meaning of life! Do not make me think so poorly of all of us women. Sure, we can rise to admire a better kind of man than Mr. Austin. We are not all to be snared with the eye, dear aunt; and those that are— Oh! I know not whether I more hate or pity them."

Ladies and gentlemen, it is not my intention to trouble you with any further extracts from this play. I should, I fear, lay myself open to a charge of unfairness by quoting scenes with the sole object of proving their ineffectiveness, even tediousness. I ask you to turn, at your leisure, to *Beau Austin* and to study the play for yourselves. I ask you to read the passages—some of them great passages—of dialogue between Dorothy and Fenwick, between Fenwick and Beau Austin, between the Beau and Dorothy; and I submit to you that while there is much in these passages that is beautiful, much that is true and subtle, there is very little that is truly and subtly ex-

pressed. The beauty the authors aimed at was, I believe you
will agree with me, the absolute beauty of words, such beauty
as Ruskin or Pater or Newman might achieve in an eloquent
passage, not the beauty of dramatic fitness to the character
and the situation.

Now, I am not attacking—and I should be sorry if you so
understood me—that poetical convention which reigns, for
instance, in our great Elizabethan drama. I am not claiming
any absolute and inherent superiority for our modern realistic
technique, though I do not think it quite so inferior as some
critics would have us believe. But what I do say is that the
dramatist is bound to select his particular form of technique,
master, and stick to it. He must not jumble up two styles
and jump from one to the other. That is what the authors
of *Beau Austin* have not realized. Their technique is neither
ancient nor modern; their language is neither poetry nor prose
—the prose, that is to say, of conceivable human life. The
period has nothing to do with it. People spoke, no doubt, a
little more formally in 1820 than they do to-day; but neither
then nor at any time was the business of life, even in its most
passionate moments, conducted in pure oratory. I say, then,
that even in *Beau Austin,* far superior though it be to his
other plays, Stevenson shows that he had not studied and
realized the conditions of the problem he was handling—the
problem of how to tell a dramatic story truly, convincingly,
and effectively on the modern stage—the problem of disclosing the workings of the human heart by methods which shall
not destroy the illusion which a modern audience expects to
enjoy in the modern theatre.

Perhaps you will tell me that the fault lay in some part,
not with Stevenson, but with the modern audience. I do not
maintain that an individual audience never makes mistakes,
or even that the theatrical public in general is a miracle of
high intelligence. But I assert unhesitatingly that the instinct
by which the public feels that one form of drama, and not
another, is what best satisfies its intellectual and spiritual
needs at this period or at that is a natural and justified instinct. Fifty years hence the formula of to-day will doubtless
be as antiquated and ineffective as the formula of fifty years
ago; but it is imposed by a natural fitness upon the dramatist
of to-day, just as, if he wants to travel long distances, he must
be content to take the railroad train, and cannot ride in a
stage-coach or fly in an air-ship. As a personal freak, of

course, he may furbish up a stage-coach or construct—at his risk and peril—an air-ship. Such freaks occur in the dramatic world from time to time, and are often interesting—sometimes, but very rarely, successful. *Deacon Brodie* and *Admiral Guinea* are what I may perhaps describe as stage-coach plays—deliberate attempts to revive an antiquated form. But *Beau Austin* is not even that. It is a costume play, I admit; but its methods are fundamentally and essentially modern. The misfortune is that the authors had not studied and mastered the formula they were attempting to use, but were for ever falling back, without knowing it, upon a by-gone formula, wholly incongruous with the matter of their play and the manner in which alone it could be presented in the theatre of their day.

Many authors, of course, have deliberately written plays "for the study," ignoring—or more often, perhaps, affecting to ignore—the possibility of stage presentation. But this was not Stevenson's case; nor did he pretend that it was. Listen to this passage from Mr. Graham Balfour's charmingly written life of his cousin and friend: "Meanwhile the first two months at Bournemouth were spent chiefly in the company of Mr. Henley and were devoted to collaboration over two new plays. The reception of *Deacon Brodie* had been sufficiently promising to serve as an incentive to write a piece which should be a complete success, and so to grasp some of the rewards which now seemed within reach of the authors. They had never affected to disregard the fact that in this country the prizes of the dramatist are out of all proportion to the payment of the man of letters; and already in 1883 Stevenson had written to his father: 'The theatre is a gold mine: and on that I must keep my eye!' " Now let me recall to your mind in this connection the "mercantile delight" which Stevenson professes to have felt in the dream-drama enacted by the "Brownies of his brain." How exactly that chimes in with his own remark to his father, and with his biographer's frank avowal of the motive which inspired his collaboration with Mr. Henley. Ladies and gentlemen, I am the last to pretend that it is a disgrace to an artist to desire an adequate, an ample, pecuniary reward for his labors. That is not at all my point. I draw your attention to these passages for two reasons. Firstly because they put out of court, once for all, any conjecture that in playwriting Stevenson obeyed a pure artistic ideal, and had no taste or ambition for success on the stage. Secondly, I draw your attention to them in order to indicate an unexpressed but clearly implied fallacy that underlies them. When Stevenson says: "The theatre is the gold mine," and when Mr. Graham Balfour tells us that Stevenson felt that "the prizes of the dramatist are out of all proportion to the payment of the man of letters," the implication obviously is that the gold mine can be easily worked, that the prizes are disproportionate to the small amount of pains necessary in order to grasp them. That was evidently the belief of these two men of distinguished talent; and that was precisely where they made the mistake. The art of drama, in its higher forms, is not and can never be easy; nor are such rewards as fall to it in any way out of proportion to the sheer mental stress it involves. No amount of talent, of genius, will, under modern conditions at any rate, enable the dramatist to dispense with a concentration of thought, a sustained intensity of mental effort, very different, if I may venture to say so, from the exertion demanded in turning out an ordinary novel. Stevenson's novels were not ordinary, and I do not for a moment imply that the amount of mental effort which produced, say, *The Master of Ballantrae* might not, if well directed, have produced a play of equal value. But Stevenson was never at the trouble of learning how to direct it well. On the contrary, he wholly ignored the necessity for so doing. What attracted him to the drama was precisely the belief that he could turn out a good play with far less mental effort than it cost him to write a good novel; and here he was radically, woefully in error. And the inadequate success of his plays, instead of bringing his mistake home to him, merely led him, I am afraid, to condemn the artistic medium which he had failed to acquire.

Towards the end of his life, while he was in Samoa, and years after his collaboration with Mr. Henley had come to a close, it seems to have been suggested by his friends at home that he should once more try his hand at drama; for we find him writing to Mr. Colvin: "No, I will not write a play for Irving, nor for the devil. Can you not see that the work of *falsification* which a play demands is of all tasks the most ungrateful? And I have done it a long while—and nothing ever came of it." It is true—it is fatally true—that he had devoted himself in his dramatic ventures to "the work of falsification"; but that was, I repeat, because he misconceived entirely the problem before him. The art—the great and fascinating and most difficult art—of the modern dramatist is nothing else than to achieve the *compression* of life which the stage undoubtedly demands *without* falsification. If Stevenson had ever mastered that art—and I do not question that if he had properly conceived it, he had it in him to master it—he might have found the stage a gold mine, but he would have found, too, that it is a gold mine which cannot be worked in a smiling, sportive, half-contemptuous spirit, but only in the sweat of the brain, and with every mental nerve and sinew strained in its uttermost. He would have known that no ingots are to be got out of this mine, save after sleepless nights, days of gloom and discouragement, and other days, again, of feverish toil the result of which proves in the end to be misapplied and has to be thrown to the winds. When you sit in your stall at the theatre and see a play moving across the stage, it all seems so easy and so natural, you feel as though the author had improvised it. The characters, being, let us hope, ordinary human beings, say nothing very remarkable, nothing, you think (thereby paying the author the highest possible compliment), that might not quite well have occurred to you. When you take up a play-book (if you ever *do* take one up) it strikes you as being a very trifling thing—a mere insubstantial pamphlet beside the imposing bulk of the latest six-shilling novel. Little do you guess that every page of the play has cost more care, severer mental tension, if not more actual manual labour, than any chapter of a novel, though it be fifty pages long. It is the height of the author's art, according to the old maxim, that the ordinary spectator should never be clearly conscious of the skill and travail that have gone to the making of the finished product. But the artist who would achieve a like feat must realize its difficulties, or what are his chances of success? Stevenson, with all his genius, made the mistake of approaching the theatre as a toy to be played with. The facts of the case were against him, for the theatre is not a toy; and facts being stubborn things, he ran his head against them in vain. Had he only studied the conditions, or in other words got into a proper relation to the facts, with what joy should we have acclaimed him among the masters of the modern stage!

[Bibliographic addenda by Clayton Hamilton begin on page 286.]

How to Write a Play

Letters by Augier, Banville, Dennery, Dumas fils, *Gondinet, Labiche, Legouvé, Pailleron, Sardou, Zola*

Translated by Dudley Miles

With an Introduction by William Gillette

Introduction

The impression has always prevailed with me that one who might properly be classed as a genius is not precisely the person best fitted to expound rules and methods for the carrying on of his particular branch of endeavor. I have rather avoided looking the matter up for fear it might not turn out to be so after all. But doesn't it sound as if it ought to be? And isn't a superficial glance about rather confirmatory? We do not—so far as I know—find that Shakespeare or Milton or Tennyson or Whitman ever gave out rules and regulations for the writing of poetry; that Michael Angelo or Raphael was addicted to formulating instructive matter as to the accomplishment of paintings and frescoes; that Thackeray or Dickens or Meredith or George Sand was known to have answered inquiries as to 'How to write a Novel'; or that Beethoven or Wagner or Chopin or Mendelssohn paused in the midst of their careers in order to tell newspaper men what they considered the true method of composing music. These fortunate people—as well as others of their time—could so easily be silent and thus avoid disclosing the fact that they could not, for the lives of them, tell about these things; but in our unhappy day even geniuses are prodded and teased and tortured into speech. In this case we may be more than grateful that they are, for the result is most delightful reading—even though it falls a trifle short of its purpose as indicated by the rather far-reaching title.

There are no workable rules for playwriting to be found here—nor, indeed, any particular light of any kind on the subject, so the letters may be approached with a mind arranged for enjoyment. I would be sorry indeed for the trying-to-be dramatist who flew to this volume for consolation and guidance. I'm sorry for him anyway, but this additional catastrophe would accelerate my sympathy, making it fast and furious. Anyone sufficiently inexperienced to consult books in order to find out how to write a play will certainly undergo a severe touch of confusion in this case, for four of the letter writers confess quite frankly that they do not know—two of these thereupon proceeding to tell us, thus forcibly illustrating their first statement. One author exclaims, "Have instinct!"—another, "Have genius!" Where these two necessaries are to be obtained is not revealed. Equally discouraging is the Dumas declaration that "Some from birth know how to write a play and the others do not and never will." That would have killed off a lot of us—if we had seen it in time.

One approaches the practical when he counsels us to "Take an interesting theme." Certainly a workable proposition. Many dramatists have done that—wherever they could find it. The method is not altogether modern. Two insist upon the necessity of a carefully considered plan, while two others announce that it is a matter of no consequence what one does; and another still wants us to be sure and begin work at the end instead of the beginning. Gondinet—most delightful of all—tells us that his method of working is simply atrocious, for all he asks when he contemplates writing a play is whether the subject will be amusing to him. Though that scarcely touches the question of how to write it, it is a practical hint on favoring conditions, for no one will dispute that one's best work is likely to be performed when he himself enjoys it. Sardou comes nearest to projecting a faint ray of practical light on the subject when he avers that there is no one necessary way to write a play, but that a dramatist must know where he is going and take the best road that leads there. He omits, however, to give instructions about finding that road —which some might think important.

The foregoing indicates to some extent the buffeting about to which a searcher for practical advice on playwriting may find himself subjected in this collection of letters. He had better go for mere instruction to those of a lower order of intellect, whose imaginative or creative faculties do not monopolize their entire mental area.

But that will hardly serve him better, for the truth is that no one can convey to him—whether by written words or orally, or even by signs and miracles—the right and proper method of constructing a play. A few people know, but they are utterly unable to communicate that knowledge to others. In one place and one only can this unfortunate person learn how to proceed, and that is the theatre; and the people to see about it there are situated in front of the footlights and not behind them.

A play or drama is not a simple and straight-told story; it is a device—an invention—a carefully adjusted series of more or less ingenious traps, independent yet interdependent, and so arranged that while yet trapping they carry forward the plot or theme without a break. These traps of scene, of situation, of climax, of acts and tableaux, or of whatever they are, require to be set and adjusted with the utmost nicety and skill so that they will spring at the precise instant and in the precise manner to seize and hold the admiration—sympathy —interest—or whatever they may be intended to capture, of an audience. Their construction and adjustment, once of the simplest, is now of necessity most complicated and intricate. They must operate precisely and effectively; otherwise the play—no matter how admirable its basic idea, no matter how well the author knows life and humanity—will fail of its appeal and be worthless; for a play is worthless that is unable to provide itself with people to play *to*. The admiration of a few librarians on account of certain arrangements of the words and phrases which it may contain can give it no value as drama. Such enthusiasm is not altogether unlike what a barber might feel over the exquisite way in which the hair has been arranged on a corpse; despite his approval it becomes quite necessary to bury it.

The playwriter's or playwright's work, then, supposing that he possesses the requisite knowledge of life as it is lived to go on with, is to select or evolve from that knowledge the basic idea, plot, or theme which, skillfully displayed, will attract; and then to invent, plan, devise, and construct the trap wherein it is to be used to snare the sympathies, etc., of audiences.

But audiences are a most undependable and unusual species of game. From time immemorial their tastes, requirements, habits, appetites, sentiments, and general characteristics have undergone constant change and modification; and this continues without pause to the present day. The dramatic trap that would work like a charm not long ago may not work at all today; the successful trap of today may be useless junk tomorrow.

It must be obvious, then, that for light and instruction on the judicious selection of the bait, and on the best method or methods of devising the trap wherein that bait is to be displayed (that is to say the play) but one thing can avail; and that one thing is a most diligent and constant study of the habits and tastes of this game which it is our business to capture—if we can. To go for information about these things to people sitting by their firesides dreaming of bygone days, or, indeed, to go to anyone sitting anywhere, is merely humorous. The information which the dramatist seeks cannot be told— even by those who know. For the gaining of such knowledge is the acquirement of an instinct which enables its possessor automatically to make use of the *effective* in playwriting and construction and devising, and automatically to shun the *ineffective*. This instinct must be planted and nourished by more or less (more if possible) *living* with audiences, until it becomes a part of the system—yet constantly alert for the necessary modifications which correspond to the changes which the tastes and requirements of these audiences undergo.

An education like this is likely to take the dramatist a great deal of time—unless he is so fortunate as to be a genius. Perhaps the main difference between the playwriting genius and the rest of us is that he can associate but briefly with audiences and know it all, whereas we must spend our lives at it and know but little. I have never happened to hear of a genius of this description; but that is no argument against the possibility of his existence.

As to the talented authors of these letters, they know excellently well—every one of them—how to write a play, or did while still alive, even though some of them see fit to deny it; but they cannot tell *us* how to do it, for the very good reason that it cannot be told. Their charming efforts to find a way out when cornered by such an inquiry as appears to have been made to them are surely worth all their trouble and annoyance—not to speak of their highly probable exasperation.

WILLIAM GILLETTE

May 1916

How to Write a Play

I

By Émile Augier

My dear Dreyfus:

You ask me the recipe for making comedies. I don't know it; but I suppose it should resemble somewhat the one given by the sergeant to the conscript for making cannon:

"You take a hole and you pour bronze around it."

If this is not the only recipe, it is at least the one most followed. Perhaps there should be another which would consist in taking bronze and making a hole through the center and an opening for light at the end. In cannon this hole is called the core. What should it be called in dramatic work? Find another name, if you don't like that one.

These are the only directions I can give you. Add to them, if you wish, this counsel of a wise man to a dramatist in a difficulty:

"Soak your fifth act in gentle tears, and salt the other four with dashes of wit."

I do not think that the author followed this advice.

Cordially yours,

E. Augier

II

By Théodore de Banville

My dear friend:

Like all questions, the question of the theatre is infinitely more simple than is imagined. All poetics, all dramatic criticism is contained in the admirable dictum of Adolphe Dennery: "It is not hard to succeed in the theatre, but it is extremely hard to gain success there with a fine play."

To see this clearly you must consider two questions which have no relation to each other:

1. How should one set about composing a dramatic work which shall succeed and make money?

2. How shall one set about composing a dramatic work which shall be fine and shall have some hope of survival?

Reply to the first question: Nothing is known about it; for if anything were known every theatre would earn six thousand francs every evening. Nevertheless, a play has some chance of succeeding and earning money if, when read to a naive person, it moves him, amuses him, makes him laugh or weep; if it falls into the hands of actors who play it in the proper spirit; and if at the public performance the leader of the claque sees no hitch in it.

Reply to the second question: To compose a dramatic work which shall be fine and shall live, have genius! There is no other way. In art talent is nothing. Genius alone lives. A poet of genius combines in himself all poets past and future, just as the first person you meet combines in himself all humanity past and present. A man of genius will create for his theatre a form which has not existed before him and which after him will suit no one else.

That, my friend, is all that I know, and I believe that anything further is a delusion. Those who are called "men of the theatre" (that is, in plain words, unlettered men who have not studied anywhere but on the stage) have decreed that a man knows the theatre when he composes comedies according to the particular formula invented by M. Scribe. You might as well say that humanity began and ended with M. Scribe, that it is he who ate the apple with Eve and who wrote the *Legendes des Siècles*. Good Luck!

Yours truly,
THÉODORE DE BANVILLE

III

BY ADOLPHE DENNERY

Take an interesting theme, a subject neither too new nor too old, neither too commonplace nor too original—so as to avoid shocking either the vulgar-minded or the delicate-souled.

ADOLPHE DENNERY

IV

BY ALEXANDRE DUMAS *fils*

My dear fellow craftsman and friend:

You ask me how a play is written. You honor me greatly, but you also greatly embarrass me.

With study, work, patience, memory, energy, a man can gain a reputation as a painter, or a sculptor, or a musician. In those arts there are material and mechanical procedures that he can make his own, thanks to which he can gain talent and particularly ability, and can attain to success. The public to whom these works are submitted, having none of the technical knowledge involved, from the beginning regard the makers of these works as their superiors: They feel that the artist can always reply to any criticism: "Have you learned painting, sculpture, music? No? Then don't talk so vainly. You cannot judge. You must be of the craft to understand the beauties," and so on. It is thus that the good-natured public is frequently imposed on, in painting, in sculpture, in music, by certain schools and celebrities. It does not dare to protest. But with regard to drama and comedy the situation is altered. The public is an interested party to the proceedings and appears, so to speak, for the prosecution in the case.

The language that we use in our plays is the language used by the spectators every day; the sentiments that we depict are theirs; the persons whom we set to acting are the spectators themselves in instantly recognized passions and familiar situations. No preparatory studies are necessary; no initiation in a studio or school is indispensable; eyes to see, ears to hear—that's all they need. The moment we depart, I will not say from the truth, but from what they think is truth, they stop listening. For in the theatre, as in life, of which the theatre is the reflection, there are two kinds of truth; first, the absolute truth, which always in the end prevails, and secondly, if not the false, at least the superficial truth, which consists of customs, manners, social conventions; the uncompromising truth which revolts, and the pliant truth which yields to human weakness; in short, the truth of Alceste and that of Philinte.

It is only by making every kind of concession to the second that we can succeed in ending with the first. The spectators, like all sovereigns—like kings, nations, and women—do not like to be told the truth, all the truth. Let me add quickly that they have an excuse, which is that they do not know the truth; they have rarely been told it. They therefore wish to be flattered, pitied, consoled, taken away from their preoccupations and their worries, which are nearly all due to ignorance, but which they consider the greatest and most unmerited to be found anywhere, because their own.

This is not all; by a curious optical effect, the spectators always see themselves in the personages who are good, tender, generous, heroic whom we place on the boards; and in the personages who are vicious or ridiculous they never see anyone but their neighbors. How can you expect then that the truth we tell them can do them any good?

But I see that I am not answering your question at all.

You ask me to tell you how a play is made, and I tell you, or rather I try to tell you, what must be put into it.

Well, my dear friend, if you want me to be quite frank, I'll own up that I don't know how to write a play. One day a long time ago, when I was scarcely out of school, I asked my father the same question. He answered: "It's very simple; the first act clear, the last act short, and all the acts interesting."

The recipe is in reality very simple. The only thing that is needed in addition is to know how to carry it out. There the difficulty begins. The man to whom this recipe is given is somewhat like the cat that has found a nut. He turns it in every direction with his paw because he hears something moving in the shell—but he can't open it. In other words, there are those who *from their birth* know how to write a play (I do not say that the gift is hereditary); and there are those who do not know at once—and these will never know. You are a dramatist, or you are not; neither will power nor work has anything to do with it. The gift is indispensable. I think that everyone whom you may ask how to write a play will reply, if he really can write one, that he doesn't know how it is done. It is a little as if you were to ask Romeo what he did to fall in love with Juliet and to make her love him; he would reply that he did not know, that it simply happened.

Truly yours,

A. Dumas *fils*

V

BY EDMOND GONDINET

My dear friend:

What is my way of working? It is deplorable. Do not recommend it to anyone. When the idea for a play occurs to me, I never ask myself whether it will be possible to make a masterpiece out of it; I ask whether the subject will be amusing 'to treat. A little pleasure in this life tempts me a great deal more than a bust, even of marble, after I am gone. With such sentiments one never accomplishes anything great.

Besides, I have the capital defect for a man of the theatre of never being able to beat it into my head that the public will be interested in the marriage of Arthur and Colombe; and nevertheless that is the key to the whole situation. You simply must suppose the public a trifle naive—and be so yourself.

I should be so willingly, but I can't bring myself to admit that others are.

For a long time I imagined that the details, if they were ingenious, would please the public as much as an intrigue of which the ultimate result is usually given in the first scene. I was absolutely wrong, and I have suffered for it more than once. But at my age one doesn't reform. When I have drawn up the plan, I no longer want to write the piece. You see that I am a detestable collaborator. Say so, if you speak to me, but don't hold me up as a model.

EDMOND GONDINET

VI

BY EUGÈNE LABICHE

Everyone writes in accordance with his inspiration and his temperament. Some sing a gay note, others find more pleasure in making people weep.

As for me, this is my procedure:

When I have no idea, I gnaw my nails and invoke the aid of Providence.

When I have an idea, I still invoke the aid of Providence —but with less fervor, because I think I can get along without it.

It is quite human, but quite ungrateful.

I have then an idea, or I think I have one.

I take a quire of white paper, linen paper—on any other kind I can imagine nothing—and I write on the first page:

PLAN

By the plan I mean the developed succession, scene by scene, of the whole piece, from the beginning to the end.

So long as one has not reached the end of his play he has neither the beginning nor the middle. This part of the work is obviously the most laborious. It is the creation, the parturition.

As soon as my plan is complete, I go over it and ask concerning each scene its purpose, whether it prepares for or develops a character or a situation, and then whether it advances the action. A play is a thousand-legged creature which must keep on going. If it slows up, the public yawns; if it stops, the public hisses.

To write a sprightly play you must have a good digestion. Sprightliness resides in the stomach.

EUGÈNE LABICHE

VII

BY ERNEST LEGOUVÉ

You ask me how a play is made.

By beginning at the end.

A novel is quite a different matter.

I could mention several illustrious novelists who have often started out without knowing where they are going.

Walter Scott, the great Walter Scott, sat down of a morning at his study table, took six sheets of paper, and wrote "Chapter One," without knowing anything else about his story than the first chapter. He set forth his characters, he indicated the situation; then situation and characters got out of the affair as best they could. They were left to create themselves by the logic of events.

Eugène Sue often told me that it was impossible for him to draw up a plan. It benumbed him. His imagination needed the shock of the unforeseen; to surprise the public he had to be surprised himself. More than once at the end of an installment of one of his serial stories he left his characters in an inextricable situation of which he himself did not know the outcome.

George Sand frequently started a novel on the strength of a phrase, a thought, a page, a landscape. It was not she who guided her pen, but her pen which guided her. She started out with the intention of writing one volume and she wrote ten. She might intend to write ten and she wrote only one. She dreamed of a happy ending, and then she concluded with a suicide.

But never have Scribe, or Dumas *père,* or Dumas *fils,* or Augier, or Labiche, or Sardou, written "Scene One" without knowing what they were going to put into the last scene. A point of departure was for them nothing but an interrogation point. "Where are you going to lead me?" they would ask it; and they would accept it only if it led them to a final point, or to a central point which determined all the stages of the route, including the first.

The novel is a journey in a carriage. You make stops, you spend a night at the inn, you get out to look at the country, you turn aside to take breakfast in some charming spot. What difference does it make to you as a traveler? You are in no hurry. Your object is not to arrive anywhere, but to find amusement while on the road. Your true goal is the trip itself.

A play is a railway journey by an express train—forty miles an hour, and from time to time ten minutes' stop for the intermissions; and if the locomotive ceases rushing and hissing you hiss.

All this does not mean that there are no dramatic masterpieces which do not run so fast or that there was not an author of great talent, Molière, who often brought about his ending by the grace of God. Only, let me add that to secure absolution for the last act of *Tartuffe* you must have written the first four.

ERNEST LEGOUVÉ

VIII

BY ÉDOUARD PAILLERON

You ask me how a play is made, my dear Dreyfus. I may well astonish you, perhaps, but on my soul and honor, before God and man, I assure you that I know nothing about it, that you know nothing, that nobody knows anything, and that the author of a play knows less about it than anyone else.

You don't believe me?

Let us see.

Here is a capable gentleman, a man of the theatre, a dramatist acclaimed a score of times, at the height of his powers, in full success. He has written a comedy. He has bestowed upon it all his care, all his time, all his ability. He has left nothing to chance.

He has just finished it, and is content. According to the consecrated expression, it is "certain to go." But as he is cautious, he does not rely entirely upon his own opinion. He consults his friends—fellow workers skillful as he, successful as he. He reads to them his piece. I will not say that they are satisfied—another word is needed—but at any rate, with more reason than ever, it is "certain to go."

He seeks out a manager, an old stager who has every opportunity for being clear-headed, because of his experience, and every reason for being exacting, because of his self-interest. He gives him the manuscript, and as soon as the manager gets a fair notion of the piece, this Napoleon of the stage, this strategist of success, is seized by a profound emotion, but one easy to comprehend in the case of a man who is convinced that five hundred thousand francs have just been placed in his hand. He exults, he shouts, he presses the author in his arms, he rains upon him the most flattering adjectives, beginning with "sublime" and mounting upward. He calls him the most honeyed names: Shakespeare, Duvert and Lauzanne, Rossini, Offenbach—according to the kind of theatre he directs. He is not only satisfied, he is delighted, he is radiant—it is "certain to go."

Wait! That is not all. It is read to the actors—the same enthusiasm! All are satisfied, if not with the play—they have not heard it yet—at least with their parts. All are satisfied! It is "certain to go."

Thereupon rehearsals are held for two months before those who have the freedom of the theatre, who sit successively in the depths of the dark hall and show the same delirium— even the sixty firemen on duty, who, during these sixty rehearsals, have invariably laughed and wept at the same passages. Yet it is well known that the fireman is the modern Laforêt of our modern Molières, as M. Prud'homme would say, and that when the fireman is satisfied—it is "certain to go!"

The dress rehearsal arrives. A triumph! Bravos! Encores! Shouts! Recalls! All the signs of success—and not that the public on this evening of rehearsal, with the exception of a small and insignificant contingent, will be the public of the first performance the next night. It is "certain to go," I tell you! Certain! Absolutely certain!

On this next night the piece is presented. It falls flat! Well, then?

If the author knows what he is doing, if he is master of his method, explain to me then why, after having written twenty good pieces, he writes a bad one?

And don't tell me that failure proves nothing—you would pain me, my friend.

I do not intend to deny, you must understand, the value of talent and skill and experience. They are, philosophically speaking, important elements. But in what proportions do they contribute to the result? That's what, let me repeat, nobody knows, the author as little as anybody else.

The author in travail with a play is an unconscious being, whatever he may think about himself; and his piece is the product of instinct rather than of intention.

Believe me, my dear Dreyfus, in this as in everything, the cleverest of us does what he can, and if he succeeds, he says that he has done exactly what he tried to do. That's the truth. In reality an author knows sometimes what he has tried to do, rarely what he has done; and as to knowing how he did it, I defy him!

Then if it is good, let him try again! I cannot recede from this view.

In our craft, you see, there is an element of unrebeginnable which makes it an art, something of genius which ennobles it, something of the fatally uncertain which renders it both charming and redoubtable. To try to pick the masterpiece to pieces, to unscrew the ideal, to pluck the heart out of the mystery, after the fashion of the baby who looks for the little insect in the watch, is to attempt a vain and puerile thing.

Ah! if I had the time—but I haven't the time. So it's just as well, or better, that I stop. To talk too much about art is not a good sign in an artist. It is like a lover's talking too much about love; if I were a woman I should have my doubts.

Well, do you wish me to disengage the philosophy of this garrulity? It is found whole and entire in an apologue of my son—he too a philosopher without knowing it. He was then seven. As a result of learning fables he was seized with the ambition of writing one, which he brought to me one fine day. It is called "The Donkey and the Canary." The verses are perhaps a trifle long, but there are only two. That's the compensation. Here they are:

"The canary once sang; and the ass asked him how he could learn this to do?

" 'I open my bill,' said the bird, 'and I say "You, you, you!" ' "

Well, the ass, that's you—don't get angry. The canary, that's I. When I sing I open my bill and I say, "You, you, you!"

That's all that I can tell you.

ÉDOUARD PAILLERON

IX

By Victorien Sardou

My dear friend:

It's not so easy to answer you as you think. . . . There is no one necessary way of writing a play for the theatre. Everyone has his own, according to his temperament, his type of intellect, and his habits of work. If you ask me for mine, I should tell you that it is not so easy to formulate as the recipe for duck *à la rouennaise* or spring chicken *au gros sel*. Not fifty lines are needed, but two or three hundred, and even then I should have told you only my way of working, which has no general significance and makes no pretense to the best. It's natural with *me,* that's all. Besides, you will find it indicated in part in the preface to *La Haine* and in a letter which I wrote to La Pommeraye about *Fédora.*

In brief, my dear friend, though there are rules, and rules that are invariable, precise, and eternal for the dramatic art, rules which only the impotent, the ignorant, blockheads, and fools misunderstand, and from which only they wish to be freed, yet there is only one true method for the conception and parturition of a play—which is, to know quite exactly where you are going and to take the best road that leads there. However, some walk, others ride in a carriage, some go by train, X hobbles along, Hugo sails in a balloon. Some drop behind on the way, others run past the goal. This one rolls in the ditch, that one wanders along a crossroad.

In short, that one goes straight to the mark who has the most common sense.

It is the gift which I wish for you—and myself also.

VICTORIEN SARDOU

X

BY ÉMILE ZOLA

My dear comrade:

You ask how I write my plays. Alas! I should rather tell you how I do not write them.

Have you noticed the small number of new writers who take their chances in the theatre? The explanation is that in reality, for our generation of free artists, the theatre is repugnant, with its cookery, its hobbles, its demand for immediate and brutal success, its army of collaborators, to which one must submit, from the imposing leading man down to the prompter. How much more independent are we in the novel! And that's why, when the glamour of the footlights makes the blood dance, we prefer to exercise it by keeping aloof and to remain the absolute masters of our works. In the theatre we are asked to submit to too much.

Let me add that in my own case I have harnessed myself to a group of novels which will take twenty-five years of my life. The theatre is a dissipation which I shall doubtless not permit myself until I am very old.

After all, if I could indulge in the theatre, I should try to *make* plays much less than is the custom. In literature truth is always in inverse proportion to the construction. I mean this: The comedies of Molière are sometimes of a structure hardly adequate, while those of Scribe are often Parisian articles of marvelous manufacture.

Very cordially yours,

ÉMILE ZOLA

A Stage Play

by

W. S. GILBERT

With an Introduction by William Archer

Introduction

It may seem rather a ponderous proceeding to write an introduction to a joke; and it is perhaps not without a spice of malice that the task has been allotted to a Scotchman. Time, however, has a Nietzschean knack of "trans-valuing all values." While it engulfs beyond recovery so many pretentious solemnities, it often confers interest and value upon the most trivial of things. So this *jeu d'esprit* of W. S. Gilbert's has become, in the space of forty-four years, a historic document of a certain importance. It sheds a curious, and to some of us a pathetic, light upon the English theatre of mid-Victorian days—days inconceivable to the youth of our time, and almost incredible even to those of us who lived through them. We can scarcely believe, what we nevertheless know to be the fact, that we not only endured, but took considerable pleasure in, the unspeakable puerilities which dominated the stage of the early seventies.

When Gilbert wrote this sketch for the *Comic Annual* of his friend Tom Hood the younger—the editor of the paper in which his *Bab Ballads* had appeared—he was at the height of his fortune as a dramatist, but had not yet come into his true kingdom as a librettist. He had produced *The Palace of Truth* in 1870, *Pygmalion and Galatea* in 1871; in 1873, the date of this paper, he had made a somewhat contested success with *The Wicked World,* and had himself burlesqued it in *The Happy Land*. Not till 1875 did *Trial by Jury* inaugurate the long series of extravaganzas which may be said to have restored the literary and musical self-respect of the English stage. And even after he had thus found his true vocation he was still eager for success in the "regular

94

drama." He attained it in *Dan'l Druce* and *Engaged,* fell very
short of it in *Gretchen;* and only when a new generation
came to the front in the eighties did he abandon (to all intents and purposes) what the Italians call the *teatro di prosa.*

Let us remember, then, that the following pages are the
work of a man who, at the time when he wrote them, was
unquestionably the leading British dramatist. T. W. Robert-
son had died three years earlier, leaving to the stage one
charming comedy and practically nothing more. James Albery,
though his vein of wit was fresher and less mechanical than
Gilbert's, had entirely failed to fulfill the promise of his *Two
Roses.* W. G. Wills, having narrowly missed writing a fine
play in *Charles I,* was degenerating into a mere rhetorical
melodramatist. For the rest, the stage was given over to the
inanities of Byron and Burnand, and to—avowed or surrep-
titious—adaptations from the French. Gilbert was the one
man who combined a certain measure of dramatic instinct
with an unquestionable literary gift. The *Bab Ballads* were
not poetry of a high order, but they were immeasurably beyond the reach of any other playwright of the period.

Well, this master of the contemporary stage sits down to
tell the world how a play is made. Writing for a *Comic Annual,* he naturally approaches his subject in a more or less
jocular mood. He chooses for purposes of illustration one of
those whimsical themes in which his soul delighted*; and he
shows a keen sense of the ridiculousness of some portions, at
any rate, of the process which he describes. Yet we cannot
but feel that, though his paper is largely comic, it is not in
the least satiric. He has not the slightest suspicion that what
he is really expounding is "how not to do it." On some points
he writes with perfect seriousness. In the last paragraph, for
instance, with its protest against the slovenly rehearsals of
the period, he practically drops the mask of "Mr. Horace
Facile." Here he is quite in the movement of his time, pleading the cause of that highly elaborated art of production
which the Bancrofts had actually introduced at the Prince
of Wales's, which Irving was soon to adopt at the Lyceum,
and which Gilbert himself carried to a notable pitch in his
extravaganzas. Again, in what he says about the difficulty of
beginning the first act, and the ten times greater difficulty of

* Long afterwards, in 1904, he actually produced a play, *The
Fairy's Dilemma,* in which a clergyman-harlequin was one of the
leading characters.

getting the second act afoot, he is evidently speaking from experience; while there can be little doubt that Mr. Horace Facile's method of writing his crucial scenes first and connecting them up afterwards was also the method of W. S. Gilbert. The whole piece, in fact, may be defined as a serious exposition in a whimsical key. The writer is quite aware that he is describing an unambitious form of art, with many ludicrous points about it; but it does not seem to cross his mind that the drama ought to be, or can be, freed from the childish conventions in which the technique of the time began and ended.

The first condition of dramatic authorship which Mr. Horace Facile accepts without a murmur is that you must fit your play to a company of which every member has his fixed *emploi* or "line of business." You must supply parts, not only for your leading man and leading lady, but for your "eccentric comedian," your "low comedian," your "first old man," and so forth. We have here an indication that Gilbert's chief successes had been written for the Haymarket Company under Buckstone's management—one of the last stock companies on the London stage. Many people—and I am one of them—are eager for a modified revival of the stock company system; but we lay the emphasis on the "modified." A revival of the old "lines of business" is the last thing to be desired. They forced the playwright to depict life in terms of a fixed set of theatrical types—which practically meant that he did not depict life at all. Even as Gilbert wrote, the system was passing away. The generation of dramatists which came to the front in the eighties were able to conceive their plays freely, draw whatever characters their observation or imagination suggested, and then select from the whole body of available artists those best fitted to realize their intentions. An author may, indeed, have in his mind's eye the actors whom he would like to secure for one or two, or even more, of his characters; but that is a totally different thing from dragging in a number of imitations of popular preachers because you want to give a "fat" part to your low comedian. With all its drawbacks, the long run system has at least freed the dramatist from the tyranny of "lines of business." The repertory system, which is the alternative to the long run system, aims, and ought to aim, not at the revival of a set of hard-and-fast types, but at giving actors such flexibility as shall enable them to answer any reasonable call an author may make upon them, instead of expecting the author to supply each of them with opportunities for showing off his own particular set of tricks.

Again, it is not at all in a satiric spirit that Gilbert represents Mr. Facile as opening the play with a servant dusting the furniture and soliloquizing as he does so. He sees that it is comic, but not that it is imbecile. He acquiesces without a murmur in the rule that leading actors must not be "discovered," but must have an effective "entrance." That every act must end with a "striking situation" is to him a law of nature, no more open to criticism than the precession of the equinoxes. He takes it for granted that the merit of dialogue resides in the "good things" with which it is sprinkled—in other words, he is entirely under the dominion of that convention of "wit" which played havoc with English comedy from the Restoration down to our own day. We see in almost every sentence that, in his eyes, art and artifice are synonymous; and that quite involuntary confession gives us the key to the all-pervading puerility of the English drama of his time.

It is noteworthy, however, and even a little surprising, that he starts from the assumption that a play should have a "general idea," a theme, or, as we should say, a problem. There he was distinctly in advance of his time. His contemporaries, as a rule, thought of nothing but the telling of a perfectly trivial story, comic or sentimental, with no more social or spiritual relevance than may be found in the legend of Mother Hubbard. The problem he selected for illustration was an exceedingly simple and safe one. In pleading for mutual tolerance between Church and Stage, the dramatist, addressing a theatrical audience, would necessarily be preaching to the converted. But here we come upon a curious point: the method of dealing with the problem which suggested itself to Gilbert exactly anticipated that of Mr. Bernard Shaw. The *scène à faire* which he had in his mind's eye was to be "a scene of haughty recrimination—the Archbishop reproaching the curate for combining the pulpit with the stage, the curate reproaching the Archbishop with his hypocritical denunciation of an institution from which he derives, in the shape of rent, an income of, say, four thousand a year." In his very first play, *Widowers' Houses,* Mr. Shaw wrote, to all intents and purposes, the scene which Gilbert here forecasts; and he has repeated it, in different disguises, over and over again.

The Gilbertianism of Mr. Shaw's methods has often been noted; but I do not remember a more convincing illustration of it than this. The truth is that both men were constitutionally predisposed to the reduction to absurdity of self-righteousness and cant. "I don't think much of our profession," says Gilbert's Pirate King, "but contrasted with respectability it is comparatively honest." There you have in a nutshell a very large part of Mr. Shaw's criticism of life, at all events in his earlier plays.

WILLIAM ARCHER

London, November 1915

A Stage Play

Most men, whatever their occupation may be, are accustomed to study mankind exclusively from their own points of view. A man who passes his life behind a tavern-bar is apt to divide the human race into those who habitually refresh themselves in public-houses, and those who do not. A policeman classifies society under two great heads—prosecutors and prisoners. In a footman's eyes, his fellow-men are either visitors or servants; in an author's, they are publishers or reviewers. Now, it is conceivable that a man may be at once a prosecutor, a visitor, and a publisher; but a policeman will take no heed of him in the two latter capacities; a footman will care nothing that he is a prosecutor and a publisher; and an author will be in no way concerned that he is a prosecutor (unless, indeed, he is prosecuting the author), or that he is a visitor, unless the visit be paid in his capacity as a publisher. Each man allows his immediate surroundings to interfere between himself and the world at large. He sees mankind, not through a distorting medium, but through a medium so circumscribed that it permits only one feature of the object looked at to be seen at one time. In short, he examines mankind, not through a field-glass, but through a microscope.

A theatre, examined through the powerful medium employed by a person whose occupation is intimately associated with theatres, is as unlike a theatre, as it appears in the eyes of the outside public, as a drop of magnified Thames water is unlike the apparently inorganic liquid that enters into the composition of almost everything we drink. Not one person in a thousand who sits in the auditorium of a theatre has any definite idea of the complicated process by which the untidy, badly-scrawled, interleaved, and interlineated manuscript of the author is transmuted into the close, crisp, bright, interesting entertainment that, in the eyes of the spectator, represents the value of the shilling he has paid for admittance. Still less does he know of the complicated mental process by which the manuscript (supposing it to have a genuine claim to the title "original") has been put together. Let us trace the progress of a modern three-act comedy from the blank-paper state to completion, and from completion to production.

We will assume that the author, Mr. Horace Facile, has such a recognized position in his profession as to justify a manager in saying to him, "Facile, I want a three-act comedy-drama from you, with parts for Jones and Brown and Robinson. Name your own terms, and get it ready, if you can, by this day two months."

Facile's engagements allow of his accepting the commission, and he sets to work on it as soon as may be.

In the first place, a "general idea" must be fixed upon, and in selecting it, Facile is guided, to a certain extent, by the resources of the company he is to write for. Jones is an excellent light comedian, with a recognized talent for eccentric parts; Brown is the leading "old man" of the establishment; Robinson is the handsome lover or *jeune premier;* and Miss Smith plays the interesting young ladies whose fortunes or misfortunes constitute the sentimental interest of every piece in which she plays. Probably one or more of these talented artists must be "exploited," and the nature of the "general idea" will depend on the powers or peculiarities of the actor or actress who is principally entitled to consideration. The motif of the comedy having been determined upon (we will suppose that it is to arise from the unnecessary and unchristian antagonism existing between the Theatre and the Church), Facile casts about for a story in which this motif can be effectively displayed. In selecting a story, Facile will probably be guided by the peculiarities of the company he is writing for. Brown (the "old man") has never played an Archbishop of Canterbury, and Facile believes such a part would afford that excellent comedian a chance of distinguishing himself in a new line of character; so the story must be put together in such a manner as to admit of an Archbishop of Canterbury taking a prominent part in it. It has often occurred to Facile that Robinson, the *jeune premier,*

could make a great deal of the part of a professional Harlequin, who, under the influence of love or some equally potent agency, has "taken orders," notwithstanding that, at the
time of his doing so, he is under engagement to play Harlequin in a forthcoming pantomime. So the story must admit,
not only of an Archbishop, but also of a serious Harlequin;
and, moreover, the interests of the Archbishop and the Harlequin must be interwoven in an interesting and yet sufficiently probable manner. However, the fact that there is a
clerical side to Harlequin's character renders this exceedingly
easy. The Harlequin loves the Archbishop's daughter; but
the Archbishop (a very haughty ecclesiastic of the Thomas
à Becket type) objects to Harlequins on principle, and determines that his daughter shall marry into the Church. Here
is at once the necessary association of the interests of the
Archbishop and the Harlequin, and here, moreover, is an
excellent reason for the Harlequin's taking holy orders. The
Archbishop admits him, in ignorance of his other professions,
and places no obstacle in the way of his courting his daughter. But a great deal of the interest of the lover's part should
obviously depend on the contrast between his duties as a
clergyman and his duties as a Harlequin (for an obdurate
manager declines to release him from his engagement in the
latter capacity), and Facile sets to work to see how the two
professions can be contrasted to the best advantage. This
requires some consideration, but he sees his way to it at last.
The Archbishop (a bitter enemy to the stage, which he denounces whenever an opportunity for doing so presents itself)
happens to be the freeholder of the very theatre in which the
Harlequin is engaged; and happening to call on the manager
one evening, with the double object of collecting his quarter's
rent and endeavouring to wean the manager from a godless
profession, he meets his daughter's lover in Harlequin costume. Here is an opportunity for a scene of haughty recrimination—the Archbishop reproaching the curate for combining the pulpit with the stage (by-the-bye, here is the title
for the piece—*The Pulpit and the Stage*), and the curate reproaching the Archbishop with his hypocritical denunciation
of an institution from which he derives, in the shape of rent,
an income of, say, four thousand a year. At this juncture the
Archbishop's daughter must be introduced. It will be difficult
to account, with anything like probability, for her presence
behind the scenes during the performance of a pantomime;

but with a little ingenuity even this may be accomplished. For instance, she may have come with a view to proselytizing the ballet; and a scene of the stage, in which she is seen proselytizing the ballet, who can't get away from her because they are all hanging on irons, ready for the transformation scene, might precede the arrival of the Archbishop. The act (the second) must end with the struggle (on the daughter's part) between filial respect for her venerable father and her love for Harlequin, resulting, of course, in her declaring for the Harlequin, and the Archbishop's renunciation of her "for ever."

This will fill two acts. The third act must show the Harlequin (now a curate) married to the Archbishop's daughter, and living in the humblest circumstances somewhere in Lambeth. They are happy, although they are extremely poor. They have many friends—some clerical, some theatrical— but all on the best of terms with each other, through the benevolent agency of the ex-Harlequin. Deans drop in from Convocation at Westminster—actors and actresses from rehearsal at Astley's; and it is shown, beyond the possibility of doubt, that the two professions have many points in common (here is an opportunity for introducing hits at High Church mummeries, with imitations of popular preachers by Wilkinson, the low comedian). Now to introduce the Archbishop. Since his renunciation of his daughter, he has become a changed man. Too haughty to admit his error frankly and take her and her husband to his Heart and Palace, he is nevertheless painfully conscious that he has acted harshly; and, in a spirit of secret self-humiliation, he disguises himself as one of the undignified clergy, and in that capacity goes through a course of house-to-house visitation. The natural course of this duty brings him to the humble abode of his daughter and son-in-law. He enters unperceived (of course in ignorance of the fact that it *is* their abode) during Wilkinson's imitations and overhears a touching scene, in which his daughter indignantly rebukes Wilkinson for giving an imitation of her Right Reverend father's pulpit peculiarities. The old man, utterly softened by this unexpected touch of filial affection, comes forward, and, in broken accents, admits both the correctness of the imitation and the filial respect that induced his daughter to check it, folds her and her husband to his heart, and gives him the next presentation to a valuable living—the present incumbent (who is present) being an aged man who cannot, in the course of nature, expect to survive many months. On this touching scene the curtain descends.

Here is an outline of a plot which Facile believes will answer every purpose. The Archbishop, the daughter, and the Harlequin will afford three excellent parts. The manager will be a bit of "character" for Jones, the eccentric comedian; the actor who gives imitations of popular preachers will fit Wilkinson's powers of mimicry to a T; the tottering old incumbent, to whose living the ex-Harlequin is to succeed, will afford Tompkins an opportunity of introducing one of his celebrated "cabinet pictures" of pathetic old men; and for the other members of the company small effective parts, arising naturally from the exigencies of the story, will readily be found.

The next thing Facile does is to arrange striking situations for the end of each act. The first act must end with announcement from the Harlequin that he has just taken holy orders, the happiness of the bishop's daughter at the information, and the entrance of the manager, who tells Harlequin that he shall nevertheless hold him to his engagement for the forthcoming pantomime. The second act must end with the renunciation of his daughter by the Archbishop, and the last with the general reconciliation. Facile then sets to work to write the dialogue. As a rule, this is not written straight off. He first tries his hand upon bits of dialogue that arise from suggestive situations—perhaps the first interview between the Archbishop's daughter and himself in Lambeth Palace. Then perhaps he will write the proselytizing scene in the second act; then the dialogue that leads to the situation at the end of Act I; and so on. After he has "settled" half-a-dozen little scenes of this description, he feels that it is time to arrange how the piece is to begin. The first act takes place in the Archbishop's library in Lambeth Palace. Shall the Archbishop and his daughter be "discovered" at breakfast? No; both the Archbishop and his daughter (that is to say, the actor and actress who are to play those parts) object to be "discovered." They want an "entrance," that they may receive special and individual "receptions," and they don't like to begin a piece, as in that case they are liable to constant interruption from the arrival of such of the audience as are not in their places when the curtain rises. Perhaps Jones (the manager) won't mind beginning, as his part is

likely to be a particularly good one; he might call on the
Archbishop about the rent of the theatre. But in this case
there must be a servant to receive him. Well, Facile tries this:
Servant discovered (dusting, of course); soliloquy (this gives
the manager an entrance); knock; servant don't answer it on
principle until several times repeated; eventually admits manager; treats manager contemptuously (or better still, as he is
an Archbishop's servant, with a grave and pitying air), as
who would say, "Poor worldly sheep (we—that is to say, the
Archbishop and I—despise you, but we don't hate you)";
servant leaves to inform Archbishop; sarcastic soliloquy by
manager; enter Archbishop; thunders of applause at Archbishop's "make-up"; and so on. Probably Facile writes and
rewrites this scene half-a-dozen times—it gives him more
trouble than all the rest of the act put together; for there
are so many ways of beginning a piece, and it is so difficult
to find sufficient reason for selecting one and rejecting all the
rest. However, Facile is eventually satisfied; the scenes that
he has already written are tacked together with dialogue of
a more commonplace order, and Act I is completed.

At this point Facile is apt to pause and to take breath.
Perhaps he will run over to Paris, or go to the sea-side for a
month, "to collect his thoughts." His thoughts collected, he
will make a tremendous effort to begin the second act; but
here all the difficulty that he experienced in beginning Act I
crops up again tenfold. We protest, from practical experience, that there is nothing in the dramatist's profession that
presents so many distasteful difficulties as the commencing
the second act of a three-act comedy. His first act is short,
sharp, crisp, and to the point—*totus teres atque rotundis*—
perfectly satisfactory in itself—artistically put together, and
telling the audience all they require to know in order to
understand what follows, but nothing more. The thread of
interest is broken at an exacting point, and it has now to be
taken up again and in such a way as not to anticipate secrets
and "situations" that require time to develop. If, in commencing the first act, Facile was bothered with the choice of
five hundred "openings," he is ten times as much bothered
now from the fact that he has only two or three, and none
of them likely to be effective when reduced to dialogue.
However, a letter from the management probably wakes him
up at this point. With a desperate effort he sets to work,
writing detached scenes as before, and tacking them together

as before, and writing the opening dialogue last as before; and, in process of time, Act II is completed. His work is now practically at an end. Act III is a simple matter enough. He has laid the train in Acts I and II, and all that remains is to bring about the catastrophe in the quickest possible manner consistent with the story he has to tell. By the time that he has finished Act II, he has cleared away all his difficulties. The different peculiarities of his principal characters have not only been irrevocably determined upon, but he has, by this time, become thoroughly saturated with their spirit; and he has no difficulty whatever in bringing the last act shortly and sharply to an effective conclusion. Facile, who knows his work pretty well, has a theory that no piece has ever yet been written which deserves to arrest the attention of an audience for more than two hours at a time, and he has not the vanity to believe that any piece of his is likely to prove an exception to the rule.

The piece, duly completed, is sent to the manager who is to produce it. That gentleman has sufficient faith in Facile to justify him in handing it over at once to his prompter, who proceeds to make a fair copy for his own use, and another for the Lord Chamberlain's inspection. He also copies the "parts" from which the actors and actresses are to study, and which contain simply the words that the actor for whom it is intended has to speak, the stage-directions that concern him, and the last three or four words of every speech that immediately precede his own. As soon as the parts are fairly copied, a "reading" is called—that is to say, the members of the company are summoned to hear the piece read by the author in the green-room. This is an ordeal that Facile particularly dreads. He reads abominably—all authors do—and he knows it. He begins well; he reads slowly and emphatically, with all the proper pauses duly marked; and he indicates the stage-directions with just the right modulation of voice. All is quite satisfactory until—say, on page 9—he comes to a "point" on which he relies for a hearty laugh. He makes his point, and dwells for a moment upon it. Nobody notices it except the stage manager, who thinks he has paused because he is hoarse and kindly pours him out a glass of water. Much abashed by this, Facile pounds through the rest of the manuscript at an astounding pace—hurrying intentionally over all the "good things" as if he were ashamed of them —which, for the moment, he is—and slurring over stirring

passages as if they were merely incidental to the general purpose of the scene—as though, in fact, the scene had not been
originally constructed in order to introduce them. As he approaches the end of the second act, he becomes quite unconscious of the fact that he is reading at all until recalled by
an enforced pause occasioned by the accident of a misplaced
leaf, or the opening or shutting of the green-room door. As
he commences the third act, he finds himself wandering into
falsetto every now and then; he becomes husky and out of
tune; he takes a copious drink of water, and the words immediately begin to babble into each other in a manner altogether incomprehensible. He falls into his old habit of slurring
over important passages, but endeavours to compensate for
this by laying such exceptional stress upon sentences of no
ultimate importance that his audience begin to wish that they
had paid more attention to the earlier passages of the play,
that they might understand more clearly the force of the old
clergyman's remark about the weather, or the subtlety of the
ex-Harlequin's invitation to the low comedian to sit down
and make himself comfortable. Facile finds the "imitations"
in the third act seem to make no impression, which is not to
be wondered at, considering he reads them "off the reel"
without any modification of voice at all. At length, very
much to his surprise, he finds himself at the last page—
which is always a tremendously long page to read; you never
seem to get to the bottom of it—and, with his heart thumping away in his mouth, he pronounces the word "curtain,"
and closes the manuscript with—"There, that's over!" and
proceeds at once to talk, with great volubility, about the sort
of day that it is—the bad business they've been doing at the
Folly—or the horrible report that Mrs. Miggleton, the wife
of Miggleton, the first surgeon of the day, never "shows" in
society, because her husband has, at different times, and
in the interests of science, cut away so much of her, by way
of experiment, that only the vital portions are left—about
anything, in short, except the piece he has just been reading.
The stage manager distributes the "parts," and the author
hurries away—in order to avoid *that row* with Miss Smith
—after appointing a day and hour for "comparing parts."

In the course of this process—a very dismal one indeed—
the members of the company who are engaged in the piece
endeavour to decipher the parts and to ascertain the context.

The copyist's errors are corrected, and every one begins to
have some idea of his or her position with reference to the
other persons engaged. It is usually a long and tedious process,
and eminently calculated to reduce Facile's self-esteem to
vanishing-point. After this preliminary canter is over Facile
thinks he may as well look up Mr. Flatting, the scene painter,
who has been at work for the last fortnight on the Archbishop's library, and who is about to begin the "behind the
scenes" scene in the second act. Facile climbs into the tall,
narrow, dingy shed called by courtesy a painting-room, and
finds Flatting describing the "model" to the carpenter and
machinist, who will have a good deal to do with it, as it
is a "set" of rather complicated description. Facile settles
matters with Flatting and goes home to dine, sleep, wake at
eleven o'clock, and set to work till three in the morning, altering this scene, polishing up that dialogue, making it crisper
here, and filling it out with business there, as the experience
of the morning may have suggested. The next day is the first
rehearsal proper. A table and three chairs are set in the middle of the stage against the footlights. One of these is for the
stage-manager, one for the prompter, and one for the author.
Very often the stage-manager and prompter are one and the
same individual, but the three chairs (one on the "prompt
side" of the table and two on the "opposite prompt") are
always there. Facile knows something of stage-management,
and invariably stage-manages his own pieces—an exceptional
thing in England, but the common custom in France. He is
nothing of an actor, and when he endeavours to show what he
wants his actors to do, he makes himself rather ridiculous,
and there is a good deal of tittering at the wings; but he con-
trives, nevertheless, to make himself understood, and takes
particularly good care that whatever his wishes are, they shall
be carried out to the letter, unless good cause is shown to the
contrary. He has his own way; and if the piece is a success, he
feels that he has contributed something more than the mere
words that are spoken. At the same time, if Facile is not a
self-sufficient donkey he is only too glad to avail himself of
,valuable suggestions offered by persons who have ten times
his experience in the details of stage management. And so
the piece flounders through rehearsal—the dingy theatre
lighted by a T-piece in front of the stage, which has no per-
ceptible effect at the back; the performers usually (at all

events during the first two or three rehearsals) standing in a row with their backs to the auditorium, that the light may fall on crabbed manuscripts they are reading from; the author endeavouring, but in vain, to arrange effective exits and entrances, because nobody can leave the T-piece; the stage-manager or prompter (who follows the performers) calling a halt from time to time that he may correct an overlooked error in his manuscript or insert a stage-direction. The actors themselves pause from time to time for the same reason. Every one has (or should have) a pencil in hand; all errors are corrected and insertions made on the spot; every important change of position is carefully marked; every "cross" indicated as the piece proceeds; and as alterations in dialogue and business are made up to the last moment—all of which have to be hurriedly recorded at the time—it will be understood that the "parts" are in rather a dilapidated condition before the rehearsals are concluded.

Eventually the piece is ready for representation—three weeks' preparation is supposed to be a liberal allowance—and with one imperfect scene rehearsal, and no dress rehearsal at all, the piece is presented to the public. It probably passes muster on the first night, whatever its merits may be; in a week or ten days actors begin to "do something" with their parts; and in a fortnight the piece is probably at its best.

There is much, very much, fault to be found (so Facile says) with the system—or rather the want of the system—that prevails at rehearsals in this country. In the first place, every actor and every person engaged in the piece should have a perfect copy of the piece, and that copy should be *printed,* not written. It costs from five to six pounds to print a three-act comedy, and in return for this trifling outlay much valuable time and an infinity of trouble would be saved, not only to the prompter, but to the actors and the author.*
It is absolutely necessary that every actor should have the context of his scenes before his eyes as he studies them. He also says (does Facile) that it is a monstrous shame and an

---

* By-the-bye, here is an invaluable hint to Messieurs the Un-acted. Never send a manuscript to a manager. Always print your play before you send it in. *It will be read;* and if rejected, it will be for a good and sufficient reason. There are thumping prizes in dramatic literature; and the five-pound outlay will be returned to you a thousand-fold, if your piece happens to turn up trumps.

unheard-of injustice to place three-act pieces on the stage
with fewer than thirty rehearsals, in ten of which the scenes
should be as they will be set at night, and in five of which
every soul engaged should be dressed and made up as they
will be dressed and made up at night. As it is now, Jones, who
is always fearfully nervous on "first nights," is embarrassed
to find himself called upon to repeat his scarcely-learnt
words in a spacious and handsomely furnished apartment,
blazing with gas and gold-foil, instead of the cold, dark,
empty stage on which he has been rehearsing them. This is
of itself enough to drive the words out of the head of Jones.
Then Jones, who has practised several scenes with Brown
(on the stage an "old man," but in private life an airy, dressy
gentleman of thirty summers), finds himself called upon to
speak his words, not to the dressy Brown, but to a white-
headed and generally venerable ecclesiastic, in gold spectacles and knee-breeches—that is to say, Brown the Archbishop. These surprises (for to a nervous man they *are* surprises) are enough to unhinge Jones altogether. He makes a
mess of his part for a night or two, picks up again after that,
and in a fortnight is the talk of the town. Now, if Jones had
had an opportunity of rehearsing with Brown the Archbishop,
instead of Brown the Swell, and if he had rehearsed his
scenes in the Archbishop's library, and not on the empty
stage, Jones might have become the talk of the town from
the first. In first-class French theatres this system is adopted.
Parts are distributed, learnt perfectly, and then rehearsed for
six weeks or two months, sometimes for three or four months.
Scene-rehearsals and dress-rehearsals occupy the last week of
preparations. Actors and actresses act at rehearsal; they have
been taught and required to do so from the first; and the
consequence is that a bad actor becomes a reasonably good
actor, and a reasonably good actor becomes an admirable
actor, by sheer dint of the microscopic investigation that his
acting receives from the stage-manager and from the author.
And until this system is in force in England; until the necessity for longer periods of preparation, for rehearsals that are
rehearsals in fact, and not merely in name—rehearsals with
scenery, dresses, and "make-up," as they are to be at night;
earnest rehearsals, with every gesture given as it is to be
given at night, every expression marked as it is to be marked
at night; until the necessity for such preparation as this is

recognized in England, the English stage will never take the position to which the intelligence of its actors and actresses, the enterprise of its managers, and the talent of its authors would otherwise entitle it. At least, so says Facile.

A Theory of the Theatre

by

Francisque Sarcey

Translated by H. H. Hughes

With an Introduction by Brander Matthews

Introduction

In the brilliant essay on the Comédie-Française which Henry James wrote forty years ago, and which had for its text the series of critical analyses of the histrionic attainments of the chief performers at the House of Molière, then recently put forth by Francisque Sarcey, the American critic declared that the French critic was so predominant in the Parisian press that he held "in his hand the fortune of a play" and that if he "devoted an encouraging line and a half to a young actress, mademoiselle immediately had a career." This may be an overstatement, but it can hardly be called a misstatement. For the final thirty years of the nineteenth century Sarcey was the most influential of all the theatrical reviewers of France, even if he could not actually make or unmake a new play or a new player.

Henry James analyzed the reasons for Sarcey's enviable influence and for the weight of his words. Sarcey was "sternly incorruptible"; he had "a religious respect for his theme"; he had a habit of taking the theatre seriously, with "unwearying attention to detail"; he had "the scenic sense, the theatrical eye"; he was "shrewd and sagacious, and almost tiresomely in earnest." And now that nearly a score of years have passed since Sarcey ceased to contribute to the *Temps* his weekly review of the passing show, a later generation has ratified the praise, even if not a few latterday critics are disposed to see Sarcey's limitations with a disenchanted eye. M. Gustave Lanson, for example, in his inestimable history of French literature, holds that Sarcey's theory of the theatre was somewhat too narrow and that it was sometimes too rigidly enforced.

But no one of the younger generation has denied that Sarcey had a theory of the theatre, that this theory has left its impress upon the contemporary French drama, and that it had been developed by Sarcey himself as the immediate consequence of his immense experience and of his indefatigable attendance in the playhouse. Sarcey's opinions about the art of the drama were the direct result of his observations in the theatre itself, just as were the opinions of Aristotle and of Lessing. He had no kinship with the erudite Italian theorists of the Renaissance who evolved their dramatic dogmas from their inner consciousness, being deprived of the privilege of persistent playgoing and having occasion only sporadically to see a good play well acted.

Sarcey was continually seeing good plays well acted; he was continually analyzing his own impressions at these performances, and he was continually investigating the impressions made upon his fellow playgoers. As a result of this relentless inquiry, pursued for twoscore years, he discovered for himself certain of the principles of the drama, just as Lessing had discovered them in like manner a century earlier. For Lessing, Sarcey had ever an exalted respect, as a critic of the keenest acumen and as a constant playgoer of alert intelligence. He said to me once that when he chanced to find in Lessing's *Hamburg Dramaturgy* an opinion which he had already arrived at by his own reflection, he felt encouraged and confirmed in his belief that his own view was sound.

When we compare Sarcey as a dramatic critic with a predecessor like Jules Janin or with a contemporary like Jules Lemaitre we cannot help noting that however inferior he may be in wit, in felicity of phrase, in charm of style, he is superior in his possession of a compact body of doctrine about the drama, which might be a little too systematic at times, but which sustained and supported his judgments upon the plays of the moment and which gave to these judgments a validity and a significance often absent from the sparkling effusions of Janin and Lemaitre, neither of whom took the theatre very seriously and both of whom now and then yielded to the temptation of accepting the play they were supposed to be criticizing either as a peg on which to hang pretty garlands of figures of speech or as a springboard from which to dive off into philosophical disquisition.

Sarcey might on occasion apply his code too rigorously; but at least he had a code to apply. He might be overemphatic at times in declaring the rigid limits of the drama and in insisting upon the futility of well-meant efforts to enlarge its scope, to broaden its mission, to bestow upon it a more significant message; but he was inexorably honest in setting forth these opinions of his, and they were founded upon an intimacy with the theatre possessed by none of his opponents. As to his critical insight and his integrity there is no room for dispute; and not a few of the principles Sarcey insisted upon, either first declared by him or by him more clearly formulated, are now among the commonplaces of dramatic criticism, employed incessantly by writers often unfamiliar with his name.

In his weekly articles Sarcey frequently mentioned the book which he proposed to devote to the History of Theatrical Conventions, but he never wrote it—and perhaps he never really intended to write it. Thirty years ago when I asked him when this long-awaited volume was to appear, he laughed and responded: "If I ever do write it, what shall I have left to fill up those long columns of my weekly article in the *Temps*?" Yet he had at least made a beginning of this book in a series of more or less connected articles published weekly in the *Temps* in the summer and fall of 1876, when there happened to be only a few new plays demanding critical consideration.

After Sarcey's death in May 1899 there was an immediate demand for a collection of his theatrical reviews. This demand had been heard during his lifetime, and he had always resisted it, on the ground that his articles contributed to a daily paper and dealing with the plays of the day were too journalistic in tone and in temper, too temporary in their illustrations and allusions, to warrant their reproduction in a series of volumes aspiring to the dignity and permanence of literature. Other Parisian dramatic reviewers, Jules Janin and Théophile Gautier, Auguste Vitu and Jules Lemaitre, might garner their newspaper sheaves and strive to rescue their hebdomadal effusions from the swift oblivion of the back number; but Sarcey resolutely refused to be tempted by the lure of this fleeting immortality.

What he had declined to do himself his son-in-law, Adolphe Brisson, piously undertook after his death; and in 1900 Brisson issued the first volume of *Quarante Ans de Théâtre*, followed in rapid succession by six other volumes, in which selections from Sarcey's weekly articles were classified under

various heads. The first volume dealt with the Comédie-Française, always the center of Sarcey's solicitude; and it contained also his discussion of the principles of dramatic criticism. More valuable than this discussion was the group of
successive articles written in 1876 in which he considered the
fundamental basis of the art of the theatre, dealt with the
necessity of conventions in the drama (as in all the other
arts), and discussed the separation of species, the setting off
of the tragic from the comic.

It is a selection from this series of papers which is here
translated, with many excisions and suppressions, due to the
desire to present Sarcey's views in a form easy of apprehension by readers not so familiar with the French stage as were
the subscribers to the *Temps* forty years ago. The excisions
have been made so as to sharpen Sarcey's points without in
any way modifying or obscuring his views; and the passages
selected for presentation here adequately reveal his method,
which was closely akin to the method of Aristotle and to
the method of Lessing. They disclose also his manner, his
intellectual integrity, his playful common sense, his total
absence of pedantic pretentiousness.

This inquiry into the aesthetic of the theatre seems to be
only a portico to an edifice which was never erected; and yet
even if it is but a beginning, it sets forth sound doctrine
about the drama. It contains at least the outline of his opinions in regard to theatrical conventions; and it is greatly to
be regretted that he never resumed the articles and that he
never supported these opinions by the host of illustrations he
employed in later years in dealing with the drama of the day.

Perhaps it may be well here to supplement the condensed
statement of the necessary conventions of the drama which
Sarcey made in the articles in the *Temps* from which these
selections have been taken, and to amplify the theory he laid
down. He began by declaring that the drama, like all the
other arts, exists and can exist only by departing from the
mere facts; and he had no difficulty in showing that the painter
is also forced to express the essential truth of nature by suppressing or altering reality. The late John La Farge, in his
very suggestive essay on "Ruskin, Art and Truth," made a
similar declaration of principles:

"When I work as an artist I begin at once by discarding
the way in which things are really done, and by translating
them at once into another material. Therein consists the

pleasure that you and I take in the work of art,—perhaps a new creation between us. The pleasure that such and such reality gives me and you has been transposed. The great depth and perspective of the world, its motion, its never resting, I have arrested and stopped upon a little piece of flat paper. That very fact implies that I consider the flatness of my paper a fair method of translating the non-existence of *any* flatness in the world that I look at. If I am a sculptor I make for you this soft, moving, fluctuating, colored flesh in an immovable hard, rigid, colorless material; and it is this transposition which delights you, as well as me in a lesser degree who have made it. Therefore at the very outset of my beginning to affect you by what is called the record of a truth, I am obliged to ask you to accept a number of the greatest impossibilities, evident to the senses, and sometimes disturbing when the convention supposed to be agreed upon between you and myself is understood by only one of the two parties in the carrying out of the matter."

In other words, the art of the painter is possible only when there is a convention, an implied contract, between the artist and his public, that he can translate and transpose in contradiction to the facts, and that he is permitted to represent as motionless (for the chosen moment) that which is in reality never still. So the art of the sculptor is based on a tacit agreement, which permits him to represent in clay or marble or bronze, in hard monochrome, that which in fact is soft and multicolored. So the art of the drama is possible only when the convention is accepted that the playwright may condense his story and omit all the needless details and all the extraneous particularities which would in real life delay and dilute the action.

The dramatist has to accept the condition that his plays are to be performed, by actors, in a theatre, and before an audience. The actor departs from the fact, and must so depart, when he makes love in tones that reach clearly to the last row of seats in the topmost gallery. The theatre can present a forest with growing trees only by the aid of painted canvas, which we must accept in accordance with our agreement. And the audience has only a limited time and a limited understanding, so that the story must move swiftly and must be made transparently clear by artifices of exposition.

The convention underlying the modern problem play in prose is that all the characters say what they have to say in

the fewest possible words and that what they say is understood by all the other characters at the first hearing. The
convention underlying the comedy of Molière is that all the
characters belong to a race of beings whose native and necessary speech is the rimed French alexandrine. In Shakespearean
tragedy this native and necessary speech is English blank
verse. In pantomime it is gesture; and in opera it is song.

When Tolstoy, in his misguided attempt to ascertain What
is Art, objected to a dying tenor in silk tights singing with
his last breath, he was simply refusing to be a party to the
convention by which alone can opera exist. This refusal was
of course within Tolstoy's right; but by it he deprived himself of the specific pleasure which only the art of the modern
music drama can bestow.

In all the forms of the drama, comedy and tragedy, problem play, pantomime, and opera, the audience gladly permits
departures from the facts of life, if this departure is for its
pleasure and for its profit. In reality Othello and Desdemona
talked to each other in Italian; yet as few of us are familiar
with any tongue but our own, we are glad to have them
speak English. But if we wish to enjoy a performance by two
great actors of different races, Othello by Salvini and Iago by
Booth, we must extend the license we have granted by our
implied contract and permit Othello to use the language which
he would have used in real life while Iago and all the others
use the language which they would not have used but which
is more satisfactory to us.

Probably this theory of the conventions by which alone the
drama is made possible had been suggested by one or another
of Sarcey's predecessors—although I have failed to find anything of the kind in all my reading in the history of theatrical
theory. Even if suggested by one or another of the earlier
critics, the theory owes its general acceptance today to the
sharpness with which Sarcey seized it, to the clearness with
which he set it forth, and to the frequency with which he
insisted on it.

Another theory of Sarcey's, not so important, perhaps, and
yet as useful, is that which asserts that there are in every
story suitable for the stage certain interviews, certain moments, certain scenes, which the dramatist must show us in
action, which he cannot merely relate, and which must not
happen between the acts. Sarcey called these the *scènes à
faire,* the scenes which must be dealt with by the dramatist,

and which can be omitted only at the risk of dumbly disappointing the spectators. Mr. William Archer has accepted this theory, and has suggested that we should term the *scènes à faire* the Obligatory Scenes.

Unfortunately M. Brisson has not replevined for us any one of Sarcey's articles in which this theory is stated. Therefore it has seemed best to devote the second half of these selections to Sarcey's characteristically logical discussion of the artistic advisability of separating the comic and the tragic. Even if Sarcey's argument is not altogether convincing to us of the Anglo-Saxon tradition, it is one which it is wise for us to consider carefully and to weigh cautiously. Attention should also be called to the fact that although Sarcey was here setting forth a dogma strenuously insisted upon by the Italian promulgators of the classicist code, he did not support it by the argument they derived from their study of Greek and Latin drama, in which they discovered that there were no humorous passages in tragedy and no strongly dramatic passages in comedy. Sarcey was consistent in basing his contention upon his analysis of the attitude of the audience, on his observation of the difficulty experienced by Parisian playgoers when they were confronted by the necessity of changing abruptly from the mood of tears to the mood of laughter.

BRANDER MATTHEWS

April 1916

A Theory of the Theatre

I

I am going to propose for your consideration the ideas which I believe should form the first chapter of a treatise on the art of the theatre. But a few words by way of preface are necessary. Most readers, when you speak to them of a treatise on the art of the theatre—or, to express it more simply as did our fathers, when you speak to them of the Rules of dramatic art—believe that you have in mind a code of precepts by the aid of which one is assured, if he writes, of composing a piece without faults, or, if he criticizes, of being able to place his finger precisely on every defect.

At bottom this prepossession is entirely French; and it does not date from yesterday. You doubtless recall the worthy Abbé d'Aubignac, who, having promulgated a code of dramatic literature, wrote a tragedy according to his own formula and made it prodigiously tiresome. This misadventure has never cured the public of its belief in the efficacy of Rules.

They were cited against Corneille when he wrote *The Cid*, and against Molière when he gave us *The School for Wives*. Poor Corneille struggled as best he could in his prefaces to release himself from these laws which threatened to strangle him. And in the *Critique de l'École des Femmes* Molière has preserved for us a record of the annoyances which the pedants of his time sought to impose on him; and it is here that he delivered his famous dictum: "There is no other Rule of the theatre than that of pleasing the public."

We have laughed at this overstatement; we have not taken it at all seriously; and less than sixty years ago our fathers saw what difficulty those who were then called the Romanticists experienced in freeing themselves from the fetters of the code of tragedy laid down by Bossu, put into verse by Boileau, commented upon and reinforced by all the critics of the eighteenth century, with Voltaire at their head and after him La Harpe and Marmontel.

This national prejudice has its root in our philosophic education. From our infancy we have been taught that there is an ideal perfection which has an existence of its own and which is like an emanation from divinity; that everybody carries about with him a conception of it more or less clear, an image more or less enfeebled; and that works of art should be declared good or bad according as they approach or depart from this type of perfection.

I will not entangle myself by affirming that there is no such beau ideal or archetype of absolute perfection. I confess simply that I do not know what is meant by this, that these are questions outside my province, which I do not comprehend. It may be that in the sublunary regions there exists a form of drama supreme and marvelously perfect of which our masterpieces are only pale counterfeits; I leave to those who have had the good fortune of beholding this, and who say they are delighted by it, the duty and the pleasure of speaking of it with competence.

Rules do not render any great service in criticizing, any more than they do in creating. The best that can be said for them is that they may serve as directions or guideposts. After all, those who have no ear never love music and always beat time out of measure when they listen. Native taste sustained and purified by training, reflection, and usage can alone help you to enjoy works of art. The first condition of having pleasure is to love; and we do not love by rule.

It is customary in seeking a definition of dramatic art to say that drama is the representation of life. Now, assuredly drama is the representation of life. But when one has said that, he has said no great thing; and he has taught nothing to those whom he has furnished with this formula.

All the arts of imitation are representations of life. All have for their purpose the placing of nature before our eyes. What other object has painting than that of portraying for us either scenes from life or places which serve as a setting for it? And does not sculpture strive to render for us the images of living creatures, now single and now joined in groups? We may say with equal truth of all the arts that they are representations of life; in other words, copies from nature. But we see just as readily (for it is an observation that does not require reflection) that each of these arts has a different means of expression, that the conditions to which it is obliged to submit in order to represent life impose on each of them the employment of particular processes. Thus painting concerns itself with the representation on a plane surface of objects which have all their dimensions and of scenes from life which in reality would require for their existence a vast depth of background. It is clear that if you wish to suggest a theory of painting you must take careful account of this condition and of all the others, if there are any others, which are essential to this art, without which the art itself could not exist.

The first question to be settled, then, is that of the conditions, material or moral, in which resides necessarily and inevitably the art of which we speak. As it is impossible to separate the art from these conditions, as it lives only through and by them, as it is not a subtle inspiration wafted from heaven or emanating from the depths of the human mind, but something wholly concrete and definite which, like all living things, cannot exist except in the environment to which it is adapted, we are moved naturally to analyze this environment to which the art has accommodated its life, from which it has sprung, so to speak, by a series of successive developments, and of which it will always retain the impress. The painter takes a bit of wood or a scrap of canvas on which to represent life. It is a plane surface, is it not? Here is a fact, sure, undeniable. We will set out from there.

In the same way let us inquire concerning dramatic art if there is not also a fact which corresponds to this fact in painting and which is in like manner the indispensable condition of its existence and development. If we find this fact, we shall be able to draw logically some conclusions as incontestable as the fact itself; and we shall discover afterwards the proof of these conclusions in the history of the art.

Now, in regard to the theatre there is one fact which cannot fail to strike the least attentive; it is the presence of an audience. The word "play" carries with it the idea of an audience. We cannot conceive of a play without an audience. Take one after another the accessories which serve in the performance of a dramatic work: they can all be replaced or suppressed except that one. Thus theatres ordinarily are provided with a platform in the form of a stage, but you can imagine one without this; in fact, comedies are played in drawing rooms without changing the arrangement of the room. This may not be very convenient, but at any rate it does not alter the meaning of the comedy. The footlights are arranged to light the actors from below; and this is a very useful device, since it places the faces of the actors in full light and makes them seem younger and more animated by suppressing the shadows of the eyebrows and the nose. But is it a necessary condition? Assuredly not. You may imagine such other lighting system as you please, to say nothing of the sun, which was the sole illumination of the ancients, who certainly had a theatre. You may even dispense with the scenery and the costumes. Corneille and Molière have been played in barns by strolling actors grotesquely costumed according to the state of their humble wardrobes. It was none the less *The Cid* or *The School for Wives*. Shakespeare, as we have been told a hundred times, did not trouble himself in the least about scenery. A board was set up on the stage which indicated in writing where the action was taking place; and the imagination of the spectator filled in the rest to suit himself. It was none the less *Othello* or *Romeo and Juliet*.

But a play without an audience is inconceivable. It is possible that a king may at some time or other indulge the fantasy of seating himself alone in a playhouse and having played for himself alone some piece commanded by him. Such an eccentricity is only the exception which proves the rule. The king represents the absent audience; he is the crowd all by himself. And likewise the famous solitary spectator at the Odéon in the old days—the one whom Lireux provided with a foot-warmer—was the representative of the absent multitude. This legendary spectator was not only a spectator, he was the public. He included in his own person the twelve hundred truants who should have occupied the vacant seats about him. They had delegated their powers to him; it was they who applauded with his hands and who bore witness of their boredom when he opened his mouth to yawn.

It is an indisputable fact that a dramatic work, whatever it may be, is designed to be listened to by a number of persons united and forming an audience, that this is its very essence, that this is a necessary condition of its existence. As far back as you can go in the history of the theatre, in all countries and in all ages, the men who have ventured to give a representation of life in dramatic form have begun by gathering the spectators—Thespis around his chariot as Dumas around his *Étrangère*. It is with a public in view that they have composed their works and had them performed. This then we can insist on: No audience, no play. The audience is the necessary and inevitable condition to which dramatic art must accommodate its means.

II

I emphasize this point because it is the point of departure, because from this simple fact we can derive all the laws of the theatre without a single exception.

A moment ago I said that the painter is constantly obliged to represent everything on a flat surface, whether objects having all their dimensions or deep perspectives. How does he accomplish this? By a series of conventions, or tricks if you prefer, some of which are indicated and imposed by the structure and habit of our eyes and can hardly be modified, while the others are mere traditions which have no foundation in the necessity of things and are constantly variable. The same is true of the theatre. Its business is to represent life to a crowd. This crowd performs in some sort for dramatic art the function of the flat surface in painting. It requires the intervention of similar tricks, or, if you like the term better, of conventions. An example or two in order to enable you better to understand this. A crowd can scarcely be held together for more than four hours; or put it at five, six, eight, ten—let us say a whole day, though that is going rather far. It is certain that the following day, if this crowd collects again, it will not be composed of the same elements. It will still be a crowd, but it will not be the same crowd. The representation of life that we can exhibit before a crowd cannot, then, exceed an average of six hours in length. That is a fact of absolute necessity, against which no argument can prevail. The reading of a book may continue two months, the reader remaining always the same. But the crowd, by the fact of being a crowd, requires that drama end in six hours or less.

The action represented evidently lasts more than six hours. Even in case it were confined within this narrow limit (which might happen after all) it would require a mass of innumerable details for which we could find no room under this compression of time. It was necessary a moment ago to resort to deceptions in order to represent perspective on a flat surface; it will be necessary to resort to conventions in order to give the impression that a long time has elapsed when we have only six hours at our disposal.

Let us take another example, drawn this time from the moral order. It is asserted that a crowd thinks and feels differently from the individuals which compose it. I do not imagine that there is need at present of proving a fact so well known and so authentic.

The distinguishing mark then of this collective being which we call the public is a certain confirmation of the eye. It has the singular privilege of seeing things from another angle, illuminated by a light different from that of reality. The crowd changes the appearance of these things; where there are certain lines it sees others; where there are colors of a certain sort it sees different shades.

Well, if you present to this collective being, whose eyes have this gift of bizarre transformation, events from life just as they happen in reality, they will strike the crowd as being false, for they appear to the spectators altogether different from what they appear to the individuals composing the audience.

Suppose a scene painter should give to his canvas backgrounds the tones he has observed in nature: his picture, lighted by the glare of the footlights, would appear grotesque. So do facts and sentiments drawn from reality and transported just as they are to the stage. It is absolutely necessary to accommodate them to the particular disposition of mind which results among people when they assemble in the form of a crowd, when they compose an audience. Therefore deceptions—conventions—are essential. Among these conventions some are permanent, others temporary and changeable. The reason is easy to understand. The audience is composed of individuals; and among individuals there are sentiments —in very small number, it is true—which are general and universal, which we find in varying degrees among all the civilized peoples who alone have developed a dramatic art. Likewise there are prejudices (in still smaller number) which we encounter in all times and in all countries. These sentiments, these prejudices, or in a word these ways of looking at things, always remaining the same, it is natural that certain conventions, certain tricks, should be inherent in all drama, and that they should be established as laws.

On the contrary there are other sentiments, other prejudices, which are changeable, which vanish every time one
civilization is succeeded by another, and which are replaced
by different ways of seeing.

When the eyes of the audience change, the conventions
invented to give the illusion of life should change also, and
the laws which the technique each epoch has promulgated
and which it has in good faith believed to be universal and
unchangeable are destined to fall. But these laws may hold
good for a long time; and they do not crumble except under
the repeated assaults of intelligent criticism and of innova-
tors of genius.

What are the universal conventions, those that have their
root in all humanity? What, on the other hand, are the temporary conventions? What has been their influence? How
have they arisen and how fallen into disuse?

It is not sufficient simply to affirm that drama is the representation of life. It would be a more exact definition to
say that dramatic art is the sum total of the conventions,
universal or local, permanent or temporary, by the aid of
which, in representing life in the theatre, the audience is
given the illusion of truth.

III

Man, by the fact of being man, in all countries and in all
ages has had the privilege of expressing his joy or his grief
by laughter or by tears. There are other animals that weep,
but of all the beings of creation man is the only one that
laughs. Why does he laugh? And what are the causes of
laughter? It is not necessary for the moment to answer this
question. Man laughs; this is a fact which cannot be dis-
puted. He weeps; that is evident. He does not laugh nor
does he weep in the same fashion or at the same things in
company as alone. A crowd laughs more heartily and boister-
ously than an individual. Tears are readier and more abundant
with an audience than with a single man.

From this disposition of the public to express the most
universal sentiments of human nature, of joy and of sorrow,
by laughter and by tears, arises the great division of the
drama into plays that are cheerful and plays that are sad;
into comedy with all its subspecies, and into tragedy and
drama with all their varieties.

I do not say that it is the mission of the dramatic author

to bring life as it actually is on the stage; that as there are in real life events, some pleasant and some unpleasant, it necessarily follows that we must have comedies and trage-dies.

I hold that reality, if presented on the stage truthfully, would appear false to the monster with the thousand heads which we call the public. We have defined dramatic art as the sum total of the conventions by the aid of which, in the theatre, we represent life and give to the twelve hundred people assembled the illusion of truth.

In themselves, events are not cheerful and they are not sad. They are neither. It is we who impregnate them with our sentiment or color them to our liking. An old man falls; the street urchin who is passing holds his sides and laughs. The woman cries out with pity. It is the same event; but the one has thought only of the ridiculousness of the fall, the other has seen only the danger. The second wept where the first found cause only for laughter.

It is with events from human life as it is with landscapes. We often say of one view that it is hideous and of another that it is agreeable. This is an abuse of words. It is we who bestow on the places we pass the sentiments that move us; it is our imagination which transforms them; and it is we who give them a soul—our own.

It is true that certain landscapes seem better adapted to harmonize with the grief of a heart which is sad; but im-agine two lovers in the most forbidding spot, in the midst of steep cliffs, surrounded by dark forests and stagnant waters. The spot would be illumined for them by their love and would remain graven in their memory in delightful outlines. This perfect indifference of nature has even become in recent times a commonplace of poetic development. There is nothing which has more inspired our poets; everybody remembers the two admirable tunes in which Victor Hugo and Alfred de Musset played upon this theme: *Tristesse d' Olympio* and *Souvenir*.

How often may we not observe in actual life that which has been pointed out to us in a well-known example in the classic repertory; viz., that the same situation may be treated by laughter or by tears, transported from the comic to the tragic. Mithridates wishes to know of Monime whether in his absence Xiphares has not made love to her, whether she does not love the young man. In order to make her tell the

truth he pretends to believe himself too old for her and offers
to marry her to the son who will be better able to take his
place in her affection. Monime allows the fatal confession to
escape and everybody shivers at the famous line:
"Sire, you change countenance."

Harpagon, in the *Miser* of Molière, uses the same artifice
with Cléante; and the whole audience laughs at the rage of
the old man when he delivers his malediction to his son, who
does not wish to surrender Marianne. It is not, then, with
events, matter inert and indifferent, that we should concern
ourselves, but with the public which laughs or weeps according as certain chords are touched in preference to others.

Having established this point, we shall answer easily a
question which has caused the spilling of a great deal of ink,
and which has been greatly obscured because those who have
discussed it have not sought out the fundamental principles.

We agreed just now that by a very natural classification
plays are divided into comedies and tragedies. May we have,
is it well that we have, pieces for the stage in which laughter
is mingled with tears, in which comic scenes succeed painful
situations?

Most of those who rebel against the sustained seriousness
of tragedy, who advocate the mixing of the tragic and the
comic in the same play, have set out with the idea that it is
thus things happen in reality and that the art of the dramatist consists in transporting reality to the stage. It is this
very simple view that Victor Hugo sets forth in his admirable
preface to *Cromwell* in that highly imaginative style which
is so characteristic of him. I prefer to quote this brilliant
passage:

"In drama, as one may conceive it, even though he is unable to write it, everything is linked together and everything
follows in sequence as in real life. The body here plays a
part as the soul does; and men and events set in action by
this double agent pass before us ludicrous and terrible by
turns, sometimes terrible and ludicrous at the same time.

"Thus the judge will say: 'Off with his head—let's to dinner.' Thus the Roman Senate will deliberate on the turbot of
Domitian. Thus Socrates, drinking the hemlock and discours-
ing of the immortality of the soul and the one god, pauses
to recommend that a cock be sacrificed to Aesculapius. Thus
Elizabeth swears and speaks Latin.

"Thus Richelieu will be companioned by the monk Joseph,

and Louis XI will be escorted by his barber, Master Olivier the Devil. Thus Cromwell will say: 'I have Parliament in my bag and the king in my pocket,' or with the hand which signs the death warrant of Charles I he will smear with ink the face of a regicide who does the same to him laughingly. Thus Caesar in the triumphal chariot is afraid of upsetting; for men of genius, however great they may be, have in them an imp which parodies their intelligence. It is by this quality that they link themselves with humanity, and it is by this that they are dramatic.

" 'From the sublime to the ridiculous is only one step,' said Napoleon when he was convicted of being human, and this flash from a fiery soul laid bare illumines at once art and history, this cry of anguish is the summing up of drama and of life."

That is superb eloquence. But the great poets are not always very exact thinkers. The question is badly put. We are not at all concerned to know whether in real life the ludicrous is mingled with the terrible; in other words, whether the course of human events furnishes by turns to those who are either spectators or participants food for laughter and for tears. That is the one truth which no one questions and which has never been questioned. But the point at issue is altogether different. Twelve hundred persons are gathered together in the same room and form an audience. Are these twelve hundred persons likely to pass easily from tears to laughter and from laughter to tears? Is the playwright capable of transporting the audience from the one impression to the other? And does he not run the risk of enfeebling both impressions by this sudden contrast?

For example, to confine ourselves to the historic incidents cited by Victor Hugo, it does not at all concern us to know whether Cromwell after having signed the death warrant of Charles I did or did not smear with ink the face of one of his colleagues; whether this coarse pleasantry did or did not give rise to a coarse laugh in the assembly. The fact is authentic; we do not attempt to question it. The only thing we ask (in dramatic art, at least) is whether the fact, if placed on the stage just as it happened, is likely to please the twelve hundred persons in the audience.

These twelve hundred persons are entirely occupied with the death of Charles I, concerning which the author has sought to stir their pity. They are shedding tears of sympathy and tenderness. Suddenly the author places before them an act of broad buffoonery, alleging that in reality the grotesque mingles artlessly with the tragic. Do they laugh? And if they laugh do they experience a genuine satisfaction? Does not this laughter spoil the grief to which they found pleasure in abandoning themselves?

IV

It has often been remarked that laughter persists long after the causes have ceased, just as tears continue to flow after the arrival of the good news which should have dried them immediately. The human soul is not flexible enough to pass readily from one extreme of sensation to the contrary one. These sudden jolts overwhelm it with painful confusion.

From this reflection, of which no one, I believe, will dispute the justice, we may conclude that if, when a man is a prey to grief, he is diverted by an idea which inclines him to laughter, he is borne suddenly far from his sorrow, and a certain lapse of time and a certain effort of will are necessary for him to return to it.

What is true of one man is even more true of a crowd. We have seen that the peculiar characteristic of an audience is that it feels more keenly than the individuals composing it. It enters more impetuously into the reasons for weeping that the poet gives it; the grief that it experiences is more intense, the tears are readier and more abundant.

I forget what tyrant it was of ancient Greece to whom massacres were everyday affairs, but who wept copiously over the misfortunes of a heroine in a tragedy. He was audience, and for the one evening clothed himself in the sentiments of the public.

It is also more difficult for an audience to return to an impression from which it has been diverted by an accident of some sort. How many performances have been interrupted, how many plays failed the first night, because of a ludicrous slip by an actor or a piquant jest shouted from the gallery. All the house bursts out laughing. At once it becomes impossible for it to recover its equilibrium. It is now launched on another tack. The most touching scenes will be turned into ridicule. The play is lost.

In real life, this mixing of laughter and tears, this difficulty of returning to your grief after having left it, has no such disadvantage. As we have already said repeatedly, nature is indifferent and so also is life. You weep; it is well. You laugh afterwards, as you please. You laugh when you should weep; you weep when it would be better to laugh. That is your affair. You may weep with one eye and laugh with the other as the weeping and laughing Jean of the legend. It makes little difference to us.

In the theatre it is not the same. The author who brings upon the stage the events of life, and who naturally desires to make them interesting to his audience, must find means to heighten and render more vivid and more enduring the impression he wishes to create.

If his intention is to provoke laughter, he will be led by that alone to guard against every incident that might induce sadness in his audience; and if, on the other hand, his purpose is to compel tears, he will discard resolutely the circumstances which, by giving rise to laughter, might tend to counteract the emotion he wishes to arouse. He is not concerned in the least to know whether in reality laughter is mingled with tears. He does not seek to reproduce the truth, but to give the illusion of truth to the twelve hundred spectators— a very different matter. When these twelve hundred spectators are entirely overwhelmed with grief they cannot believe that joy exists; they do not think about it; they do not wish to think about it; it displeases them when they are torn suddenly from their illusion in order to be shown another aspect of the same subject.

And if you do show it to them against their will, if you force them to change abruptly from tears to laughter, and this last impression once becomes dominant, they will cling to it, and a return to the mood they have abandoned will be almost impossible. In life minutes are not counted, and we have all the time we need to bring about the transition from one sentiment to the other. But in the theatre, where we have at our disposal at most only four hours to exhibit all the series of events composing the action, the changes must take place swiftly and, so to speak, on the minute. This a man would resist if he were by himself; all the more will he resist it when he is one of a crowd.

To be strong and durable an impression must be single. All dramatists have felt this instinctively; and it is for this reason that the distinction between the comic and the tragic is as old as art itself.

It would seem that when drama came into being the writ-

ers of ancient times would have been led to mingle laughter
with tears, since drama represents life, and in life joy goes
hand in hand with grief, the grotesque always accompanying
the sublime. And yet the line of demarcation has been drawn
from the beginning. It seems that, without realizing the philosophic reasons we have just set forth, the dramatic poets
have felt that in order to sound the depths of the soul of
the audience they must strike always at the same spot; that
the impression would be stronger and more enduring in proportion as it was unified.

Do you find the least little word to excite laughter in the
grand conceptions of Aeschylus or the simple and powerful
dramas of Sophocles? It is true that in Sophocles the characters of humble condition express themselves in familiar
language which may seem comic to those of us who have
been nourished in the tradition of a necessary dignity in
tragedy. But this style has nothing of the comic in itself, any
more, for example, than the chattering of the Nurse in Shakespeare's *Romeo and Juliet.*

These characters speak as they would speak naturally; but
what they say does not alter in any way the impression of
sadness that is to result from the whole. They do not give
a turn to the events different from what the author intended.
They do not divert the attention of the audience either to
themselves or to ludicrous incidents. They contribute in the
measure of their ability, with the qualities peculiar to their
minds and their temperaments, to the general impression. We
hardly find except in Euripides, innovator and decadent genius, buffoonery deliberately mingled with drama, the grotesque
invading tragedy. The drunken scene between Hercules and
Admetus, who is mourning the death of Alcestis, is a celebrated example of this kind.

I need not say that with us more than with any other people this distinction of species has been marked from the beginning, until recent times. We have even carried it to the
extreme, for we have an exaggerated love of logic.

In the *Malade Imaginaire,* which is a comedy and which
consequently should turn entirely on laughter, Argan stretches
himself on his couch and pretends to be dead, and Angélique
is told that she has lost her father. Angélique in tears throws
herself beside her father, whom she really believes to be
dead. Suppose that Molière, forgetting that he was writing
a comedy, had insisted on this situation, which after all is

very touching. Suppose that he had prolonged it, that he had shown Angélique overcome with grief, ordering mourning, arranging for the funeral, and finally, by dint of the tenderness expressed and the tears shed, wringing tears from the audience. He could have done it assuredly. It would not have been difficult for him to move the twelve hundred spectators with these displays of filial grief. And likewise in the scene in *Tartuffe* in which Marianne kneels before her angry father to beg him to allow her to enter a convent.

If Molière had not restrained himself, he might have committed the precise fault into which Shakespeare, as I understand it, did not fall. He would have changed the aspect of events; I mean by this that he would have changed the mood in which he had led us to believe that the events would be treated. What was his intention? It was to show us, in contrast to Bélise punished for her avarice, Angélique rewarded for her filial piety, and the audience roaring with laughter at the sight of her father raised from the dead to marry her to her lover.

It was an impression of gaiety that he sought. He would have destroyed this impression had he dwelt too long on the grief of the young girl. From the same events he had meant to make use of in arousing laughter he could have extracted tears, and the audience would no longer be in the mood for laughter at the proper moment. The shock would have been too strong for the transition to be made easily.

Try to recall your past theatrical experience; you will find that in all the melodramas, in all the tragedies, whether classic or romantic, into which the grotesque has crept, it has always been obliged to take an humble place, to play an episodic part; otherwise it would have destroyed the unity of impression which the author always strives to produce. Wherever this does not hold, it is because it was the secret design of the author to extract mirth from a situation which is sad in appearance. Thus in *La Joie Fait Peur;* it is true that the situation in this play is that of a young man mourned by his mother, his *fiancée,* his sister, his friends, and his old servant. But the action is arranged in such a way that the entire audience is admitted at once to the secret that the young man is not dead. Everybody finally discovers this— except the mother, who remains disconsolate till the very end.

But who does not see that the joy of the others is one of

the important elements in this amusing play, that it consequently occupies an important place in the mind of the audience and adds a certain mysterious savor of humor to the tears shed by the poor mother? The impression here, then, remains single, since, far from being spoiled by the laughter which it arouses on its way, the dramatic quality of the situation is really heightened. The principle is this: The impression must be single; any mingling of laughter and tears tends to destroy this. It is better therefore to avoid it. There is nothing more legitimate than the absolute distinction of the comic from the tragic, of the grotesque from the sublime. Yet nowadays every rule is subject to many exceptions. It is an exception when the playwright feels himself strong enough to subordinate particular impressions to the general impression, when he can so control the temper of his spectators as to turn them all at once from laughter to tears, when the public he is seeking to please is capable of passing easily from one attitude to another, because of its advanced civilization, its racial instincts, its prejudices due to its education.

It depends on whether the author believes himself able to subordinate the particular to the general impression which he wishes to produce, whether he is sufficiently master of the psychology of his audience to transport them by a single stroke from laughter to tears, and on whether the audience to which he addresses himself is, by reason of the state of civilization at which it has arrived, either by prejudice of education or instinct of race, likely to pass easily from one sentiment to the other.

The rule remains intact. The impression must be single; and it cannot be this if the characters brought in for the comic scenes are anything more than episodic, if their pleasantries are anything more than accessories which can be easily supported.

Nature itself and life are impartial in the presence of joy and sorrow, laughter and tears, and pass with perfect indifference from one sentiment to the other. But to have demonstrated this, as did Victor Hugo in the admirable passage which we cited above, proves nothing, since a play is not a reproduction of life but an aggregate of conventions designed to produce upon the spectators the illusion of life; and they cannot have this illusion if the author disconcerts them by changing the sentiments which he inspires—if he disarranges their pleasure.

V

The conclusion is that the distinction between the comic and the tragic rests, not on a prejudice, but on the very definition of drama; that this distinction may remain absolute without disadvantage; that there are disadvantages on the contrary if it is not observed; that nevertheless it may be disregarded—not without peril, however—on this condition, that the disturbing element shall not interfere with the first impression, which should remain single, and that it shall even heighten that impression by a slight effect of contrast.

Consider for a moment that we must come down to the middle of the eighteenth century to find in our literature a single comedy in which a situation turns toward the pathetic and is treated in a manner to bring tears to the eyes of the spectators.

There is no doubt that the founders of our drama, and above all the immortal Molière, had made the very simple observation that in life it often happens that the most joyful events face about suddenly and change joy into despair. After a good dinner you embark with some comrades in a boat for a fishing party. Your spirits are a little flushed with wine; somebody is guilty of an imprudence. A single person has preserved his good sense and warns you of the danger you are inviting. You laugh him to ridicule; he himself yields to the general hilarity. A puff of wind catches the boat crosswise; it capsizes; everybody falls into the water. Two or three remain there and are not recovered till the next day. Is there an accident of more common occurrence? It is the terrible and the pathetic breaking in abruptly and imposing silence on laughter and changing it to tears. This is seen every day; it is the regular course of life.

If the masters of the drama, who could not have failed to make so simple an observation, have nevertheless written as if it had been unknown to them, it is apparent that their sole purpose was not to exhibit life as it really is on the stage, that they had in view another object—that of showing life in a certain aspect to twelve hundred persons assembled in a theatre, and of producing on the multiple soul of this audience a certain impression.

They must have said to themselves, or rather they felt instinctively, that every sensation is stronger the more it is prolonged without being opposed by any other; that an in-

dividual, and still more an audience, does not pass easily
from laughter to tears in order to return immediately from
tears to laughter; that they cling to the first impression; that
if you wrench them violently from one sentiment and throw
them into a contrary, it will be almost impossible to bring
them back later on; that these jolts threaten to destroy their
pleasure for them, and are especially wrong because they
give the impression that in the theatre all is false, the events
as well as the lighting, thus destroying the illusion.

As we do not pass in real life suddenly from laughter to
tears and return immediately, or almost immediately, from
tears to laughter, as the suddenness of these changes, however abrupt they may be, is relieved by intervals of time
more or less considerable, which the authors cannot preserve
in the theatre, the rapidity of these movements, aside from
the fact that they tire the audience, has this curious disadvantage, that in pretending to give us life in all its reality
they destroy the illusion of this same reality.

You may search all Molière, all Regnard, all Dufresny, all
Dancourt, and the rest of the dramatists of the beginning of
the eighteenth century, without finding in them a scene which
is not in the key suitable to comedy. If not all the scenes
are comic, all at least are amiable and pleasant. You will find
in them often tender conversations between lovers, scenes of
jealousy, lovers opposed by parents; but these scenes present
to the mind only the agreeable images of youth and hope. If
there is mingled with them some shadow of sadness, it is a
grief which is not without sweetness; the smile is always just
beneath the tears, as in that admirable account of Hector's
farewell to Andromache, which remains the best example of
these mingled sentiments of sun and shower.

Molière never wrote, or wished to write, anything but comedies which were comedies from beginning to end. And if
you will go back to classic antiquity you will see that he was
not an innovator. Show me a passage in Plautus to weep over;
and even Terence restricts himself to this scale of tempered
sentiments—to scenes in which, if he allows the tears sometimes to form on the eyelashes, they never fall, and are wiped
away at once with a smile.

Everywhere the characteristic of comedy in the great periods in which it flourished is to be comic.

And even today, look at the pieces truly worthy of the
name, from those of Augier to the marvelous farces of the

Palais Royal by Labiche, Meilhac, and Gondinet. Do you find in them any mixture of the pathetic? Is the unity of impression destroyed by a tearful scene? Can you easily imagine in *Célimare le Bien-Aimé,* the *Effrontés,* the *Testament de César Girodot,* the *Faux-Bonshommes,* the *Gendre de M. Poirier,* or *Mercadet* a situation which brings tears to the eyes?

I have here chosen purposely as examples works very diverse in tone and in style in order to show that this great law of the unity of impression—without which there is no possibility of illusion for an audience of twelve hundred persons —has been observed instinctively by all the playwrights who were truly endowed with the comic genius.

Goethe on the Theatre

Selections from the Conversations with Eckermann

Translated by John Oxenford

With an Introduction by William Witherle Lawrence

Introduction

In 1823, nine years before Goethe's death, Johann Peter Eckermann, a young man in his early thirties, journeyed on foot from Hanover to Weimar in order to meet face to face the poet and dramatist, whose works he had deeply admired. He was cordially received, and soon became an almost daily visitor at Goethe's house. His modest and gentle disposition, and his genuine enthusiasm for literature and art, and particularly for the drama, seem to have endeared him to the aging poet, who admitted him to an intimacy denied to far abler men. Eckermann's somewhat passive nature was no doubt more agreeable than a more assertive character would have been. Despite his mental vigor, Goethe was in his last years frequently unwell, and there are occasional hints in the *Conversations* of the ruses which he adopted to avoid wearying himself with uncongenial visitors. Probably, too, he had a shrewd idea that this sensitive adorer might transmit to posterity a portrait worth the having, and more flattering than one from the hand of a more vigorous artist. Many years before, Goethe had met Madame de Staël, who made no secret of the fact that she intended to immortalize their conversation in print. But Goethe was repelled rather than stimulated by the brilliant Frenchwoman, and he might well have feared that the outlines of a likeness of himself etched by her hand would be unduly sharpened. Certainly he had nothing of the sort to fear from Eckermann. He knew quite well what his disciple was doing; the writing and publication of the *Conversations* was agreed upon by the two men some years before Goethe's death. It was a happy inspiration; few

138

books throw more light upon the convictions of Goethe's maturity, or give a more vivid impression of his personality.

The literary reputation of Eckermann himself rests solely
upon this work. He had, at various times in his life, grandiose
plans for literary achievement, but such other material as he
actually produced is of no consequence. He is interesting
solely as the interpreter of Goethe. Although he was well
fitted by temperament for this task, he was indifferently educated. Born of peasant parents, he had, by virtue of his
quickness as a child, received schooling superior to his station,
but the necessity of earning his own living prevented him
from following his scholarly inclinations. After some experience in the army, and in a subordinate governmental post, he
finally enrolled at Göttingen as a student of law. But, as he
says in the little account of his early life which he has left us,
he was like a maiden who finds good reason to object to a
proposed marriage because she cherishes another in her heart.
Eckermann's real love was not law, but poetry and the drama.
He had also bestowed his affections upon a girl, Johanna
Bertram, whom Goethe does not seem to have encouraged
him to marry. Even when he did marry her, in 1831, after
many years of waiting, his devotion to Goethe and his frequent visits at the poet's house seem hardly to have been
interrupted. During all these years, his means of making a
living were somewhat precarious. Although he asserted with
vigor that he was not Goethe's secretary, but his pupil and
coworker, his services seem to have been in part those of
literary assistant, with the customary remuneration. He also
gave lessons to English visitors and residents in Weimar,
which helped him to gain a knowledge of English and an
ability to read the English classics—a valuable addition to
his incomplete education. Six years after Goethe's death he
was made Librarian to the Grand Duchess in Weimar, with
the title of Court Councilor; and in this pleasant sinecure
lived out the remaining years of his life until his death in
1854, a gentle, conceited, unimportant man, to whom the
reflected glory of a great personality has lent a kind of immortality.

Eckermann was not a Boswell; the *Conversations* have not
the vigor and piquancy of the immortal biography of Johnson. Nor does Goethe appear before us with the directness
and sincerity of the great lexicographer. Despite many charming glimpses of the poet's home life in Weimar, of his kind-

ness of heart and simplicity of taste, there are constant suggestions that he is posing for his admirer and for posterity. One must take Eckermann's record of their intimacy, too, with a grain of salt. The entries in Goethe's own diary are singularly laconic when compared with the enthusiastic expressions in Eckermann's pages. Goethe had been too long in the public eye to reveal himself without reserve. But this very element of calculation gives to his views an authority and finality which less considered utterances might have lacked. It is here, indeed, that the greatest value of the *Conversations* lies. They are chiefly important as a record of Goethe's convictions on a wide variety of subjects. In recording these utterances, in reproducing dialogue, Eckermann was singularly happy. Goethe's personality stands forth with wonderful vividness, and his words, even when oracular, seem easy and unconstrained. We can forgive the occasional self-satisfaction with which the biographer sets down his own views beside those of his master, in view of the greater naturalness which they lend to the dialogue. And if Eckermann has not the alluringly inquisitive toadiness of a Boswell, he is not too colorless a character to engage the sympathy and interest of the reader on his own account. But there are no other full-length portraits, not even of Goethe's family. An occasional visitor passes before our eyes, but he is only sketched in. Eckermann saw only his idol; he was not the man to portray a variety of personalities. It is only fair to add that neither the visitors to Weimar nor the dwellers in the little grand-ducal capital were at all comparable to the brilliant circle which gathered about Johnson and is immortalized in the pages of Boswell.

The biographer's chief passion was for the theatre—a passion so intense that Goethe has many a sly hit at his friend's ardor. The Weimar theatre in the decade before Goethe's death, while far from having the renown which the activity of Goethe and Schiller had earlier lent to it, was a good one as the times went, and it was supported with considerable enthusiasm. One of the most interesting passages in the *Conversations* describes the fire which destroyed the building in 1825, and there are further accounts of the new structure immediately planned and erected to take its place. The Weimar theatre had once before, like the phoenix, arisen from its ashes. A fire in 1774 had consumed it; and the new playhouse, the so-called Altes Theater, shown in the old prints as a long barracklike building of two stories, with a small portico in front, was the scene of most of Goethe's practical experience with the drama. A consideration of his connection with the stage, then, must deal chiefly with his career as director of this theatre.

When Goethe came to Weimar in 1775, at the invitation of Duke Karl August, he found a pleasure-loving court devoted to stage plays, but possessing no regular theatre. Private dramatic entertainments were a favorite form of amusement, and much care was lavished upon elaborate pieces in which the court circle took part. In these amateur theatricals Goethe naturally became prominent. He had shown himself to be a writer of distinction, and he was manifesting much executive ability in the affairs of the duchy. So when the theatre was finally built and opened for dramatic performances, Goethe was made director. The expenses of its maintenance were chiefly borne by the Duke; while the public was provided for, it was essentially a house for the court and the intellectuals. Actors of ability were engaged, and great care was taken with the production of ambitious works. Over all these performances Goethe ruled with a rod of iron. From 1800 on, the genius of Schiller co-operated with that of Goethe in making the Weimar theatre memorable. The untimely death of his brother poet was a great blow to Goethe's interest in the active stage, but he continued as director, though not in full activity, until 1817, when an unlucky quarrel with the Duke caused his retirement, together with that of his son August, who had recently become associated with him in the direction of the theatre. The rawness of the breach with Karl August was soon salved over, but it was an unfortunate end to Goethe's distinguished career as a theatrical manager, and a melancholy break in a long and intimate friendship. Karl August, though ruling over a duchy small in territory, had made it notable through his own ability and the talents of the men whom he had gathered about him.

The theatre under Goethe's direction was, however, by no means wholly successful. The trouble seems to have been that he was primarily a poet rather than a playwright, and that as a director he often sacrificed theatrical effectiveness to other considerations. Like Byron, whom he greatly admired, and like Tennyson and Browning, Goethe wrote much which was unsuited for production on the stage, though cast in dramatic form. With all his greatness, he belongs in a different category from Shakespeare or Molière, or even from Holberg or Goldoni, in that his plays are often not essentially dramatic. He was much occupied with moral issues, with setting forth an ideal; and he was much concerned in reviving masterpieces of the past, and in imitating the technique of great dramatists of other countries and other ages. He apparently allowed himself to forget that drama lives because it tells a story effectively, in a manner suited to the audience and to the playhouse in which it is acted. His *Iphigenia*, molded upon Greek tragedy, is a noble work, despite its long speeches and lack of action; but it suffers in the modern theatre because the audience lacks that intimate acquaintance with the story which enabled the Greeks to concentrate their attention upon motivation and upon analysis of character. His *Götz von Berlichingen*, one of his best plays, obviously influenced by the chronicle histories of Shakespeare, cuts the action up into many scenes, an arrangement easy enough upon the bare stage of the Elizabethans, but unsuited to the more elaborate scenery of modern days, which must be shifted for each change of locality. Goethe dreamed of founding a German drama, as he tells Eckermann, and to that end wrote *Iphigenia* and *Tasso*, but was disheartened at the lack of enthusiasm in his audience. He criticized Lessing for choosing the quarrels of Saxony and Prussia as a background for *Minna von Barnhelm*, but it was a wiser choice for an audience of German people than episodes of classical tragedy or Renaissance idealism. Goethe's greatest work, *Faust*, is a perfect illustration of great drama which is unsuited to the theatre. The Second Part, though often given in Germany, needs only to be seen on the stage to be adjudged a piece to be read; and the First Part, with all its glorious poetry, and with all the effectiveness of single scenes, is really a succession of episodes rather than a connected drama. It lacks the cohesion which binds together even the loosest of Shakespeare's dramatic romances, like the *Winter's Tale* or *Cymbeline*. The plays of Schiller are far superior to those of Goethe in dramatic effectiveness, but even Schiller was not wholly free from the fault which has just been noted. Goethe himself speaks in the *Conversations* of the difficulty which Schiller experienced in subduing his material to dramatic form. The soaring imagination of each great poet was hardly to be confined within the somewhat arbitrary limits of dramatic technique. It may be questioned whether some of Goethe's plays which are given in Germany at the present day would not have lost their place in the playhouse long since, were it not for the greatness of Goethe as a master of literature and the piety with which the Germans regard even the minor works of a genius. Probably few Germans would agree with Scherer's conclusion that Goethe lacked the fiber of a dramatist.

It is interesting to observe that if Goethe was not always successful in practice, he was generally correct in precept. He recognized very clearly the difficulty of composition for the stage. Upon this point he expressed himself in no uncertain terms to Eckermann. "Writing for the stage," he said, "is an art by itself, and he who does not understand it thoroughly had better leave it alone. Everyone thinks that an interesting fact will appear interesting in the theatre—nothing of the kind! Things may be very pretty to read, and very pretty to think about; but as soon as they are put upon the stage the effect is quite different, and what has charmed us in the closet will probably fall flat on the boards. When one reads my *Hermann and Dorothea*, he thinks it might be brought out at the theatre. Töpfer has been inveigled into the experiment, but what is it, what effect does it produce, especially if it is not played in a first-rate manner? And who can say that it is in every respect a good piece? Writing for the stage is a trade that one must understand, and requires a talent that one must possess. Both are uncommon, and where they are not combined, we shall scarcely have any good result." Such suggestive observations as these on the business of playmaking and play-producing are scattered through the *Conversations*. Goethe loved to crystallize his knowledge into pungent phrases, but he perceived clearly the futility of attempting to reduce theatrical management to a series of aphorisms. "The theatre," he says in a short paper on the Weimar stage, "is one of those affairs which can least of all be managed according to rules; one is entirely dependent upon the times in which he lives and upon his contemporaries. What the author chooses to write, the actors to perform, and the public to hear—these are the things that tyrannize over the directors of theatres, and in the face of which they can preserve hardly any will of their own." The history of the Weimar theatre scarcely bears this out. Goethe was, it appears, rather a tyrannical director himself; his imperious will often aroused opposition. Possibly the very force of the circumstances of which he speaks—the demands made by author, actors, and public—roused his naturally vigorous temperament to a more intense activity.

To select for reprinting passages which deal with only one subject does an injustice to the *Conversations* as a whole. Perhaps the most remarkable thing about Goethe was the variety of his interests and the diversity of the pursuits in which he attained distinction. Of this versatility and virtuosity the *Conversations* give a very striking illustration. The keenest interest in art, letters, science, politics, and philosophy is there revealed. It is the record of a mind of the widest sympathy with many different forms of human endeavor. The picture is no doubt too much idealized; we know well enough that Goethe was neither a saint nor a demigod, but a man with many human weaknesses. But we can forgive some suppression of his defects in the general truth of the portrait drawn by Eckermann. The *Conversations* indeed confirm Napoleon's terse characterization of Goethe—an unconscious echo of Antony's words over the dead Brutus, and doubly significant because of Napoleon's own intellectual eminence —"*Voilà un homme!*"

John Oxenford's translation of the *Conversations*, completed midway in the nineteenth century, while not without faults, is fairly adequate.* The original German, which would sometimes be clumsy if rendered literally into English, is often paraphrased, with a slight flavor of mid-Victorian elegance quite in keeping with Eckermann's rather conscious style. The present editor has taken the liberty of making a few alterations, in order to secure greater accuracy, clearness, or smoothness.

It seems incomparably the better plan to arrange the *Con-*

* *Conversations of Goethe with Eckermann and Soret, translated from the German by John Oxenford.* Revised edition, Bell and Sons, London, 1913. The original edition of Oxenford's work appeared in 1850. A useful critical edition of the original is that by Dr. H. H. Houben: *Gespräche mit Goethe in den letzten Jahren seines Lebens, von Johann Peter Eckermann.* Brockhaus, Leipzig, 1909. The first German edition of the *Conversations* was published in two volumes in 1836. In 1848 Eckermann added a third volume containing additional material, some of it furnished by a Swiss gentleman named Soret, who had been a frequent visitor at Goethe's house. A translation of some portions of the *Conversations* by Margaret Fuller was published in 1839.

versations in the order in which they are reported as having taken place, irrespective of the date of their appearance in print. To indicate the arrangement in the original editions serves only the purpose of the special student of Goethe bibliography. In general, only those passages which have a direct bearing on the drama are here reprinted, although no attempt has been made to include them all. Enough of the narrative of life in Weimar has been given to make the discussions of the theatre and its people more vivid and comprehensible.

The purpose of the present selections is not to offer a commentary on Goethe, or on the theatrical conditions of his day; its aim is rather to bring together in convenient form the dramatic convictions of a great poetic genius who was both a prolific writer for the theatre and a dramatic director of long and varied experience.

WILLIAM WITHERLE LAWRENCE

Goethe on the Theatre

Tuesday, October 14th. This evening, I went for the first time to a large tea-party at Goethe's. I arrived first, and enjoyed the view of the brilliantly lighted apartments, which, through open doors, led one into another. In one of the furthest, I found Goethe, who came to meet me with a cheerful air. He was dressed in black, and wore his star, which became him so well. We were for a while alone, and went into the so-called "ceiling room" (*Deckenzimmer*), where the picture of the Aldobrandine Marriage, which was hung above a red couch, especially attracted my attention. On the curtains being drawn aside, the picture was before my eyes in a strong light, and I was delighted to contemplate it quietly. . . .

Goethe himself appeared very amiable in society. He went about from one to another, and always seemed to prefer listening and hearing his guests talk, to talking much himself. . . .

He came to me with Frau von Goethe. "This is my daughter-in-law," said he; "do you know each other?"

We told him that we had just become acquainted.

"He is as much a child about a theatre as you, Ottilie!" said he; and we exchanged congratulations upon the taste which we had in common. "My daughter," continued he, "never misses an evening."

"That is all very well," said I, "as long as they give good lively pieces; but when the pieces are bad, they try the patience."

"But," said Goethe, "it is a good thing that you cannot leave, but are forced to hear and see even what is bad. By this means, you are penetrated with the hatred for the bad, and come to a clearer insight into the good. In reading, it is not so—you throw aside the book, if it displeases you; but at the theatre you must endure."

Saturday, October 25th. We talked of the theatre, which was one of the topics which chiefly interested me this winter. The *Erdennacht* of Raupach was the last piece I had seen. I gave it as my opinion that the piece was not brought before us as it existed in the mind of the poet; that the Idea was more predominant than Life; that it was rather lyric than dramatic; and that what was spun out through five acts would have been far better in two or three. Goethe added that the idea of the whole turned upon aristocracy and democracy, and that this was by no means of universal interest to humanity.

I then praised those pieces of Kotzebue's which I had seen—namely, his *Verwandschaften,* and his *Versöhnung.* I praised in them the quick eye for real life, the dexterity at seizing its interesting sides, and the occasionally genuine and forcible representation of it. Goethe agreed with me. "What has kept its place for twenty years, and enjoys the favour of the people," said he, "must have something in it. When Kotzebue contented himself with his own sphere, and did not go beyond his powers, he usually did well. It was the same with him as with Chodowiecky, who always succeeded perfectly with the scenes of common citizens' life, while if he attempted to paint Greek or Roman heroes, he failed."

Goethe named several other good pieces of Kotzebue's, especially *Die beiden Klingsberge.* "No one can deny," said he, "that Kotzebue has looked about a great deal in life, and kept his eyes open.

"Intellect, and some poetry," continued Goethe, "cannot be denied to our modern tragic poets, but most of them are incapable of an easy, living representation; they strive after something beyond their powers; and for that reason I might call them *forced* talents."

"I doubt," said I, "whether such poets could write a piece in prose, and am of the opinion that this would be the true touchstone of their talent." Goethe agreed with me, adding that verification enhanced, and even called forth, poetic feeling.

1824

Friday, January 2nd. We talked of English literature, the greatness of Shakespeare, and the unfavourable position held by all English dramatic authors who had appeared after that poetical giant.

"A dramatic talent of any importance," said Goethe, "could not forbear to notice Shakespeare's works, nay, could not forbear to study them. Having studied them, he must be aware that Shakespeare has already exhausted the whole of human nature in all its tendencies, in all its heights and depths, and that, in fact, there remains for him, the after-comer, nothing more to do. And how could one get courage to put pen to paper, if one were conscious, even in a spirit of earnestness and appreciation, that such unfathomable and unattainable excellences were already in existence!

"It fared better with me fifty years ago in my own dear Germany. I could soon come to an end with all that then existed; it could not long awe me, or occupy my attention. I soon left behind me German literature, and the study of it, and turned my thoughts to life and to production. So gradually advancing I proceeded in my natural development, and formed myself for the work which from one time to another I was able to produce. And at every step of life and development my standard of excellence was not much higher than what at such step I was able to attain. But had I been born an Englishman, and had all those diverse masterpieces been brought before me in all their power at my first dawn of youthful consciousness, they would have overpowered me, and I should not have known what to do. I could not have gone on with such fresh light-heartedness, but should have had to bethink myself, and look about for a long time, to find some new outlet."

I turned the conversation back to Shakespeare. "When one, to some degree, disengages him from English literature," said I, "and considers him transformed into a German, one cannot fail to look upon his gigantic greatness as a miracle. But if one seeks him in his home, transplants oneself to the soil of his country, and to the atmosphere of the century in which he lived; further, if one studies his contemporaries, and his immediate successors, and inhales the force wafted to us from Ben Jonson, Massinger, Marlowe, and Beaumont and

Fletcher, Shakespeare still, indeed, appears a being of the most exalted magnitude; but one arrives at the conviction that many of the wonders of his genius are, in some measure, accessible, and that much in his work is due to the powerful and productive atmosphere of his age and time."

"You are perfectly right," returned Goethe. "It is with Shakespeare as with the mountains of Switzerland. Transplant Mont Blanc at once into the large plain of Lüneburg Heath, and you would find no words to express your wonder at its magnitude. Visit it, however, in its gigantic home, go to it over its immense neighbours, the Jungfrau, the Finsteraarhorn, the Eiger, the Wetterhorn, St. Gothard, and Monte Rosa; Mont Blanc will, indeed, still remain a giant, but it will no longer produce in us such amazement.

"Besides, let him who will not believe," continued Goethe, "that much of Shakespeare's greatness belongs to his great vigorous time only ask himself the question, whether he thinks so astounding a phenomenon would be possible in the present England of 1824, in these evil days of journals that criticize and destroy?"

Tuesday, March 30th. This evening I was with Goethe. I was alone with him; we talked on various subjects, and drank a bottle of wine. We spoke of the French drama, as contrasted with the German.

"It will be very difficult," said Goethe, "for the German public to come to a kind of right judgment, as they do in Italy and France. We have a special obstacle in the circumstance that on our stage a medley of all sorts of things is represented. On the same boards where we saw Hamlet yesterday, we see Staberle to-day; and if to-morrow we are delighted with *The Magic Flute,* the day after we shall be charmed with the oddities of the favourite of the moment. Hence the public becomes confused in its judgment, mingling together various species, which it never learns rightly to appreciate and to understand. Furthermore, every one has his own individual demands and personal wishes, and returns to the spot where he finds them realised. On the tree where he has plucked figs to-day, he would pluck them again to-morrow, and would make a long face if sloes had grown in their stead during the night. But if any one is a friend to sloes, he turns to the thorns.

"Schiller had the happy thought of building a house for

tragedy alone, and of giving a piece every week for the male sex exclusively. But this notion presupposed a very large city, and could not be realised in our humble circumstances."

We talked about the plays of Iffland and Kotzebue, which, in their way, Goethe highly commended. "From this very fault," said he, "that people do not perfectly distinguish between *kinds* in art, the pieces of these men are often unjustly censured. We may wait a long time before a couple of such popular talents come again."

Sunday, May 2nd. Goethe had sent me this morning a roll of papers relative to the theatre, among which I had found some detached remarks, containing the rules and studies which he had carried out with Wolff and Grüner to qualify them for good actors. I found these details important and highly instructive for young actors, and therefore proposed to put them together, and make from them a sort of theatrical catechism. Goethe consented, and we discussed the matter further. This gave us occasion to speak of some distinguished actors who had been formed in his school; and I took the opportunity to ask some questions about Frau von Heigendorf. "I may," said Goethe, "have influenced her, but, properly speaking, she is not my pupil. She was, as it were, born on the boards, and was as decided, ready, and adroit in anything as a duck in the water. She did not need my instruction, but did what was right instinctively, perhaps without knowing it."

We then talked of the many years he had superintended the theatre, and the infinite time which had thus been lost to literary production. "Yes," said he, "I may have missed writing many a good thing, but when I reflect, I am not sorry. I have always regarded all I have done solely as symbolical; and, in fact, it has been pretty much a matter of indifference to me whether I have made pots or dishes."

1825

Tuesday, January 18th. Reimer spoke of Schiller's personal appearance. "The build of his limbs, his gait in the street, all his motions," said he, "were proud; his eyes only were soft."

"Yes," said Goethe, "everything else about him was proud and majestic, only the eyes were soft. And his talent was like his outward form. He seized boldly on a great subject, and turned it this way and that, and looked at it now on one side, now on another, and handled it in diverse ways. But he saw his object, as it were, only on the outside; a quiet development from within was not within his province. His talent was desultory. Thus he was never decided—could never bring things to an end. He often changed a part just before a rehearsal.

"And, as he went boldly to work, he did not take sufficient pains about *motives*. I recollect what trouble I had with him, when he wanted to make Gessler, in *Tell*, abruptly break an apple from the tree, and have it shot from the boy's head. This was quite against my nature, and I urged him to give at least some motive to this barbarity by making the boy boast to Gessler of his father's dexterity, and say that he could shoot an apple from a tree at a hundred paces. Schiller, at first, would have nothing of the sort; but at last he yielded to my arguments and intentions, and did as I advised him. I, on the other hand, by too great attention to motives, kept my pieces from the theatre. My *Eugenie* is nothing but a chain of motives, and this cannot succeed on the stage.

"Schiller's genius was really made for the theatre. With every piece he progressed, and became more finished; but, strange to say, a certain love for the horrible adhered to him from the time of *The Robbers*, which never quite left him even in his prime. I still recollect perfectly well that in the prison scene in my *Egmont*, where the sentence is read to him, Schiller would have made Alva appear in the background, masked and muffled in a cloak, enjoying the effect which the sentence would produce on Egmont. Thus Alva was to show himself insatiable in revenge and malice. I, however, protested, and prevented his appearance. Schiller was a great and wonderful man."

Thursday, February 24th. "If I were still superintendent of the theatre," said Goethe this evening, "I would bring out Byron's *Doge of Venice*. The piece is indeed too long and would require shortening. Nothing, however, should be cut out, but the import of each scene should be taken, and expressed more concisely. The piece would thus be brought close together, without being damaged by alterations, and it would gain a powerful effect, without any essential loss of beauty."

This opinion of Goethe's gave me a new view as to how we might proceed on the stage, in a hundred similar cases. . . .

We talked more about Lord Byron, and I mentioned how, in his conversations with Medwin, he had said there was something extremely difficult and unthankful in writing for the theatre. "The great point is," said Goethe, "for the poet to strike into the path which the taste and interest of the public have taken. If the direction of his talent accords with that of the public, everything is gained. Houwald hit this path with his *Bild*, and hence the universal applause he received. Lord Byron, perhaps, would not have been so fortunate, inasmuch as his tendency varied from that of the public. The greatness of the poet is by no means the important matter. On the contrary, one who is little elevated above the general public may often gain the most general favour precisely on that account."

We continued to converse about Byron, and Goethe admired his extraordinary talent. "That which I call invention," said he, "I never saw in any one in the world to a greater degree than in him. His manner of loosing a dramatic knot is always better than one would anticipate."

"That," said I, "is what I feel about Shakespeare, especially when Falstaff has entangled himself in such a net of falsehoods, and when I ask myself what I should do to help him out I find that Shakespeare far surpasses all my ideas. That you say the same of Lord Byron is the highest praise that can be bestowed on him. Nevertheless," I added, "the poet who takes a clear survey of beginning and end has, by far, the advantage with the experienced reader."

Goethe agreed with me, and laughed to think that Lord Byron, who, in practical life, could never adapt himself, and never asked about a law, finally subjected himself to the stupidest of laws—that of the *three unities*.

"He understood the purpose of this law," said he, "no better than the rest of the world. Comprehensibility is the purpose, and the three unities are only so far good as they conduce to this end. If the observance of them hinders the comprehension of a work, it is foolish to treat them as laws, and try to observe them. Even the Greeks, from whom the rule was taken, did not always follow it. In the *Phaëthon* of Euripides, and in other pieces, there is a change of place, and it is obvious that good representation of their subjects was with them more important than blind obedience to a law, which, in itself, is of no great consequence. The pieces of Shakespeare deviate, as far as possible, from the unities of time and place; but they are comprehensible—nothing is more so—and on this account the Greeks would have found no fault with them. The French poets have endeavoured to follow more rigidly the laws of the three unities, but they sin against comprehensibility, inasmuch as they show a dramatic law, not dramatically, but by narration."

Tuesday, March 22nd. Last night, soon after twelve o'clock, we were awakened by an alarm of fire; we heard cries: "The theatre is on fire!" I at once threw on my clothes, and hastened to the spot. The universal consternation was very great. Only a few hours before we had been delighted with the excellent acting of La Roche in Cumberland's *Jew*, and Seidel had excited universal laughter by his good humour and jokes. And now, in the place so lately the scene of intellectual pleasures, raged the most terrible element of destruction.

The fire, which was occasioned by the heating apparatus, appears to have broken out in the pit; it soon spread to the stage and the dry lath-work of the wings, and, as it increased fearfully by the great quantity of combustible material, it was not long before the flames burst through the roof, and the rafters gave way. . . .

I saw in beautiful eyes many tears, which flowed for its downfall. I was no less touched by the grief of a member of the orchestra. He wept for his burnt violin. As the day dawned, I saw many pale countenances. I remarked several young girls and women of high rank, who had awaited the result of the fire during the whole night, and who now shivered in the cold morning air. I returned home to take a little rest, and in the course of the forenoon I called upon Goethe.

The servant told me that he was unwell and in bed. Still Goethe called me to his side. . . .

"I have thought much of you, and pitied you," said he. "What will you do with your evenings now?"

"You know," returned I, "how passionately I love the theatre. When I came here, two years ago, I knew nothing at all, except three or four pieces which I had seen in Hanover. . . . All was new to me, actors as well as pieces; and twice, according to your advice, I have given myself up entirely to the impression of the subject, without much thinking or reflecting. I can say with truth that I have, during these two winters, passed at the theatre the most innocent and most agreeable hours that I have ever known. I was, moreover, so infatuated with the theatre that I not only missed no performance, but also obtained admission to the rehearsals; nay, not contented with this, if, as I passed in the daytime, I chanced to find the doors open, I would enter, and sit for half an hour upon the empty benches in the pit, and imagine scenes which might at some time be played there."

"You are a crazy fellow," returned Goethe, laughing; "but that is what I like. Would to God that the whole public consisted of such children! And in fact you are right. Any one who is sufficiently young, and who is not quite spoiled, could not easily find any place that would suit him so well as a theatre. No one makes any demands upon you; you need not open your mouth unless you choose; on the contrary, you sit quite at your ease like a king, and let everything pass before you, and recreate your mind and senses to your heart's content. There is poetry, there is painting, there are singing and music, there is acting and what not besides. When all these arts, and the charm of youth and beauty heightened to a considerable degree, work together on the same evening, it is an occasion to which no other can compare. But, even when part is bad and part is good, it is still better than looking out of the window, or playing a game of whist in a close party amid the smoke of cigars. The theatre at Weimar is, as you feel, by no means to be despised; it is still an old trunk from our best time, to which new and fresh talents have attached themselves; and we can still produce something which charms and pleases, and at least gives the appearance of an organised whole."

"Would I had seen it twenty or thirty years ago!" answered I.

"That was certainly a time," replied Goethe, "when we were assisted by great advantages. Consider that the tedious period of the French taste had not long gone by; that the public was not yet spoiled by overexcitement; that the influence of Shakespeare was in all its first freshness; that the operas of Mozart were new; and, lastly, that the pieces of Schiller were first produced here year after year, and were given at the theatre of Weimar in all their first glory, under his own superintendence. Consider all this, I say, and you will imagine that, with such dishes, a fine banquet was given to old and young, and that we always had a grateful public."

I remarked, "Older persons, who lived in those times, cannot praise highly enough the elevated position which the Weimar theatre then held."

"I will not deny that it was of some account," returned Goethe. "The main point, however, was this, that the Grand Duke left my hands quite free, and I could do just as I liked. I did not look to magnificent scenery, and a brilliant wardrobe, but I looked to good pieces. From tragedy to farce, every species was welcome; but a piece was obliged to have something in it to find favour. It was necessary that it should be great and clever, cheerful and graceful, and, at all events, healthy and containing some pith. All that was morbid, weak, lachrymose and sentimental, as well as all that was frightful, horrible and offensive to decorum, was utterly excluded; I should have feared, by such expedients, to spoil both actors and audience.

"By means of good pieces I educated the actors; for the study of excellence, and the perpetual practice of excellence, must necessarily make something of a man whom nature has not left ungifted. I was, also, constantly in personal contact with the actors. I attended the readings of plays, and explained to every one his part; I was present at the chief rehearsals, and talked with the actors as to any improvements that might be made; I was never absent from a performance, and pointed out the next day anything which did not appear to me to be right. By these means I advanced them in their art. But I also sought to raise the whole class in the esteem of society by introducing the best and most promising into my own circle, and thus showing to the world that I considered them worthy of social intercourse with myself. The result of this was that the rest of the higher society in Weimar did not remain behind me, and that actors and actresses gained soon an honourable admission into the best circles. By all this they acquired a great personal as well as external culture. My pupil Wolff, in Berlin, and our Dürand are people of the finest tact in society. Oels and Graff have enough of the higher order of culture to do honour to the best circles.

"Schiller proceeded in the same spirit as myself. He had a great deal of intercourse with actors and actresses. He, like me, was present at every rehearsal; and after every successful performance of one of his pieces, it was his custom to invite the actors, and to spend a merry day with them. All rejoiced together at that which had succeeded, and discussed how anything might be done better next time. But even when

Schiller joined us, he found both actors and the public already cultivated to a high degree; and it is not to be denied that this conduced to the rapid success of his pieces."

It gave me great pleasure to hear Goethe speak so circumstantially upon a subject which always possessed great interest for me, and which, in consequence of the misfortune of the previous night, was uppermost in my mind.

"This burning of the house," said I, "in which you and Schiller, during a long course of years, effected so much good, in some degree closes a great epoch, which will not soon return for Weimar. You must at that time have experienced great pleasure in your direction of the theatre and its extraordinary success."

"And not a little trouble and difficulty," returned Goethe with a sigh.

"It must be difficult," said I, "to keep such a many-headed being in proper order."

"A great deal," said Goethe, "may be done by severity, more by love, but most by clear discernment and impartial justice, which pays no respect to persons.

"I had to beware of two enemies, which might have been dangerous to me. The one was my passionate love of talent, which might easily have made me partial. The other I will not mention, but you can guess it. At our theatre there was no want of ladies, who were beautiful and young, and who were possessed of great mental charms. I felt a passionate inclination towards many of them, and sometimes it happened that I was met half way. But I restrained myself, and said, No further! I knew my position, and also what I owed to it. I stood here, not as a private man, but as chief of an establishment, the prosperity of which was of more consequence to me than a momentary gratification. If I had involved myself in any love affair, I should have been like a compass, which cannot possibly point right, if it has a powerful magnet beside it."

Sunday, March 27th. . . . The conversation then turned upon actors, and much was said about the use and abuse of their powers.

"I have, during my long practice," said Goethe, "found that the main point is never to allow any play, or scarcely any opera, to be prepared for representation unless one can look forward with some certainty to a good success for years. No one sufficiently considers the expenditure of power, which is demanded for the preparation of a five-act play, or even an opera of equal length. Yes, my good friends, much is required before a singer has thoroughly mastered a part through all the scenes and acts, much more before the choruses go as they ought. . . .

"And then, when a good play or a good opera has once been prepared for the stage, it should be represented at short intervals—be allowed to run as long as it draws, and continues at all to fill the house. The same plan would be applicable to a good old play, or a good old opera, which has, perhaps, been long laid aside, and which now requires not a little fresh study to be reproduced with success. Such a representation should be repeated at short intervals, as frequently as the public shows any interest in it. The desire always to have something new, and to see only once, or at the most twice, a good play or opera, which has been studied with excessive pains, or even to allow the space of six or eight weeks to elapse between such repetitions, in which time a new study becomes necessary—all this is a real detriment to the theatre, and an unpardonable misuse of the talents of the performers engaged in it."

Goethe appeared to consider this matter very important, and it seemed to lie so near his heart that he became more excited than, with his calm disposition, is often the case.

"In Italy," continued Goethe, "they perform the same opera every evening for four or six weeks, and the Italians —big children—by no means desire any change. The polished Parisian sees the classical plays of his great poets so often that he knows them by heart, and has a practised ear for the accentuation of every syllable. Here, in Weimar, they have done me the honour to perform my *Iphigenia* and my *Tasso,* but how often? Scarcely once in three or four years. The public finds them tedious. Very probably. The actors are not in practice to play the pieces, and the public is not accustomed to hear them. If, through more frequent repetitions, the actors entered so much into the spirit of their parts that their representation gained life, as if it were not the result of study, but as though everything flowed from their own hearts, the public would, assuredly, no longer remain uninterested and unmoved.

"I really had the illusion once upon a time that it was possible to form a German drama. Nay, I even fancied that I myself could contribute to it, and lay some foundation-stones for such an edifice. I wrote my *Iphigenia* and my *Tasso,* and thought, with a childish hope, that thus it might be brought about. But there was no emotion or excitement— all remained as it was before. If I had produced an effect, and met with applause, I would have written a round dozen of such pieces as *Iphigenia* and *Tasso.* There was no deficiency of material. But, as I said, actors were wanting to represent such pieces with life and spirit, and a public was wanting to hear and receive them with sympathy."

Thursday, April 14th. This evening at Goethe's. Since conversations upon the theatre and theatrical management were now the order of the day, I asked him upon what maxims he proceeded in the choice of a new member of the company.

"I can scarcely say," returned Goethe; "I had various modes of proceeding. If a striking reputation preceded the new actor, I let him act, and saw how he suited the others; whether his style and manner disturbed our ensemble, or whether he would supply a deficiency. If, however, he was a young man who had never trodden a stage before, I first considered his personal qualities; whether he had about him anything prepossessing or attractive, and, above all things, whether he had control over himself. For an actor who possesses no self-possession, and who cannot appear before a stranger in his most favourable light, has, in any case, little talent. His whole profession requires continual self-concealment, and a continual existence in a foreign mask.

"If his appearance and his deportment pleased me, I made him read, in order to test the power and extent of his voice, as well as the capabilities of his mind. I gave him some sublime passage from a great poet, to see whether he was capable of feeling and expressing what was really great; then something passionate and wild, to prove his power. I then went to something marked by sense and smartness, something ironical and witty, to see how he treated such things, and whether he possessed sufficient versatility. Then I gave him something in which was represented the pain of a wounded heart, the suffering of a great soul, that I might learn whether he had it in his power to express pathos.

"If he satisfied me in all these numerous particulars I had a well-grounded hope of making him a very important actor. If he appeared more capable in some particulars than in others, I remarked the line to which he was most adapted. I also now knew his weak points, and, above all, endeavoured to work upon him so that he might strengthen and cultivate himself here. If I remarked faults of dialect, and what are called provincialisms, I urged him to lay them aside, and recommended to him social intercourse and friendly practice with some member of the stage who was entirely free from them. I then asked him whether he could dance and fence; and if this were not the case, I would hand him over for some time to the dancing and fencing masters.

"If he were now sufficiently advanced to make his appearance, I gave him at first such parts as suited his individuality, and I desired nothing but that he should represent himself. If he now appeared to me of too fiery a nature, I gave him phlegmatic characters; if too calm and slow, I gave him fiery and hasty characters, that he might thus learn to lay aside himself and assume a foreign individuality."

The conversation turned upon the casting of plays, upon which Goethe made, among others, the following remarkable observations.

"It is a great error to think," said he, "that an indifferent piece may be played by indifferent actors. A second- or third-rate play can be incredibly improved by the employment of first-rate powers, and be made something really good. But if a second- or third-rate play be performed by second- or third-rate actors, no one can wonder if it is utterly ineffective. Second-rate actors are excellent in great plays. They have the same effect that the figures in half shade have in a picture; they serve admirably to show off more powerfully those which have the full light."

Wednesday, April 20th. A poet who writes for the stage must have a knowledge of the stage, that he may weigh the means at his command, and know what is to be done, and what is to be left alone; the opera-composer, in like manner, should have some insight into poetry, that he may know how to distinguish the bad from the good, and not apply his art to something impracticable.

"Carl Maria von Weber," said Goethe, "should not have composed *Euryanthe*. He should have seen at once that this was a bad material, of which nothing could be made. So much insight we have a right to expect of every composer, as belonging to his art."

Thus, too, the painter should be able to distinguish subjects; for it belongs to his department to know what he has to paint, and what to leave unpainted.

"But when all is said," observed Goethe, "the greatest art is to limit and isolate oneself."

Friday, April 29th. The building of the new theatre up to this time had advanced very rapidly; the foundation walls had already risen on every side, and gave promise of a very beautiful building.

But to-day, on going to the site of the building, I saw, to my horror, that the work was discontinued; and I heard it reported that another party, opposed to Goethe and Cowdray's plan, had at last triumphed; that Cowdray had retired from the direction of the building, and that another architect was going to finish it after a new design, and alter accordingly the foundation already laid.

I was deeply grieved at what I saw and heard, for I had rejoiced, with many others, at the prospect of seeing a theatre arise in Weimar executed according to Goethe's practical view of a judicious internal arrangement, and, as far as beauty was concerned, in accordance with his cultivated taste.

But I also grieved for Goethe and Cowdray, who must both, more or less, feel hurt by this event.

Sunday, May 1st. Dined with Goethe. It may be supposed that the alteration in the building of the theatre was the first subject we talked upon. I had, as I said, feared that this most unexpected measure would deeply wound Goethe's feelings; but there was no sign of it. I found him in the mildest and most serene frame of mind, quite raised above all sensitive bitterness. . . .

"The Grand Duke," said Goethe, "disclosed to me his opinion that a theatre need not be of architectural magnificence, which could, in general, not be contradicted. He further said that it was nothing but a house for the purpose of getting money. This view appears at first sight rather material; but, rightly considered, it is not without a higher purport. For if a theatre is not only to pay its expenses, but is, besides, to make and save money, everything about it must be excellent. It must have the best management at its head; the actors must be of the best; and good pieces must continually be performed, that the attractive power required to draw a full house every evening may never cease. But that is saying a great deal in a few words—almost what is impossible."

"The Grand Duke's view," said I, "of making the theatre gain money appears to be very practical, since it implies a necessity of remaining continually on a summit of excellence."

"Even Shakespeare and Molière," returned Goethe, "had no other view. Both of them wished, above all things, to make money by their theatres. In order to attain this, their principal aim, they necessarily strove that everything should be as good as possible, and that, besides good old plays, there should be some clever novelty to please and attract. The prohibition of *Tartuffe* was a thunderbolt to Molière; but not so much for the poet as for the director Molière, who had to consider the welfare of an important troupe, and to find some means to procure bread for himself and his actors.

"Nothing," continued Goethe, "is more dangerous to the well-being of a theatre than when the director is so placed that a greater or less receipt at the treasury does not affect him personally, and he can live on in careless security, knowing that, however the receipts at the treasury may fail in the course of the year, at the end of that time he will be able to indemnify himself from another source. It is a property of human nature soon to relax when not impelled by personal advantage or disadvantage. Now, it is not desirable that a theatre, in such a town as Weimar, should support itself, and that no contribution from the Prince's treasury should be necessary. But still everything has its bounds and limits, and a thousand thalers yearly, more or less, is by no means a trifling matter, particularly as diminished receipts and deteriorations are dangers natural to a theatre; so that there is a loss not only of money, but also of honour.

"If I were the Grand Duke, I would in future, on any change in the management, once for all appoint a fixed sum for an annual contribution. I would strike the average of the contributions during the last ten years, and according to that I would settle a sum sufficient to be regarded as a proper support. With this sum the house would have to be run. But then I would go a step further, and say, that if the director and his stage-managers contrived, by means of judicious and energetic management, to have an overplus in the treasury at the end of the year, this overplus should be shared, as a remuneration, between the director, the stage-managers, and the principal members of the company. Then you would see what activity there would be, and how the establishment would awaken out of the drowsiness into which it must gradually fall.

"Our theatrical laws," continued Goethe, "contain various penalties; but there is no single law for the encouragement and reward of distinguished merit. This is a great defect. For if, with every failure, I have a prospect of a deduction from my salary, I should also have the prospect of a reward, whenever I do more than can be properly expected of me. And it is by every one's doing more than can be hoped or expected of him that a theatre attains excellence."

We walked up and down the garden, enjoying the fine weather; we then sat upon a bench with our backs against the young leaves of a thick hedge. We spoke about the bow of Ulysses, about the heroes of Homer, then about the Greek tragic poets, and lastly about the widely diffused opinion that Euripides caused the decline of the Greek drama. Goethe was by no means of this opinion.

"Altogether," said he, "I am opposed to the view that any single man can cause the decline of an art. Much, which it is not so easy to set forth, must co-operate to this end. The decline of the tragic art of the Greeks could no more have been caused by Euripides than could that of sculpture by any great sculptor who lived in the time of Phidias, but was inferior to him. For when an epoch is great, it proceeds in the path of improvement, and an inferior production is without results. But what a great epoch was the time of Euripides! It was the time, not of a retrograde, but of a progressive taste. Sculpture had not yet reached its highest point, and painting was still in its infancy.

"If the pieces of Euripides, compared with those of Sophocles, had great faults, it was not necessary that succeeding poets should imitate these faults, and be spoilt by them. But if they had great merits, so that some of them were even preferable to plays of Sophocles, why did not succeeding poets strive to imitate their merits; and why did they not thus become at least as great as Euripides himself? But if after the three celebrated tragic poets, there appeared no equally great fourth, fifth, or sixth—this is, indeed, a matter difficult to explain; nevertheless, we may have our own conjectures, and approach the truth in some degree.

"Man is a simple being. And however rich, varied, and

unfathomable he may be, the cycle of his conditions is soon run through.

"If the same circumstances had occurred, as with us poor Germans, for whom Lessing has written two or three, I myself three or four, and Schiller five or six passable plays, there might easily have been room for a fourth, fifth, and sixth tragic poet.

"But with the Greeks and the abundance of their productions—for each of the three great poets has written a hundred or nearly a hundred pieces, and the tragical subjects of Homer, and the heroic traditions, were some of them treated three or four times—with such abundance of existing works, I say, one can well imagine that by degrees, subjects were exhausted, and that any poet who followed the three great ones would be puzzled how to proceed.

"And, indeed, for what purpose should he write? Was there not, after all, enough for a time? And were not the productions of Æschylus, Sophocles, and Euripides of that kind and of that depth that they might be heard again and again without being esteemed trite or put on one side? Even the few noble fragments which have come down to us are so comprehensive and of such deep significance that we poor Europeans have already busied ourselves with them for centuries, and shall find nutriment and work in them for centuries still."

Thursday, May 12th. Goethe spoke with much enthusiasm of Menander. "I know no one, after Sophocles," said he, "whom I love so well. He is thoroughly pure, noble, great, and cheerful, and his grace is unattainable. It is certainly to be lamented that we possess so little of him, but that little is invaluable, and highly instructive to gifted men.

"The great point is, that he from whom we would learn should be congenial to our nature. Now, Calderón, for instance, great as he is, and much as I admire him, has exerted no influence over me for good or for ill. But he would have been dangerous to Schiller—he would have led him astray; and hence it is fortunate that Calderón was not generally known in Germany until after Schiller's death. Calderón is infinitely great in the technical and theatrical; Schiller, on the contrary, far more sound, earnest, and great in his intentions, and it would have been a pity if he had lost any of these virtues, without, after all, attaining to the greatness of Calderón in other respects."

We spoke of Molière. "Molière," said Goethe, "is so great, that one is astonished anew every time one reads him. He is a man by himself—his pieces border on tragedy; they are enthralling; and no one has the courage to imitate them. His *Avare*, where vice destroys all the natural piety between father and son, is especially great, and in a high sense tragic. But when, in a German paraphrase, the son is changed into a relation, the whole is weakened, and loses its significance. They feared to show vice in its true nature, as he did; but what is tragic there, or indeed anywhere, except what is intolerable?

"I read some pieces of Molière's every year, just as, from time to time, I contemplate the engravings after the great Italian masters. For we little men are not able to retain the greatness of such things within ourselves; we must therefore return to them from time to time and renew our impressions.

"People are always talking about originality; but what do they mean? As soon as we are born, the world begins to work upon us, and this goes on to the end. And, after all, what can we call our own except energy, strength, and will? If I could give an account of all that I owe to great predecessors and contemporaries, there would be but a small balance in my favour."

Sunday, December 25th. Goethe then showed me a very important English work, which illustrated all Shakespeare in copper plates. Each page embraced, in six small designs, one piece with some verses written beneath, so that the leading idea and the most important situations of each work were brought before the eyes. All these immortal tragedies and comedies thus passed before the mind like processions of masks.

"It is even terrifying," said Goethe, "to look through these little pictures. Thus are we first made to feel the infinite wealth and grandeur of Shakespeare. There is no motive in human life which he has not exhibited and expressed! And all with what ease and freedom! But we cannot talk about Shakespeare; everything is inadequate. I have touched upon the subject in my *Wilhelm Meister*, but that is not saying much. He is not a theatrical poet; he never thought of the stage; it was far too narrow for his great mind: nay, the whole visible world was too narrow. He is even too rich and too powerful. A productive nature ought not to read more than one of his dramas in a year if it would not be wrecked entirely. I did well to get rid of him by writing *Götz von Berlichingen* and *Egmont,* and Byron did well by not having too much respect for him, but going his own way. How many excellent Germans have been ruined by him and Calderón!

"Shakespeare gives us golden apples in silver dishes. We get, indeed, the silver dishes by studying his works; but, unfortunately, we have only potatoes to put into them."

I laughed, and was delighted with this admirable simile.

Goethe then read me a letter from Zelter, describing a representation of *Macbeth* at Berlin, where the music could not keep pace with the grand spirit and character of the piece, as Zelter set forth by various intimations. By Goethe's reading, the letter gained its full effect, and he often paused to admire with me the point of some single passage.

"*Macbeth*," said Goethe, "I consider Shakespeare's best acting play, the one in which he shows most understanding with respect to the stage. But would you see his mind unfettered, read *Troilus and Cressida,* where he treats the materials of the *Iliad* in his own fashion."

1826

Sunday, January 29th. The conversation now turned upon the theatre, and the weak, sentimental, gloomy character of modern productions.

"Molière is my strength and consolation at present," said I; "I have translated his *Avare,* and am now busy with his *Médecin malgré lui.* Molière is indeed a great, a real (*reiner*) man."

"Yes," said Goethe, "a real man; that is the proper term. There is nothing distorted about him. And such greatness! He ruled the manners of his day, while, on the contrary, our Iffland and Kotzebue allowed themselves to be ruled by theirs, and were limited and confined in them. Molière chastised men by drawing them just as they were."

"I would give something," said I, "to see his plays acted in all their purity! Yet such things are much too strong and natural for the public, so far as I am acquainted with it. Is not this over-refinement to be attributed to the so-called ideal literature of certain authors?"

"No," said Goethe, "it has its source in society itself. What business have our young girls at the theatre? They do not belong to it—they belong to the convent; and the theatre is only for men and women, who know something of human affairs. When Molière wrote, girls were in the convent, and he was not forced to think about them. But since we cannot get rid of these young girls nowadays, and pieces which are weak and therefore suited to girls continue to be produced, be wise and stay away, as I do. I was really interested in the theatre only so long as I could have a practical influence upon it. It was my delight to bring the establishment to a high degree of perfection; and when there was a performance, my interest was not so much in the pieces as in observing whether the actors played as they ought. The faults I wished to point out I sent in writing to the stage-manager, and was sure they would be avoided on the next representation. Now that I can no longer have any practical influence in the theatre I feel no call to enter it; I should be forced to endure defects without being able to amend them; and that would not suit me. And with the reading of plays, it is no better. The young German poets are eternally sending me tragedies; but what am I to do with them? I have never read German plays except with the view of seeing whether I could have them acted; in every other respect they were indifferent to me. What am I to do now, in my present situation, with the pieces of these young people? I can gain nothing for myself by reading how things ought not to be done; and I cannot assist the young poets in a matter which is already finished. If, instead of their printed plays, they would send me the plan of a play, I could at least say, 'Do it,' or 'Leave it alone,' or 'Do it this way,' or 'Do it that'; and in this there might be some use."

Wednesday, July 26th. This evening I had the pleasure of hearing Goethe say a great deal about the theatre.

I told him that one of my friends intended to arrange Lord Byron's *Two Foscari* for the stage. Goethe doubted his success.

"It is indeed a temptation," he said. "When a piece makes a deep impression on us in reading, we think it will do the same on the stage, and that we could obtain such a result with little trouble. But this is by no means the case. A piece that is not originally, by the intent and skill of the poet, written for the boards will not succeed; but whatever is done to it will always remain somewhat unmanageable and unacceptable. What trouble have I taken with my *Götz von Berlichingen!* yet it will not go right as an acting play, but is too long; and I have been forced to divide it into two parts, of which the last is indeed theatrically effective, while the first is to be looked upon as a mere introduction. If the first part were given only once as an introduction, and then the second repeatedly, it might succeed. It is the same with *Wallenstein:* the *Piccolomini* does not bear repetition, but *Wallenstein's Death* is always seen with delight."

I asked how a piece must be constructed so as to be fit for the theatre.

"It must be symbolical," replied Goethe; "that is to say, each incident must be significant in itself, and lead to another still more important. The *Tartuffe* of Molière is, in this respect, a great example. Only think what an exposition the first scene is! From the very beginning everything is highly significant, and leads us to expect something still more important which is to come. The exposition of Lessing's *Minna von Barnhelm* is also admirable; but that of the *Tartuffe* comes only once into the world: it is the greatest and best thing that exists of the kind."

We then came to the pieces of Calderón.

"In Calderón," said Goethe, "you find the same perfect adaptation to the theatre. His pieces are throughout fit for the boards; there is not a touch in them which is not directed towards the required effect. Calderón is a genius who had also the finest understanding."

"It is singular," said I, "that the dramas of Shakespeare are not theatrical pieces, properly so called, since he wrote them all for his theatre."

"Shakespeare," replied Goethe, "wrote those pieces direct from his own nature. Then, too, his age, and the existing arrangements of the stage, made no demands upon him; people were forced to put up with whatever he gave them. But if Shakespeare had written for the court of Madrid, or for the theatre of Louis XIV, he would probably have adapted himself to a severer theatrical form. This, however, is by no means to be regretted, for what Shakespeare has lost as a theatrical poet he has gained as a poet in general. Shakespeare is a great psychologist, and we learn from his pieces the secrets of human nature."

We then talked of the difficulties in managing a theatre.

"The difficulty of it," said Goethe, "is so to deal with contingencies that we are not tempted to deviate from our higher maxims. Among the higher maxims is this: to keep a good repertory of excellent tragedies, operas, and comedies, which can be adhered to, and which may be regarded as permanent. Among contingencies, I reckon a new piece about which the public is anxious, a starring engagement, and so forth. We must not be led astray by things of this kind, but always return to our repertory. Our time is so rich in really good pieces that nothing is easier to one who knows how than to form a good repertory; but nothing is more difficult than to maintain one.

"When Schiller and I superintended the theatre, we had the great advantage of playing through the summer at Lauchstedt. There we had a select audience, who would have nothing but what was excellent; so we always returned to Weimar thoroughly practised in the best plays, and could repeat all our summer performances in the winter. Besides, the Weimar public had confidence in our management, and, even in the case of things they could not appreciate, they were convinced that we acted in accordance with some higher view.

"When the nineties began," continued Goethe, "the proper period of my interest in the theatre was already past, and I wrote nothing for the stage, but wished to devote myself to epic poetry. Schiller revived my extinct interest, and for the sake of his works, I again took part in the theatre. At the time of my *Clavigo*, I could easily have written a dozen theatrical pieces. I had no want of subjects, and production was easy to me. I might have written a piece every week, and I am sorry I did not."

Wednesday, November 8th. To-day, Goethe spoke again of Lord Byron with admiration. "I have," said he, "read once more his *Deformed Transformed*, and must say that to me his talent appears greater than ever. His devil was suggested by my Mephistopheles; but it is no imitation—it is thoroughly new and original, and everywhere compact, genuine, and spirited. There are no weak passages—not a place where you could put the head of a pin, where you do not find invention and thought. Were it not for his hypochondriacal negative turn, he would be as great as Shakespeare and the ancients."

Wednesday, December 20th. The Berlin papers were brought in, and Goethe sat down to read them. He handed one of them to me, and I found in the theatrical intelligence that at the opera house and the Theatre Royal they gave just as bad pieces as they gave here. "How should it be otherwise?" said Goethe. "There is no doubt that with the help

of good English, French, and Spanish pieces, a repertory can
be formed sufficiently abundant to furnish a good piece every
evening. But what need is felt by the nation always to see
good pieces? The time in which Æschylus, Sophocles—and
Euripides wrote was different. Then there was mind enough
to desire only what was really greatest and best. But in our
miserable times, where is felt a need for the best? Where are
the organs to appreciate it?

"And then," continued Goethe, "people wish to have something new. In Berlin or Paris, the public is always the same.
A quantity of new pieces are written and brought out in Paris,
and you must endure five or six thoroughly bad ones before
you are compensated by a single good one. The only expedient to keep up a German theatre at the present time is that
of starring. If I had the direction of a theatre now, the whole
winter should be provided with excellent stars. Thus, not
only would all the good pieces be repeated, but the interest
of the audience would be led more from the pieces to the
acting; a power of comparing and judging would be acquired;
the public would gain in penetration, and the superior acting
of a distinguished star would maintain our own actors in a
state of excitement and emulation. As I said before, keep on
with your starring, and you will be astonished at the benefit
that will accrue both to the theatre and the public. I foresee
a time when a clever man, who understands the matter, will
take four theatres at once, and provide them with stars by
turn. And I am sure he will keep his ground better with these
four than if he had only one."

1827

Wednesday, January 17th. We talked of Schiller's *Fiesco*,
which was acted last Saturday. "I saw it for the first time,"
said I, "and have been much occupied with thinking whether
those extremely rough scenes could not be softened; but I
find very little could be done to them without spoiling the
character of the whole."

"You are right—it cannot be done," replied Goethe. "Schiller often talked with me on the matter; for he himself could
not endure his first plays, and would never allow them to be
acted while he had the direction of the theatre. At last we
were in want of pieces, and would willingly have gained those
three powerful firstlings for our repertory. But we found it
impossible; all the parts were too closely interwoven one

with another; so that Schiller himself despaired of accomplishing the plan, and found himself constrained to give it up, and leave the pieces just as they were."

" 'Tis a pity," said I; "for, notwithstanding all their roughness, I love them a thousand times better than the weak, forced, and unnatural pieces of some of the best of our later tragic poets. A grand intellect and character is felt in everything of Schiller's."

"Yes," said Goethe, "Schiller might do what he would, he could not make anything which would not come out far greater than the best things of these later people. Even when he cut his nails, he showed he was greater than these gentlemen." We laughed at this striking metaphor.

"But I have known persons," continued he, "who could never be content with those first dramas of Schiller. One summer, at a bathing place, I was walking through a very secluded, narrow path, which led to a mill. There Prince —————— met me, and as at the same moment some mules laden with mealsacks came up to us we were obliged to get out of the way and enter a small house. Here, in a narrow room, we fell, after the fashion of that prince, into deep discussion about things divine and human; we also came to Schiller's *Robbers,* when the prince expressed himself thus: 'If I had been the Deity on the point of creating the world, and had foreseen, at the moment, that Schiller's *Robbers* would have been written in it, I would have left the world uncreated.' " We could not help laughing. "What do you say to that?" said Goethe; "that is a dislike which goes pretty far, and which one can scarcely understand."

"There is nothing of this dislike," I observed, "in our young people, especially our students. The most excellent and matured pieces by Schiller and others may be performed, and we shall see but few young people and students in the theatre; but if Schiller's *Robbers* or Schiller's *Fiesco* is given, the house is almost filled by students alone."

"So it was," said Goethe, "fifty years ago, and so it will probably be fifty years hence. What a young man has written is always best enjoyed by young people. Do not let us imagine that the world will so much advance in culture and good taste that young people will pass over the ruder epoch. Even if the world progresses generally, youth will always begin at the beginning, and the epochs of the world's accomplishment will be repeated in the individual. This has ceased to irritate me, and a long time ago I made a verse in this fashion:

> Still let the bonfire blaze away,
> Let pleasure never know decay;
> Old brooms to stumps are always worn,
> And youngsters every day are born.

Wednesday, January 31st. We talked of Alexander Manzoni; and Goethe told me that Count Reinhard, not long since, saw Manzoni at Paris, where, as a young author of celebrity, he had been well received in society, and that he was now living happily on his estate, in the neighbourhood of Milan, with a young family and his mother.

"Manzoni," continued he, "lacks nothing except to know what a good poet he is, and what rights belong to him as such. He has too much respect for history, and on this account is always adding notes to his pieces, in which he shows how faithful he has been to detail. Now, though his facts may be historical his characters are not so, any more than my Thoas and Iphigenia. No poet has ever known the historical characters which he has painted; if he had, he could scarcely have made use of them. The poet must know what effects he wishes to produce, and regulate the nature of his characters accordingly. If I had tried to make Egmont as history represents him, the father of a dozen children, his light-minded proceedings would have appeared very absurd. I needed an Egmont more in harmony with his own actions and my poetic views; and this is, as Clärchen says, my Egmont.

"What would be the use of poets if they only repeated the record of the historian? The poet must go farther, and give us, if possible, something higher and better. All the characters of Sophocles bear something of that great poet's lofty soul; and it is the same with the characters of Shakespeare. This is as it ought to be. Nay, Shakespeare goes farther, and makes his Romans Englishmen; and there, too, he is right; for otherwise his nation would not have understood him.

"Here, again," continued Goethe, "the Greeks were so great that they regarded fidelity to historic facts less than the treatment of them by the poet. We have, fortunately, a fine example in Philoctetes, which subject has been treated by all three of the great tragedians, and last and best by Sophocles."

Thursday, February 1st. Goethe had a volume of the *Theory of Colours* before him.

I read as far as those interesting paragraphs where it is taught that the eye has need of change, since it never willingly dwells on the same colour, but always requires another, and that so urgently that it produces colours itself if it does not actually find them.

This remark led our conversation to a great law which pervades all nature, and on which all life and all the joy of life depend. "This," said Goethe, "is the case not only with all our other senses, but also with our higher spiritual nature; and it is because the eye is so eminent a sense, that this 'law of required change' is so striking and so especially clear with respect to colours. We have dances which please us in a high degree on account of the alternation of major and minor, while dances in only one of these modes weary us at once."

"The same law," said I, "seems to lie at the foundation of a good style, where we like to avoid a sound which we have just heard. Even on the stage a great deal might be done with this law, if it were well applied. Plays, especially tragedies, in which a uniform tone uninterrupted by change prevails, have always something wearisome about them; and if the orchestra plays melancholy, depressing music during the intermissions of a melancholy piece, we are tortured by an insupportable feeling, which we would escape by all possible means."

"Perhaps," said Goethe, "the lively scenes introduced into Shakespeare's tragedies rest upon this 'law of required change,' but it does not seem applicable to the higher tragedy of the Greeks, where, on the contrary, a certain fundamental tone pervades the whole."

"The Greek tragedy," said I, "is not of such a length as to be rendered wearisome by one pervading tone. Then there is an interchange of chorus and dialogue; and the sublime spirit is of such a kind that it cannot become fatiguing since a certain genuine reality, which is always of a cheerful nature, constantly underlies it."

"You may be right," said Goethe; "and it would be well worth the trouble to investigate how far the Greek tragedy is subject to the general 'law of required change.' You see how all things are connected with each other, and how a law respecting the theory of colours can lead to an inquiry into

Greek tragedy. We must only take care not to push such a
law too far, and make it the foundation for much besides.
We shall go more safely if we only apply it by analogy as an
example."

Wednesday, February 7th. To-day Goethe spoke severely
of certain critics who were not satisfied with Lessing, and
made unjust demands upon him. "When people," said he,
"compare the pieces of Lessing with those of the ancients,
and call them paltry and miserable, what is one to say?
Rather let us pity the extraordinary man for being obliged
to live in a pitiful time, which afforded him no better materials than are treated in his pieces; pity him, because in
his *Minna von Barnhelm,* he found nothing better to do than
to occupy himself with the squabbles of Saxony and Prussia.
His constant political turn, too, resulted from the badness of
his time. In *Emilia Galotti,* he vented his pique against
princes; in *Nathan,* against the priests."

Wednesday, March 28th. . . . "When we," continued
Goethe, "for our modern purposes, wish to learn how to
conduct ourselves upon the stage, Molière is the man to
whom we should apply. Do you know his *Malade Imaginaire?*
There is a scene in it which, as often as I read the piece,
appears to me the symbol of a perfect knowledge of the
boards. I mean the scene where the malade imaginaire asks
his little daughter Louison if there has not been a young
man in the chamber of her eldest sister. Now, any other who
did not understand his craft so well would have let the little
Louison plainly tell the fact at once, and there would have
been the end of the matter.

"But what various motives for delay are introduced by
Molière into this examination, for the sake of life and effect!
He first makes the little Louison act as if she did not understand her father; then she denies that she knows anything;
then, threatened with the rod, she falls down as if dead;
then, when her father bursts out in despair, she springs up
from her feigned swoon with roguish hilarity, and at last,
little by little, she confesses all. My explanation can only
give you a very meagre notion of the animation of the scene;
but read this scene yourself till you become thoroughly impressed with its theatrical worth, and you will confess that
there is more practical instruction contained in it than in all
theories in the world.

"I have known and loved Molière," continued Goethe,

"from my youth, and have learned from him during my whole life. I never fail to read some of his plays every year, that I may keep up a constant intercourse with what is excellent. It is not merely the perfectly artistic treatment which delights me; but particularly the amiable nature, the highly formed mind, of the poet. There is in him a grace and a feeling for the decorous, and a tone of good society, which his innate beautiful nature could only attain by daily intercourse with the most eminent men of his age. Of Menander, I only know the few fragments; but these give me so high an idea of him, that I look upon this great Greek as the only man who could be compared to Molière."

"I am happy," returned I, "to hear you speak so highly of Molière. This sounds a little different from Herr von Schlegel! I have to-day, with great repugnance, swallowed what he says concerning Molière in his lectures on dramatic poetry. He quite looks down upon him as a vulgar buffoon who has only seen good society at a distance, and whose business it was to invent all sorts of farces for the amusement of his lord. In these low farces Schlegel admits he was most happy, but thinks he stole the best of them, that he was obliged to force himself into the higher school of comedy, and never succeeded in it."

"To a man like Schlegel," returned Goethe, "a genuine nature like Molière's is a veritable thorn in the eye; he feels that he has nothing in common with him, he cannot endure him. The *Misanthrope*, which I read over and over again, as one of my most favourite pieces, is repugnant to him; he is forced to praise *Tartuffe* a little, but he lets him down again as much as he can. Schlegel cannot forgive Molière for ridiculing the affectation of learned ladies; he feels, probably, as one of my friends has remarked, that he himself would have been ridiculed if he had lived with Molière.

"It is not to be denied," continued Goethe, "that Schlegel knows a great deal, and one is almost terrified at his extraordinary attainments and his extensive reading. But this is not enough. All the learning in the world is still no judgment. His criticism is completely one-sided, because in all theatrical pieces he merely regards the skeleton of the plot and arrangement, and only points out small points of resemblance to great predecessors without troubling himself in the least as to what the author brings forward of graceful life and the culture of a noble soul. But of what use are all

the arts of a talent if we do not find in a theatrical piece
an amiable or great personality of the author? This alone
influences the cultivation of the people. I look upon the
manner in which Schlegel has treated the French drama as
a sort of recipe for the formation of a bad critic, who is
wanting in every organ for the veneration of excellence, and
who passes over a sound nature and a great character as if
they were chaff and stubble."

"Shakespeare and Calderón, on the other hand," I replied,
"he treats justly, and even with decided affection."

"Both," returned Goethe, "are of such a kind that one
cannot say enough in praise of them, although I should not
have wondered if Schlegel had scornfully deprecated them
also. Thus he is also just to Æschylus and Sophocles; but
this does not seem to arise so much from a lively conviction
of their extraordinary merit as from the tradition among
philologists to place them both very high; for, in fact,
Schlegel's own little person is not sufficient to comprehend
and adequately to appreciate such lofty natures. If this had
been the case, he would have been just to Euripides too, and
would have gone to work with him in a different manner. But
he knows that philologists do not estimate him very highly,
and he therefore feels no little delight that he is permitted,
upon such high authority, to fall foul of this mighty ancient,
and to schoolmaster him as much as he can. I do not deny
that Euripides has his faults; but he was always a very respectable competitor with Sophocles and Æschylus. If he
did not possess the great earnestness and the severe artistic
completeness of his two predecessors, and as a dramatic poet
treated things a little more leniently and humanely, he probably knew his Athenians well enough to be aware that the
chord which he struck was the right one for his contemporaries.
A poet whom Socrates called his friend, whom Aristotle
lauded, whom Menander admired, and for whom Sophocles
and the city of Athens put on mourning on hearing of his
death, must certainly have amounted to something. If a
modern man like Schlegel must pick out faults in so great an
ancient, he ought only to do it upon his knees."

Sunday, April 1st. In the evening with Goethe. I con-
versed with him upon the yesterday's performance of his
Iphigenia, in which Herr Krüger, from the Theatre Royal at
Berlin, played Orestes with great applause.

"The piece," said Goethe, "has its difficulties. It is rich

in internal but poor in external life; the point is to make the internal life come out. It is full of the most effective means, arising from the various horrors which form the foundation of the piece. The printed words are indeed only a faint reflex of the life which stirred within me during the composition of the piece, but the actor must bring us back to this first fire which animated the poet with respect to his subject. We wish to see the vigorous Greeks and heroes, with the fresh sea-breezes blowing upon them, who, oppressed and tormented by various ills and dangers, speak out strongly as their hearts prompt them. But we want none of those feeble, sentimental actors who have only just learned their part by rote, and least of all do we want those who are not even perfect in their parts.

"I must confess that I have never succeeded in witnessing a perfect representation of my *Iphigenia*. That was the reason why I did not go yesterday; for I suffer dreadfully when I have to do with these spectres who do not manifest themselves as they ought." . . .

"An actor," said Goethe, "should properly go to school to a sculptor and a painter; for, in order to represent a Greek hero, it is necessary for him to study carefully the antique sculptures which have come down to us, and to impress on his mind the natural grace of their sitting, standing, and walking. But the merely bodily is not enough. He must also, by diligent study of the best ancient and modern authors, give a great cultivation to his mind. This will not only assist him to understand his part, but will also give a higher tone to his whole being and his whole deportment. But tell me more! What else did you see good in him?"

"It appeared to me," said I, "that he possessed great love for his subject. He had by diligent study made every detail clear to himself, so that he lived and moved in his hero with great freedom; and nothing remained which he had not made entirely his own. Thence arose a just expression and a just accentuation for every word, together with such certainty, that the prompter was for him a quite superfluous person."

"I am pleased with this," said Goethe; "this is as it ought to be. Nothing is more dreadful than when the actors are not masters of their parts, and at every new sentence must listen to the prompter. By this their acting becomes a mere nullity, without any life and power. When the actors are not perfect in their parts in a piece like my *Iphigenia*, it is better

not to play it; for the piece can have success only when all
goes surely, rapidly, and with animation. However, I am
glad that it went off so well with Krüger. Zelter recommended him to me, and I should have been annoyed if he
had not turned out so well as he has. I will have a little joke
with him, and will present him with a prettily bound copy of
my *Iphigenia*, with some verses inscribed in reference to his
acting."

The conversation then turned upon the *Antigone* of Sophocles, and the high moral tone prevailing in it; and, lastly,
upon the question—how the moral element came into the
world?

"Through God himself," returned Goethe, "like everything
else which is good. It is no product of human reflection, but
a beautiful natural quality inherent and inborn. It is, more
or less, inherent in mankind generally, but to a high degree
in a few eminently gifted minds. These have, by great deeds
or doctrines, manifested their divine nature; which, then, by
the beauty of its appearance, won the love of men, and powerfully attracted them to reverence and emulation.

"A consciousness of the worth of the morally beautiful
and good could be attained by experience and wisdom, inasmuch as the bad showed itself in its consequences as a
destroyer of happiness, both in individuals and the whole
body, while the noble and right seemed to produce and secure the happiness of one and all. Thus the morally beautiful could become a doctrine, and diffuse itself over whole
nations as something plainly expressed."

"I have lately read somewhere," answered I, "the opinion
that the Greek tragedy had made moral beauty a special object."

"Not so much morality," returned Goethe, "as pure humanity in its whole extent; especially in such positions where,
by falling into contact with rude power, it could assume a
tragic character. In this region, indeed, even the moral stood
as a principal part of human nature. The morality of Antigone, besides, was not invented by Sophocles, but was contained in the subject, which Sophocles chose the more readily, as it united so much dramatic effect with moral beauty."

Goethe then spoke about the characters of Creon and
Ismene, and on the necessity of these two persons for the
development of the beautiful soul of the heroine.

"All that is noble," said he, "is in itself of a quiet nature, and appears to sleep until it is aroused and summoned forth by contrast. Such a contrast is Creon, who is brought in, partly on account of Antigone, in order that her noble nature and the right which is on her side may be brought out by him, partly on his own account, in order that his unhappy error may appear odious to us.

"But, as Sophocles meant to display the elevated soul of his heroine even before the deed, another contrast was requisite by which her character might be developed; and this is her sister Ismene. In this character the poet has given us a beautiful standard of the commonplace, so that the greatness of Antigone, which is far above such a standard, is the more strikingly visible."

The conversation then turned upon dramatic authors in general, and upon the important influence which they exerted, and could exert, upon the great mass of the people.

"A great dramatic poet," said Goethe, "if he is at the same time productive, and is actuated by a strong, noble purpose, which pervades all his works, may succeed in making the soul of his pieces become the soul of the people. I should think that this was something well worth the trouble. From Corneille proceeded an influence capable of forming heroes. This was something for Napoleon, who had need of an heroic people; on which account, he said of Corneille that if he were still living he would make a prince of him. A dramatic poet who knows his vocation should therefore work incessantly at its higher development, in order that his influence on the people may be noble and beneficial.

"One should not study contemporaries and competitors, but the great men of antiquity, whose works have, for centuries, received equal homage and consideration. Indeed, a man of really superior endowments will feel the necessity of this, and it is just this need for an intercourse with great predecessors which is the sign of a higher talent. Let us study Molière, let us study Shakespeare, but above all things, the old Greeks, and always the Greeks."

Wednesday, April 18th. At dinner we were very cheerful. . . .

"I will treat you to something good, by way of dessert," said Goethe. With these words he placed before me a landscape by Rubens.

"You have," said he, "already seen this picture; but one

cannot look often enough at anything really excellent; besides, there is something very particular attached to this. Will you tell me what you see?"

"I begin from the distance," said I. "I see in the remotest background a very clear sky, as if after sunset. Then, still in the extreme distance, a village and a town, in the light of evening. In the middle of the picture there is a road, along which a flock of sheep is hastening to the village. At the right hand of the picture are several haystacks, and a wagon which appears well laden. Unharnessed * horses are grazing near. On one side, among the bushes, are several mares with their foals, which appear as though they were going to remain out of doors all night. Then, nearer to the foreground, there is a group of large trees; and lastly, quite in the foreground to the top, there are various labourers returning homewards. . . .

"But," continued I with surprise, "the figures cast their shadows into the picture; the group of trees, on the contrary, cast theirs towards the spectator. We thus have light from different sides, which is contrary to Nature."

"That is the point," returned Goethe with a smile. "It is by this that Rubens proves himself great, and shows to the world that he, with a free spirit, stands *above* Nature, and treats her unfavourably to his high purposes. The double light is certainly a violent expedient, and you are certainly justified in saying that it is contrary to Nature. But if it is contrary to Nature, I still say that it is superior to Nature; I say it is the bold stroke of the master, by which he, in a genial manner, proclaims to the world that art is not entirely subject to natural necessities, but has laws of its own." . . .

"Are there not," said I, "bold strokes of artistic fiction similar to this double light of Rubens to be found in literature?"

"We need not go far," said Goethe, after some reflection; "I could show you a dozen of them in Shakespeare. Only take *Macbeth*. When the lady would animate her husband to the deed, she says—

> I have given suck, and know
> How tender 'tis to love the babe that milks me.

---

* Obviously, as Oxenford notes, the proper word here, though the text has *angeschirrt*—harnessed.

Whether this be true or not does not appear; but the lady says it, and she must say it in order to give emphasis to her speech. But in the course of the piece, when Macduff hears of the account of the destruction of his family, he exclaims in wild rage—

He has no children!

These words of Macduff contradict those of Lady Macbeth; but this does not trouble Shakespeare. The grand point with him is the force of each speech; and as the lady, in order to give the highest emphasis to her words, must say 'I have given suck,' so, for the same purpose, Macduff must say 'He has no children.'

"Generally," continued Goethe, "we must not judge too exactly and narrowly of the pencil touches of a painter, or the words of a poet; we should rather contemplate and enjoy a work of art that has been produced in a bold and free spirit, with the same spirit, if we possibly can. Thus it would be foolish, if, from the words of Macbeth—

Bring forth men children only!

the conclusion was drawn that the lady was a young creature who had not yet borne any children. And it would be equally foolish if we were to go still further, and say that the lady must be represented on the stage as a very youthful person.

"Shakespeare by no means makes Macbeth say these words to show the youth of the lady; but these words, like those of Lady Macbeth and Macduff, which I quoted just now, are merely introduced for rhetorical purposes, and prove nothing more than that the poet always makes his character say whatever is proper, effective, and good in each *particular place,* without troubling himself to calculate whether these words may, perhaps, fall into apparent contradiction with some other passage.

"Shakespeare, in writing his pieces, could hardly have thought that they would appear in print, so as to be told over, and compared one with another; he had rather the stage in view when he wrote; he regarded his plays as a lively and moving scene, that would pass rapidly before the eyes and ears upon the stage, not as one that was to be held firmly, and carped at in detail. Hence, his only point was to be effective and significant for the moment."

1829

Wednesday, February 4th. "If the Genasts stay here" [said Goethe], "I shall write two pieces for you, both in one act and in prose. One will be of the most cheerful kind, and end with a wedding; the other will be shocking and terrible, and two corpses will be on the stage at the end. The latter dates from Schiller's time, who wrote a scene of it at my request. I have long thought over both these subjects, and they are so completely present to my mind that I could dictate either of them in a week, as I did my *Bürgergeneral.*" . . .

"Do so," said I; "write the two pieces at all events; it will be a recreation to you after the *Wanderjahre,* and will operate like a little journey. And how pleased the world would be, if, contrary to the expectation of every one, you did something more for the stage."

"As I said," continued Goethe, "if the Genasts stay here, I am not sure that I shall not indulge in this little pleasantry. But without this prospect there is but small inducement; for a play upon paper is nought. The poet must know the means with which he has to work, and must adapt his characters to the actors who are to play them. If I can reckon upon Genast and his wife, and take besides La Roche, Herr Winterberger, and Madame Seidel, I know what I have to do, and can be certain that my intentions will be carried out.

"Writing for the stage," he continued, "is an art by itself, and he who does not understand it thoroughly had better leave it alone. Every one thinks that an interesting fact will appear interesting in the theatre—nothing of the kind! Things may be very pretty to read, and very pretty to think about; but as soon as they are put upon the stage the effect is quite different, and what has charmed us in the closet will probably fall flat on the boards. When one reads my *Hermann and Dorothea,* he thinks it might be brought out at the theatre. Töpfer has been inveigled into the experiment; but what is it, what effect does it produce, especially if it is not played in a first-rate manner, and who can say that it is in every respect a good piece? Writing for the stage is a trade that one must understand, and requires a talent that one must possess. Both are uncommon, and where they are not combined, we shall scarcely have any good result."

Thursday, Februray 19th. Dined with Goethe alone in his study. . . . We talked a great deal about *Egmont,* which had been represented, according to Schiller's version, on the preceding evening, and the injury done to the piece by this version was brought under discussion.

"For many reasons," said I, "the Regent should not have been omitted; on the contrary, she is thoroughly necessary to the piece. Not only does this princess impart to the whole a higher, nobler character, but the political relations especially of the Spanish court are brought much more clearly in view by her conversation with Machiavelli."

"Unquestionably," said Goethe. "And then Egmont gains in dignity from the lustre which the partiality of this princess casts upon him, while Clärchen also seems exalted when we see that, vanquishing even princesses, she alone has all Egmont's love. These are very delicate effects, which cannot be obliterated without compromising the whole."

"It seems to me, too," said I, "that where there are so many important male parts, a single female personage like Clärchen appears too weak and somewhat overpowered. By means of the Regent the picture is better balanced. It is not enough that the Regent is talked of; her personal entrance makes the impression."

"You judge rightly," said Goethe. "When I wrote the piece I well weighed everything, as you may imagine; and hence it is no wonder that the whole materially suffers, when a principal figure is torn out of it, which has been conceived for the sake of the whole, and through which the whole exists. But Schiller had something violent in his nature; he often acted too much according to a preconceived idea, without sufficient regard to the subject which he had to treat."

"You may be blamed also," said I, "for allowing the alteration, and granting him such unlimited liberty in so important a matter."

"We often act more from indifference than kindness," replied Goethe. "Then, at that time, I was deeply occupied with other things. I had no interest for *Egmont* or for the stage, so I let Schiller have his own way. Now it is, at any rate, a consolation for me that the work exists in print, and that there are theatres where people are wise enough to perform it, as I wrote it, without abbreviation."

1830

Sunday, February 14th. We . . . spoke of the theatre,
and dramatic poetry.

"Gozzi," said Goethe, "would maintain that there are only
six-and-thirty tragical situations. Schiller took the greatest
pains to find more, but he did not find even so many as
Gozzi."

Wednesday, February 17th. We talked of the theatre—
of the colour of the scenes and costumes. The result was as
follows:

Generally, the scenes should have a tone favourable to
every colour of the dresses, like Beuther's scenery, which
has more or less of a brownish tinge, and brings out the
colour of the dresses with perfect freshness. If, however,
the scene-painter is obliged to depart from so favourable
an undecided tone, and to represent a red or yellow chamber,
a white tent or a green garden, the actors should be clever
enough to avoid similar colors in their dresses. If an actor
in a red uniform and green breeches enters a red room, the
upper part of his body vanishes, and only his legs are seen;
if, with the same dress, he enters a green garden, his legs
vanish, and the upper part of his body is conspicuous. Thus
I saw an actor in a white uniform and dark breeches, the
upper part of whose body completely vanished in a white
tent, while the legs disappeared against a dark background.

"Even," said Goethe, "when the scene-painter is obliged
to have a red or yellow chamber, or a green garden or wood,
these colours should be somewhat faint and hazy, that every
dress in the foreground may be relieved and produce the
proper effect."

Wednesday, March 17th. This evening at Goethe's for a
couple of hours. By order of the Grand Duchess I brought
him back *Gemma von Art,* and told him the good opinion I
entertained of this piece.

"I am always glad," returned he, "when anything is produced which is new in invention and bears the stamp of talent." Then taking the volume between his hands, and looking
at it somewhat askance, he added, "But I am never quite
pleased when I see a dramatic author make pieces too long
to be represented as they are written. This imperfection

takes away half the pleasure that I should otherwise feel. Only see what a thick volume this *Gemma von Art* is."

"Schiller," returned I, "has not managed much better, and yet he is a very great dramatic author."

"He too has certainly committed this fault," returned Goethe. "His first pieces particularly, which he wrote in the fullness of youth, seem as if they would never end. He had too much on his mind, and too much to say to be able to control it. Afterwards, when he became conscious of this fault, he took infinite trouble, and endeavoured to overcome it by work and study; but he never perfectly succeeded. It really requires a poetical giant, and is more difficult than is imagined, to control a subject properly, to keep it from over-powering one, and to concentrate one's attention on that alone which is absolutely necessary."

1831

Tuesday, February 15th. Dined with Goethe. I told him about the theatre; he praised the piece given yesterday— *Henry III*, by Dumas—as very excellent, but naturally found that such a dish would not suit the public.

"I should not," said he, "have ventured to give it, when I was director; for I remember well what trouble we had to smuggle upon the public *The Constant Prince*, which has far more general human interest, is more poetic, and in fact lies much nearer to us, than *Henry III*."

I spoke of *The Grand Cophta*, which I had been lately reperusing. I talked over the scenes one by one, and, at last, expressed a wish to see it once on the stage.

"I am pleased," said Goethe, "that you like that piece. and find out what I have worked into it. It was indeed no little labour to make an entirely real fact first poetical, and then theatrical. And yet you will grant that the whole is properly conceived for the stage. Schiller was, also, very partial to it; and we gave it once, with brilliant effect, for the higher or-der of persons. But it is not for the public in general; the crimes of which it treats have about them an *enthralling* character, which produces an uncomfortable feeling in the people. Its bold character places it, indeed, in the sphere of *Clara Gazul;* and the French poet might really envy me for taking from him so good a subject. I say *so good a subject*, because it is in truth not merely of moral, but also of great historical significance; the fact immediately preceded the

French Revolution, and was, to a certain extent, its foundation. The Queen, through being implicated in that unlucky story of the necklace, lost her dignity, and was no longer respected, so that she lost, in the eyes of the people, the ground where she was unassailable. Hate injures no one; it is contempt that casts men down. Kotzebue had been hated long; but before the student dared to use his dagger upon him it was necessary for certain journals to make him contemptible."

Thursday, December 1st. We then spoke of Victor Hugo, remarking that his too great fertility had been highly prejudicial to his talent.

"How can a writer help growing worse, and destroying the finest talent in the world," said Goethe, "if he has the audacity to write in a single year two tragedies and a novel; and, further, when he only appears to work in order to scrape together immense sums of money? I do not blame him for trying to become rich, and to earn present renown; but if he intends to live long in futurity, he must begin to write less and to work more."

Goethe then went through *Marie de Lorme,* and endeavoured to make it clear to me that the subject only contained sufficient material to make one single good and really tragical act; but that the author had allowed himself, by considerations of quite a secondary nature, to be misled into stretching out his subject to five long acts. "Under these circumstances," said Goethe, "we have merely the advantage of seeing that the poet is great in the representation of details, which certainly is something, and indeed no trifle."

1832

March (no date). We talked of the tragic idea of Destiny among the Greeks.

"It no longer suits our way of thinking," said Goethe, "it is obsolete, and is also in contradiction with our religious views. If a modern poet introduces such antique ideas into a drama, it always has an air of affectation. It is a costume which is long since out of fashion, and which, like the Roman toga, no longer suits us.

"It is better for us moderns to say with Napoleon, 'Politics is Destiny.' But let us beware of saying, with our latest literati, that politics is poetry, or a good subject for the poet. The English poet Thomson wrote a very good poem on the seasons, but a very bad one on liberty, and that not from want of poetry in the poet, but from want of poetry in the subject.

"If a poet would work politically, he must give himself up to a party; as soon as he does that, he is lost as a poet; he must bid farewell to his free spirit, his unbiased view, and draw over his ears the cap of bigotry and blind hatred.

"The poet, as a man and a citizen, will love his native land; but the native land of his *poetic* powers is the good, the noble, the beautiful, which is confined to no particular province or country, and which he seizes upon and forms wherever he finds it. Therein is he like the eagle, who hovers with free gaze over whole countries, and to whom it is of no consequence whether the hare on which he pounces is running in Prussia or Saxony.

"And then, what is meant by love of one's country? What is meant by patriotic deeds? If the poet has employed a life in battling with pernicious prejudices, in setting aside narrow views, in enlightening the minds, purifying the tastes, ennobling the feelings and thoughts of his countrymen, what better could he have done? How could he have acted more patriotically?"

[*This is the last conversation recorded by Eckermann. Goethe died on March 22, 1832.*]

Goldoni on Playwriting

Translated and compiled by F. C. L. van Steenderen

With an Introduction by H. C. Chatfield-Taylor

Introduction

Among the writers of whom Italy is justly proud, Carlo Goldoni, the Venetian dramatist, holds a commanding place. Though not a world genius such as Dante, Petrarch, or Boccaccio, he is nevertheless the foremost playwright of his native land. Furthermore, he is the pioneer poet of a people, no previous dramatist having painted the life of the common people in colors so truthful as his.

Being simply a naturalist, he had no avowed purpose, such as Molière's, to correct the vices of his time; his ambition was merely "not to spoil nature." Yet he spoiled it whenever he transplanted some exotic story to the soil of his native Italy; since only when he painted the life of Venice was he *Gran Goldoni,* the tribune of her people.

His work fairly covers the entire range of the drama—tragedy, tragicomedy, comedy, farce, extravaganza, opera, and opéra bouffe; yet he is eminent only in comedy. Through this dramatic form, he blazed a virgin path; for although he has been called the Italian Molière, his dramatic naturalism is peculiarly his own, his genius being quite apart from that of *Le Grand Comique.*

Goldoni's merit lies in his fidelity to nature. When using the plots of Molière and other Frenchmen or in attempting to emulate them, as he sometimes did. he forgot his own dictum that "every clime has its national taste"; and whenever he strayed into a land to which his southern blood was not acclimated, his work became insignificant.

His ambition was to reform the Italian stage; yet his reform was brought about so gradually and he wandered away from his beloved Venice so frequently that perhaps no writer of a world-wide repute has ever written so unevenly. He wrote not only many kinds of plays, but many kinds of comedies as well, his dramatic output, roughly speaking, being a hundred and fifty comedies and a hundred tragedies, operatic tragedies, and opéras bouffes. Indeed, his comedies in verse alone fairly vie in number with all the plays of Shakespeare and equal those of Molière; therefore, in judging him, the terrific pace at which he worked should be borne in mind.

He wrote comedies in Tuscan and comedies wholly or partly in the Venetian dialect; comedies in prose and comedies in verse; some dealt with the life of Venice, others were exotic in subject; some were comedies of character, others of intrigue; some were serious, others light; some dealt with fashionable life, others with the bourgeoisie or the common people. At no time, however, in his long career did he confine his work to any particular style; his choice of subject was determined either by his mood or the demands of his managers. Prose was the natural medium of his art; verse a form of expression forced upon him by the exigencies of contemporaneous literary taste.

He was not a palpable imitator; yet there are points of similarity between the creator of French comedy and himself which justify to a certain degree his sobriquet of "the Italian Molière." Both he and the great Frenchman, for instance, learned their technique in the same school—the Italian Commedia dell'Arte, or Improvised Comedy—and by discarding the stereotyped characters and farcical intrigues of that comedy for true characterization and human situations, each created a national comedy of manners. Certain coincidences, too, can be found in their lives, since both dramatists attended a school taught by Jesuits, and both studied law; although Goldoni alone practiced at the bar. Moreover, each of these masters of comedy, when harassed by the critics of his day, defended his art by a dramatic skit in which he set forth his theories of the drama; Molière's was the *Critique de l'Ecole des femmes,* and Goldoni's the *Teatro comico.*

Although these coincidences establish a casual relationship between the two dramatists, such occurrences are merely fortuitous, Goldoni's character being as different from Molière's as his genius is foreign to the Frenchman's. The one was lighthearted by nature, the other overborne at times by sorrow or misfortune; Molière's views, like his experiences, were deeper and farther-reaching than those of his transalpine rival. Yet both were at heart optimists, else they could not have expressed themselves best in comedy. There is a serious phase in Molière's work, however, indicative of the tragedy he lived—a sadder note than is ever sounded by his Venetian rival. The Frenchman, moreover, is broader in his vision and more suggestive, a greater poet, too, and a greater philosopher. Therefore it is an unkindness to Goldoni to compare him with Molière.

The genial cleanser of Italian comedy viewed life optimistically and wore a helpful smile upon his lip. "Lovable painter of nature," Voltaire called him, and today he remains the most wholesome writer in the entire dramatic realm. Indeed, to the wholesomeness of his mind quite as much as to his humor is due the truly tender affection in which he is held throughout Italy. It is this lovable human quality in Goldoni which Browning depicts in the following sonnet, written at the time the playwright's statue was unveiled in Venice:

Goldoni—good, gay, sunniest of souls,—
   Glassing half Venice in that verse of thine,—
   What though it just reflect the shade and shine
   Of common life, nor render, as it rolls,
Grandeur and gloom? Sufficient for thy shoals
   Was Carnival; Parini's depths enshrine
   Secrets unsuited to that opaline
   Surface of things which laughs along thy scrolls.
There throng the people; how they come and go,
   Lisp the soft language, flaunt the bright garb,—see,—
   On Piazza, Calle, under Portico
And over Bridge! Dear King of Comedy,
   Be honoured! thou that didst love Venice so,—
   Venice, and we who love her, all love thee!

Born in Venice at the beginning of the eighteenth century, Goldoni died in Paris barely a fortnight after Louis XVI mounted the scaffold, the span of his life being eighty-four years, during forty-six of which he was a writer for the professional stage of Italy and France. During his happy-go-lucky youth he was ever in amorous adventure or college boy scrapes. At the age of fourteen, for instance, he ran away from school to join a band of strolling players, and at eighteen he was expelled from college for writing a satire upon the inhabitants of Pavia. Indeed, save in its last moments, his life was a continuous comedy.

During his earlier years his vagrant spirit led him into many channels and through many adventures. From 1721, when he ran away from school at Rimini and traveled to his home at Chioggia with a band of strolling players, until the autumn of 1748, when he appeared in Venice as the playwright of a troupe managed by an actor named Medebac, he led a fitful life as a student, diplomatist, and lawyer, a life at once adventurous and unsuccessful. From 1734 until 1748 he wrote plays for the troupe of an actor named Imer; yet during a part of this time he was Genoese consul at Venice, so it cannot be said that he had adopted playwriting as his profession. It was his avocation rather than his vocation; furthermore he abandoned the stage in 1744 to practice law at Pisa. During this first period of his life he wrote some thirty dramatic pieces: tragedies, tragicomedies, operas, operatic interludes, opéras bouffes, written comedies, and improvised comedies. It was a period of essay during which he was groping in dramatic darkness and still dubious of dramatic writing as a profession.

Burning his legal bridges entirely in 1747 by signing a contract with Medebac, he appeared in Venice during the following year as a professional dramatist and, to quote his own words, "abandoned himself without reflection to the comic genius that had lured him." For fourteen years he wrote professionally for the stage of Venice; his life, except for quarrels with managers, actresses, and critics, was joyously lived in the tranquillity of domestic peace. During that happy time he penned fully a hundred comedies and about half as many opéras bouffes. Graced by nearly all his masterpieces, this was the most prolific period of his life, as well as the period of his greatest achievement.

When the indifference of the public and the attacks of rivals and critics drove him into exile in Paris in 1762, he began again in France, as the playwright of the Comédiens du roi de la troupe italienne, the reform of comedy he had accomplished in Italy; yet he fought less valiantly for his ideals. Though he penned some fifty comedies, scenarî, and opéras bouffes in France, once only did his genius shine with its full splendor, and then in a foreign tongue.

At the age of forty-three when he was still striving for

Venetian success, Goldoni performed the herculean task of writing sixteen comedies in a single year, exactly double the number he was under contract with Medebac to supply annually. Two or three of his plays had failed at the Sant'-Angelo Theatre, and its leading comedian had announced his intention of leaving it to take service with the King of Poland; whereupon the box holders began to refuse to renew their subscriptions for the ensuing season.

This state of affairs called for drastic action, and Goldoni stepped into the breach in the bold manner he thus describes: "Offended on my side by the ill temper of the public, and being blindly confident that I amounted to something, I wrote for the leading actress the Complimento with which the season ended, and made her say in bad verse, but very clearly and very positively, that the author who worked for her and her comrades agreed to present sixteen new comedies during the ensuing year. The troupe on the one hand and the public on the other at once gave me a certain and very flattering proof of their confidence, for the actors did not hesitate to accept an engagement upon my word, and a week later all the boxes were let for the ensuing year. When I made this agreement I had not a single subject in mind; yet I had to keep my word or die. My friends trembled, my enemies laughed. I comforted the former, I made game of the latter. . . . It was a terrible year for me, which I cannot recall without trembling again. Sixteen comedies in three acts, each requiring for its performance, according to Italian usage, two hours and a half!"

That theatrical season (1750–51) was indeed "terrible," and the wonder is that Goldoni did not die in the attempt to keep his defiant promise to the Venetian public. He had agreed to produce sixteen new comedies, which, in addition to the labor of writing, meant the onerous task of rehearsal. In length, including stage directions, his comedies average about twenty-five thousand words; hence he had contracted to write four hundred thousand words, or the equivalent of a newspaper column a day of the most difficult kind of imaginative work. Not only was he called upon to pen the average daily stint of the modern newspaperman, but he must accomplish it in dialogue that would unfold a dramatic story vivaciously and entertainingly. He had, moreover, to invent the subjects for his sixteen comedies, as well as to construct their plots. The physical task he had set himself was the equivalent of writing five novels of the present day, but in imaginative requirements it was far greater. When it is borne in mind that a prolific novelist produces no more than two novels a year, and that a popular playwright, the late Clyde Fitch, placed upon his stage, if we count both original plays and adaptations, a few more than forty dramatic pieces in twenty years, some idea can be gained of the gigantic nature of Goldoni's undertaking.

Not only did he produce sixteen new plays at the Sant' Angelo Theatre during a single theatrical season, but he was writing the libretti of five comic operas as well, which were performed at other theatres, and he had, besides, orders for comedies from other cities. Moreover, in spite of this abnormal work, there were only two failures among the sixteen plays; and three, *Femmine puntigliose*, the *Bottega del caffè*, and the *Dama prudente*, take a high if not a commanding rank in their author's work.

The first of this remarkable series of plays is the *Teatro comico*, which, as I have already stated, Goldoni wrote to defend himself against his critics. A confession of faith rather than a play, in which he took occasion to berate the antiquated methods of the Improvised Comedy and prepare the public for the suppression of the mask actor's hackneyed tricks, it is in reality a bold polemic intended by its author to be the prologue to his reform of Italian comedy.

So flimsy in plot that dramatically it is the merest skit, *The Comic Theatre* nevertheless abounds in both atmosphere and characterization. A company of actors are discovered on their stage rehearsing a comedy. They are interrupted by a playwright who tries to dispose of his antiquated wares to a canny manager and, failing in his purpose, decides that rather than starve he will become an actor himself. An opera singer out of employment appears, seeking an engagement to sing intermezzi, and she too descends to histrionism as a last resort. The incidents of *The Comic Theatre* are too attenuated to constitute more than a slender sketch; yet it pictures life behind the scenes so candidly and portrays stage folk so ruthlessly, that the wonder is that Medebac's players did not refuse to appear in this exposure of the egotism that distinguishes their calling. Here are shown all the vagabond types that compose a theatrical troupe—the overbearing leading lady and her harassed manager, the pert soubrette, the vain *jeune premier*, and the coarse comedian hungering for laughs, each as clamorous for a "fat part" as any modern star; for, as one of them says: "There are some actors who have the conceit to judge a comedy by their part. If it is short, they say that the comedy is poor. They would all like to play the leading role, since the actor rejoices and is glad when he hears laughter and handclapping:

> For if the public's hands clap hard,
> The actor's worthy of regard."

While stripping his actors of their pretensions and exposing their artistic leanness to the public, Goldoni gives them considerable wise counsel. "Don't you see that it isn't right to address the audience?" he makes the manager in this play say to a member of his company. "When he is alone on the stage, an actor should pretend that no one hears or sees him, for this habit of speaking to the audience is an intolerable fault that should not be permitted on any ground whatever." In the following speech from this skit Goldoni vies with Shakespeare in artistic sanity: "See to it that you pronounce clearly the last syllables, so they can be heard. Recite slowly, but not too slowly; and in strong passages speak louder, and accelerate your speech. . . . Guard especially against drawling and against declamation; speak naturally, as if you were talking; since comedy is an imitation of nature, everything that is done must be likely and probable."

Though dramatically *The Comic Theatre* is but a gossamer, in biographical texture it is so durable that from its lines much insight into Goldoni's literary life is gained; for besides presenting its author's theories of writing and acting, it shows the difficulties that lay in his progress toward fame. For instance, when a hack writer in this play declares that he intends to write comedies as good as Goldoni's, the manager, speaking ex cathedra, says: "Ah, my lad, you must first spend on the stage as many years as he has passed there, and then you may hope to be able to do something. Do you think he became a writer of comedies all at once? He did so little by little, and succeeded in being appreciated by the public only after long study, long practice, and a continuous and untiring observation of the stage and of the manners and customs as well as the genius of nations."

At the time when Goldoni began to write for the stage of his day, the Improvised Comedy was in its decadence. In its prime this stage parody of life, unexcelled in spontaneity and truth to nature, was allied to the fine arts; in its decline it became the base medium of anathematized buffoons, forbidden by law to enter decent houses.

Goldoni has been accused of never escaping from the influence of the Improvised Comedy. But when he discards the masks and their lazzi entirely and presents the life of his beloved Venice just as it appears to his artistic eyes, his work is as free from the stereotyped devices of the Improvised Comedy as that of Molière; and then he appears as a consummate naturalist depicting actual life in truthful colors, even though only a few times in his long dramatic career did he liberate himself wholly from the hackneyed tricks of the native comedy, or the stilted artifice of the French comedy of his day.

His ambition was to reform the Improvised Comedy by creating from its elements a national written comedy. His method was to accustom the public to written plays constructed in the old style with some or all of the stereotyped characters, then to discard this style and these characters entirely and present to his countrymen a written comedy along traditional French lines. Yet so little did he appreciate his true genius that his memoirs teem with defense of artificial comedies that he had written under French influence, while his naturalistic masterpieces often receive scant mention. Nevertheless, he seems to have understood that his ability to reproduce the life about him was the source of his immediate success; for while he scolded his countrymen for their inability to appreciate refined comedy, he catered to their taste. He had, moreover, a definite purpose in view, which he expressed in these words: "Now there was within me this selfsame spirit, which making me a most attentive observer of the comedies that were being performed in the various theatres of Italy, caused me to recognize and lament their corrupted taste, while comprehending at the same time that the public would derive no little benefit, and he who should succeed, no small praise, if some man of talent inspired by the comic spirit should attempt to uplift the abased Italian theatre. This hope of glory finally enlisted me in the undertaking."

When Goldoni began to reform Italian comedy there were seven regular playhouses in operation in his native city— more than there were in Paris then, and more than are to be found in Venice now. Three of these were devoted to comedy, and at each of them he was in turn employed; first at the San Samuele, when Imer was his manager, then at the Sant' Angelo under Medebac, and finally at the San Luca, the property of two brothers named Vendramin, where his Venetian theatrical career terminated.

These Venetian theatres were owned by wealthy patricians who retained the receipts of the boxes, which, like the opera boxes of today, were rented for the season. A ticket to a box did not include admission to the house, a box holder being required to pay the entrance fee, which, according to Goldoni, "never exceeded the value of a Roman *paolo,* or ten French *sous.*" "As the daily receipts could not be large," he continues, "they were not worth being run after by a playwright."

With the apparent intention of permitting play lovers to attend several performances on the same day, the Venetian theatres opened at different hours. Their performances, however, were not seemly events such as we are accustomed to in our modern playhouses. The boxes were the scene of frivolity and amours. Many of their occupants wore masks, and sometimes carnival costumes of indecent scantiness; indeed, in the words of an Italian writer, "almost every box was a temple of Venus." In them the fashionable world met, or young men of wealth flaunted their mistresses boldly in the public gaze. The boxes belonged to the owners of the theatres and were let by them for the season to fellow patricians. Besides being lovers' trysts, they were the rendezvous of groups of intimate friends who gossiped and flirted while pelting hoi polloi in the pit below with oranges, or even spitting on them.

The denizens of Goldoni's pit, like those of Molière's parterre, applauded and hissed at will or rent the fetid air with coarse laughter and catcalls, while the patricians above them giggled, sneezed, and yawned. The benches were of wood, well polished by use, and they were scorned by ladies, though women of the people occupied them. During the entr'actes a ticket taker with a candle end in hand passed among them, collecting the modest price of the seats. At a popular play the gondoliers, who ordinarily were admitted to the pit, were forced to wait outside the theatre, since long before the performance began the seats were filled by servants holding them for masters or by speculators ready to sell them at a profit. An hour before the performance two wretched candles were lighted. No lights glowed in the auditorium even after the curtain rose, except an occasional candle in the region of the upper boxes or the smudging tallow dips of the musicians.

Between the acts girls with baskets on their arms passed between the rows of benches selling oranges, anisette, cakes, fritters, and chestnuts, while in the boxes coffee and ices were served. "At six or seven paces from the entrance to the pit," its classic missiles, baked apples and pears, were sold, although the actor who won its favor had little to fear from its wrath, since he enjoyed in the affections of the public the same unmerited ascendancy over the dramatist that is held by his modern compeer, the matinée idol. Though the authorities proclaimed him to be "a person detested of God," the popular actor was received familiarly in patrician households, and when he appeared on the stage he was greeted by such affectionate cries as "Blessed be thou! Blessed be he who fathered thee!" or "Darling, I throw myself at thy feet!" In his wake swarmed his cronies, all of whom were deadheads, and some of whom "got in his way on the stage, only to speak ill of the play."

At the end of the performance it was the privilege of a popular actor to announce the next play; but if the one that had first been given happened to have pleased the audience, his voice was drowned by cries of "The same, give us the same!" On the first and the last night of the season a favorite actress would recite to the audience complimentary verses; but it was not customary for the mere author to appear before the curtain in response to applause.

In such an atmosphere Goldoni learned his craft. Small wonder that he pronounces "the World and the Stage" to be "the two books upon which I have meditated most," experience being a better training for a dramatist than erudition.

To attain his fame he was obliged to tread a stony path. Wearied by the antiquated and obscene lazzi of the Improvised Comedy, the intelligent public of Venice had become wedded to the melodrama of Zeno and Metastasio; therefore Goldoni was obliged to create a following for the new comedy. His actors were only wretched outcasts beyond the social pale, whose voices, when their efforts failed to please, were drowned by the hisses and catcalls of ribald audiences. No Richelieu or Louis XIV sustained him; yet this patient Venetian plunged courageously into the task of cleansing the filthy comedy of his day. Making his theatre a wholesome resort for his fellow townsmen, he mirrored them truly there in the hope that his humorous expositions of their vices and foibles might turn them from their degeneracy back to the glory of their ancestors.

Though experience is a bitter school, it is the only one in which practicality is taught. Thus the lesson to be learned from Goldoni's ideas on playwriting is the fact that the stage-craft of his day was precisely like that of our own. Indeed, I know of no better guide for an aspiring dramatist of the present time to follow than Goldoni's precepts of the dramatic art, as collected and translated by Dr. van Steenderen, his ideas about playwriting being as sane and timely now as when they were penned, nearly two centuries ago.

In gathering them together and presenting them in their present form, Dr. van Steenderen is more than a translator, for his task has been to cull a paragraph here, a phrase there, and put ideas thus collected from a number of sources together in a way that will make them read like a spontaneous treatise on the art of playwriting.

Knowing both the delicacy and the intricacy of his task, I feel that it has been admirably accomplished, for it will be difficult, I believe, for the reader of the pages which follow to realize that they have been collected from memoirs, prefaces, plays, and letters, since they are strung together so deftly that they read like a continuous narrative. Save for a connecting link here and there, the words are all Goldoni's, and thus formulated they express all his theories and beliefs regarding the dramatist's art.

In penning these introductory words, I have culled freely, I confess, from the pages of my *Goldoni, a Biography,* published in 1913. It was my intention to write about this gentle lover of mankind in language wholly different from that which I had used in my book about him; yet, owing to some curious mental process which I am unable to explain, my mind refused at times to respond to the calls made upon it for new words with which to clothe my ideas. Former phrases came back to mind so persistently that I could not evade them. The result has been that, in expressing my convictions regarding Goldoni and his work, I have found myself unable in a number of instances to avoid using the very phraseology I used six years ago. Plagiarism being defined as "the use of *another person's* thoughts or writings as one's own," I feel that the only literary offense which may be charged against me is repetition. Of this I am guilty to a considerable degree; yet in the instances in which I have quoted from myself, I know that it has been to the benefit of the reader; my knowledge of Goldoni having been far more intimate, as well as more thorough, six years ago than it is today.

H. C. CHATFIELD-TAYLOR

1919

Goldoni on Playwriting

God forbid that I should set up for a teacher! I purpose merely to confide to my readers what little I may have learned or may be trying to do, reminding them, meanwhile, that even in the least important books one sometimes finds little matters deserving attention.[1] I have no mind to write an academic treatise on the Art of Comedy. Why offer oracularly, like a pedant, what has so often been repeated by valiant men of every cultured nation?[2] Nor do I mean to lay down rules for others to follow. My plan is just to make known that I have at last, through long-continued observation and practice, succeeded in blazing a path for myself which I can travel with some degree of security, offering as proof for the statement the favor which my plays enjoy among the frequenters of theatres.[3]

It must be confessed that all men carry with them from their birth a natural disposition peculiar to themselves, which leads them rather into one than another sort of study or profession, and in which they may succeed with admirable facility if they will apply themselves. As for me, I certainly have felt since my tenderest childhood the forward drive of an internal, almost insuperable power toward theatrical af-

[1] *Memoirs,* p. 313. Memoirs = *Memorie di Carlo Goldoni riprodotte integralmente dalla edizione francese. Con prefazione e note di Guido Mazzoni.* Two vols., Florence, 1907.
[2] Pasquali I, p. ix. Pasquali = Giambattista Pasquali's edition of Goldoni's Works in 17 vols., begun in 1761 and finished sometime after 1777. Only the Introduction in Vol. I is cited here.
[3] *Teatro comico,* Introduzione. *Il teatro comico* is a play first performed October 5, 1750. It embodies the author's ideas about playwriting.

fairs. Whenever a play fell into my hands, I found delight in
it. I remember that I wrote, merely as a result of reading
some of Cicognini's dramatic works at the age of nine, a
comedy, such as it was, before ever having seen one performed on the stage.

This native inclination became still stronger when I began
to go to the theatres, nor did it abandon me in my various
journeys among Italian cities, undertaken either for reasons
of study, or to accompany my father in the course of his
wanderings as a physician. At Perugia, Rimini, Milan, or
Pavia, while in the midst of the disgusting work of that calling which he wished to compel me by main force to enjoy,
as well as later, during my study and profession of the law,
my pleasure in dramatic poetry was always finding an outlet,
whether through the writing of dialogues and comedy sketches
or by representing some dramatic character at an aristocratic
academy.

Having finally returned to Venice, I was obliged to devote
myself to the legal profession in order to earn a living, my
father having departed this life. My genius continued to lead
me to the theatre, however, and I fulfilled with painful reluc-
tance the duties of my calling and the really honorable positions which were derived from it.[4] Thus, three or four times,
I have lost the luckiest opportunities for bettering my state,
but, abandoning myself without reflection to the blandish-
ments of the stage, I always allowed myself to be caught in
the same trap.[5] In fact, I never applied myself with more
delight and diligence to dramatic writing than in those far-
away days of my youth. So it came about that, though I
could hope for a prosperous future in the noble profession
of advocate in an important court, I nevertheless denied
myself to the city of my birth, resolved as I was to yield
wholly to the power within me which claimed me outright for
Dramatic Poetry. Intent upon learning the various usages
and customs which flourish in plentiful variety in this our
delightful corner of Europe, I visited many Italian cities;
and, stopping finally in Milan, I began to write seriously for
the Italian stage.

I have ingenuously related all this with the single view of
emphasizing the true and only incentive I felt for devoting
myself to the drama. It was nothing short of an invincible

[4] Pasquali I, p. ix.
[5] *Memoirs* I, p. 291.

call of nature. I could not withstand it. Is it a wonder then that in all my journeys, amid all the vicissitudes of life, in my amusements even, my mind remained fixed and observant in the direction of this interest? Involuntarily I gathered abundant material, an inexhaustible mine of substance, ready and adapted for eventual use on the stage.[6]

What, you may ask, can be accomplished by one not naturally endowed with this spontaneous inclination? After developing through ample study a fair knowledge of the drama, he may be able to judge correctly other men's plays, but this by no means insures his producing a successful one himself. He may, it is true, succeed in constructing plays according to rule, he may even write in the purest vernacular; yet he will have the misfortune of not pleasing on the stage. Neither, as a consequence, can he teach, for if the spectator, coming as he does to the theatre primarily for recreation, is to be induced to accept a moral lesson, it must be conveyed to him *en passant,* sweetened by poetic grace and comic wit. In short, whoever does not possess the comic genius will be unable to exercise that joyous animation which sustains the sprightliness of the characters; moreover, he will be at a loss in trying to infuse his work with that humor which is the flower of a fine mind, as well as of the peculiar talent which comedy demands.[7]

However, the selfsame ardor which made me a most attentive observer of the plays which were being performed in the various theatres of Italy made me recognize and also lament their corrupted taste. I fancied, besides, that the public would derive no little benefit, and he who should succeed no small praise, if some man of talent, inspired by the spirit of comedy, should attempt to lift the Italian stage out of its abasement. The hope of this glory finally enlisted me in the undertaking.

Indeed, the Comic Stage in our Italy had been so corrupt for more than a century that among the transalpine nations it had become an object of contempt. Upon her public boards only unseemly harlequinades and scandalous jests were in vogue. The plots were poor in conception and worse—even uncivil and ill ordered—in the performance, since far from correcting vice as the first and most noble aim of comedy, they but fomented it. Arousing the laughter of the ignorant

[6] Pasquali I, p. ix.
[7] Pasquali I, p. xi.

plebeians, dissolute youths, and the most debauched of the
population, the comic stage disgusted, then irritated the educated and the well-bred, who, if they sometimes attended so
poor a theatre, and were there dragged out of boredom, took
good care not to take with them their innocent families, lest
their hearts should be corrupted. The Fathers of the Church
justly anathematized such plays, and they were in fact very
proper subjects for the loathing of the wise.

Many tried to purify the stage and bring back good taste
to it. Some attempted to do so by means of comedies translated from the Spanish or the French; but mere translations
cannot be successful in Italy.[8] The stage must be imbued
with national life, brought within the sphere of everybody,[9]
for national points of view differ as do customs and languages.
Seeing, in spite of their purblindness, the force of this truth,
our mercenary actors set about altering these foreign pieces
and reciting them in improvised form; yet they so disfigured
them that they could no longer be recognized as works of
such celebrated authors as Lope de Vega and Molière, who,
beyond the mountains where better taste flourished, had happily written them. They treated with the same cruelty the
comedies of Plautus and Terence; nor did they spare any of
the other ancient and modern comedies which chanced to
fall into their hands. Meanwhile the educated chafed, the
public wearied. All exclaimed in accord against bad comedies;
yet most people had no idea of what good ones were like.

Noticing this universal discontent, actors tried to find profit
in innovation. They introduced elaborate paraphernalia, transformation scenes and magnificent stage sets, but beyond in-
creasing their expenses inordinately, they did not succeed at
all, for the attendance of the public soon decreased. Then
they tried to save comedy by means of musical interludes.
This expedient succeeded well for a time, and I was among
the first to contribute to the number of such pieces. Since
actors are not musicians, however, it was not long before it
became evident how little relation there is between comedy
and music. What kept the theatres open was tragedies and
operas, the applause lavished upon them signifying the abasement of comedy, and offering convincing proof of its extreme
decadence.[10]

[8] Pasquali I, p. xii.
[9] *Memoirs* I, p. 354.
[10] Pasquali I, p. xii.

The germ of comedy, however, had not been utterly killed in the prolific heart of Italy. Those who were among the first to strive toward its revival, unable as they were to find in a century of ignorance the necessary skillful writers, boldly constructed plots themselves, divided them into acts and scenes, and recited extempore the phrases, thoughts, and witticisms they had agreed upon among themselves. During the last two centuries this kind of play had amused all Italy; in fact, my country had become distinguished because of it, no nation having been able to imitate Improvised Comedy. In my time it was the Bolognese who clung more tenaciously than other Italians to this form of play. There were among them people of merit who found pleasure in constructing these *commedie dell'arte,* and certain of their citizens played them very well, giving delight to their countrymen.

Before explaining what I think about this matter, I should like to entertain my readers for a few minutes with remarks on the origin, the use, and the effect of Improvised Comedy and the Four Masks which constituted its staple cast.

Those who knew how to read Latin found that in the comedies of Plautus and Terence there were always duped fathers, debauched sons, amorous daughters, rascally valets, and doltish servants. As they traveled through Italy, the actors took the fathers from Venice and Bologna, the valets from Bergamo, the lovers—male and female—and the soubrettes from Rome and Tuscany. Indeed, I have in my possession a manuscript of the sixteenth century, well preserved and bound in parchment, containing one hundred and twenty plots of Italian plays, called Art Comedies, and the dramatic foundation of them is always Pantaloon, Merchant of Venice; the Doctor, Jurisconsult of Bologna; Brighella and Harlequin, Bergamesque Valets, the one clever, the other dull.

Pantaloon is a merchant of Venice, because Venice was in former days the state which carried on the richest and most extensive commerce in Italy. He has always worn the ancient Venetian costume; the black cloak and woollen bonnet being still in use in that city, while the red waistcoat, the breeches resembling drawers, the red stockings and slippers represent in a lifelike way the habiliments of the Lagoons of the Adriatic. Nowadays his beard, which in remote times was an adornment, is scorned and ridiculed.

The second old man, called the Doctor, was taken from among the gentlemen of the robe in order to contrast the educated man with the man of commerce, and Bologna was adopted as his home because there existed in that city a university which, in spite of the ignorance of the times, continued to conserve the duties and emoluments of the professors. The costume of the Doctor is nearly the dress still in use at the University and the Law Court of Bologna, while the singular mask which covers his forehead and nose is supposed to imitate a purple birthmark which marred the face of a certain jurisconsult of earlier days. Lovers of this sort of comedy are attached to this red spot as to a tradition.

Brighella and Harlequin, also called the two Zani, were taken from Bergamo because, the first being extremely adroit and the second completely dull, it is only in that region that one finds these extremes among the lower classes. Brighella represents an intriguing, tricky, cunning valet. His costume is a species of livery; his tawny mask exaggerates the complexion of the mountaineers of Bergamo, burned by the heat of the sun. Harlequin's costume shows him to be a poor devil who will pick up pieces of divers colors in order to mend his coat; his hat corresponds to his beggarly habits, while the rabbit's scut which is its ornament is even to this day the trimming common to the headgear of Bergamesque peasants.

This will explain sufficiently the origin and the use of the four principal masks. It remains for me to speak of the effects they produce.

The masks cannot but hamper the art of the actor. Whether he try to express joy or grief, whether he show passionate or gentle love, it is always the same leather that intrudes. He may gesticulate and vary the tone of his voice as much as he will; yet he can never express through his features, which are the interpreters of the heart, such passions as the character he represents may feel. The public demands that the actor interpret a soul, but a soul under a mask is like fire under ashes. Any plan of reform must therefore include a gradual obliteration of the masks, as well as a substitution of pure comedy for slapstick farce.[11]

My first play, *Belisario,* was performed amid extraordinary silence, an almost unknown phenomenon in Italian theatres. Yet, used as it was to hubbub, the audience made up between the acts for its quiet with cries of joy, handclappings, and reciprocal signals repeated from the pit to the boxes. At the end of the performance the unusual outbursts of satisfaction

[11] *Memoirs* II, p. 37.

increased to such a din that the actors wept and laughed in turn. When the leading man appeared to make the customary announcement for the following evening, the audience cried in chorus: "No, this one, this one!" and the curtain fell. The play was not worth all this admiration. I myself think so little of it that it shall never appear in the printed collection of my works. But my heroes were men, not demigods. They showed human foibles in the way we all know them to be; they did not carry their virtues and vices to fantastic excess.[12]

I had, however, not yet acquired sufficient experience to do aught but ponder the ways and means of reform. But I observed. And, for instance, I saw that even in poor comedies there is often something that will call forth applause from the pit and approval from the boxes; I noticed that this occurs mostly at a moment of intense seriousness, of delicate humor, or when a good situation is shown, when some noteworthy character is being truthfully revealed, or some contemporary custom worth correcting is being exposed in its results. Above all I remarked that, more than the marvelous, it was the simple, the natural that won the heart of an audience.[13]

When I brought my bride home to Venice, the company of actors for whom I had been writing more or less were glad to see me, the more so since I brought them a new play.[14] What made this troupe exceptional was the presence in it of a famous Harlequin, Sacchi by name, whose wife played the Second Lady very well, and whose sister was a good soubrette.

"There you are," I said to myself; "you can now give free rein to your imagination. You have worked on hackneyed material long enough; now you must create, invent. You have promising actors, but in order to get out of them what is in them, you must study them, for each has his own natural bent. Success will almost be assured if you give them characters to act which are analogous to their own. Come," I went on reflecting, "this is perhaps your chance to attempt the reform you have had in mind so long. Yes, you must handle character subjects, they being the source of all good comedy. This is what Molière did, thus developing his art to a degree

[12] *Memoirs* I, p. 204.
[13] Pasquali I, p. xii.
[14] *Memoirs* I, p. 228.

which the ancients only indicated, and which the moderns have not yet equaled."

In accordance with these musings I searched in the company for the actor best suited to playing a maskless character. I chose the Pantaloon Colinetti, because I had formed a high opinion of his manner in the society of people among whom I had studied him. I believed I could make him an excellent portrayer of a gentleman, and I was not mistaken. Therefore I wrote for him a comedy entitled *Momolo Cortesan* or *L'Uomo di Mondo, The Man of the World.* "Are there many such in Venice?" you will ask. Yes, there are not a few, and some possess, more or less, the very qualities I depicted in Momolo. To present such a character to the public, however, one has to pad it, and I dressed mine in all the perfection of the species.

In order to bring out a character I have always thought it necessary to place it in direct contrast with another whose nature is the opposite of it. I therefore introduced into my play a Venetian good-for-nothing. My Gentleman defends the dupes of this scoundrel against his snares, finally unmasking him. Thus the Harlequin in this piece is no longer a slapstick valet, but becomes a rascal fundamentally characterized by the fact that he insists upon his sister's maintaining him in his vices by her shame.

This comedy enjoyed excellent success, and I was content. My compatriots were beginning to give up their antiquated taste for farce. My reform was started. Yet I could not boast of it. The play was not dialogued. Nothing but the part of the leading man was written out, all the rest being left in improvised form. Indeed, the smoothness of style which distinguishes classical authors was not there. I could not reform everything at once without antagonizing the lovers of Improvised Comedy; but I awaited the favorable moment for a frontal attack, when I could deliver it with more vigor and greater effect.[15]

My experience goes to prove that the reputation of a playwright often depends upon the performance of the actors. There is no use hiding this truth from oneself.[16] I always took time, therefore, and sought opportunity to study the divers natures of my players. When I began to work for Medebac's troupe, I soon observed in Darbes, one of its members, two

[15] *Memoirs* I, p. 230.
[16] *Memoirs* I, p. 239.

contrasting but habitual facial expressions, to which his manner and action corresponded. He would be the jolliest, wit-
tiest, and most energetic man in the world, then suddenly
assume the expression, the speech, and the ways of an imbecile or bumpkin, and these changes would take place in
him quite naturally, without apparent effort. This discovery
gave me the idea of making him appear under these two
different aspects in the same play. Another successful comedy,
I due Gemelli Veneziani, was the result.[17]

As long as I continued working over the time-worn materials of the Improvised Comedy and produced only partly
written plays, I was permitted to enjoy in peace the applause
of the pit; but as soon as I laid claim to being a regular
author, a poet, a creator, people awoke from their lethargy
and considered me worthy of their criticism. Indeed, my
countrymen, for so long a time accustomed to trivial farces
and elaborate scenery, suddenly became severe censors of
my work. They made the names of Aristotle, Horace, and
Castelvetro resound throughout their clubs, and my plays became the talk of the town.

I might today refrain from recalling these verbose disputes,
which drifted away with the wind and which my successes
made harmless, but I am glad to refer to them now, because
of the opportunity thus afforded of telling my readers about
my way of thinking in regard to the rules of comedy and the
method I planned to follow when writing a play.

The unities, required for the greater perfection of theatrical work, were at all times open to discussion among authors
and critics. The censors of my character comedies had no
reproach to make concerning the unity of action, nor in
regard to the unity of time, but they asserted that I had
failed to satisfy the requirements of the unity of place. Yet
the action in my comedies always transpired in one city.
The characters might move about, it is true, in different parts
of it, but they remained within the limits of the same walls.
I believed then, and believe now, that the unity of place is
thereby satisfactorily observed.

In every art, in every discovery, experience has ever preceded precept. Authors have later laid down methods for the
practical guidance of inventiveness, but the moderns have
ever reserved the right to interpret these methods of the
ancients. As for me, since I do not find either in Aristotle's or

[17] *Memoirs* I, p. 301.

Horace's *Poetics* a clear, absolute, and vigorously worked-out principle regarding the unity of place in comedy, I have indeed been glad to conform whenever my subject lent itself to the idea, but I have never sacrificed a comedy which had a chance to turn out well to a prejudice which would have rendered it unsatisfactory.[18] If Aristotle were now alive, he would cancel the obnoxious rule, for a thousand absurdities, a thousand blunders and improprieties are caused by it.

There are, it seems to me, two kinds of comedy, pure comedy and comedy of intrigue. The first can be written while observing the unity of place, the second cannot be thus constructed without crudity and incongruity. The ancients had not, as we have, a way to shift scenery, and for this reason they observed all the unities. We comply with the unity of place when the action occurs in the same city, and all the more when it remains in the same house. I conclude, therefore, that if comedy can be constructed in compliance with the unity of place without hairsplitting and unseemliness, it should be done; but if, because of it, absurdities must be introduced, it is better to change the plot and observe the rules of probability.[19]

Like Aristotle, Horace has been made to say more than he intended. I refer particularly to the precept that not more than three persons should act at the same time in one scene. He says: *"Nec quarta loqui persona laboret."* Some think this to mean: "Let no more than three work." What he must have intended to say is that, if there are four persons, one of them should not exert himself; that is, the four actors should not be simultaneously in action with one another, as happens in improvised scenes, in which four or five persons immediately cause confusion. For that matter, scenes may be arranged for eight or ten persons, provided their action is carefully regulated and that they allow one another to speak in turn.[20]

For this reason, when certain fanatic admirers of antiquity demand of me either a scrupulous application of the unity of place or an adherence to the idea that not more than three persons should speak in one scene, or any similar finicality which has no relation to the constituent beauty of comedy, I answer them by pointing to the contrary usage of many au-

[18] *Memoirs* I, p. 310.
[19] *Teatro comico*, Act III, Scene 3.
[20] *Teatro comico*, Act III, Scene 9.

thors approved by the fame of centuries. There are things in ancient comedy which, though pleasing in their day, would prove intolerable in ours. I hold, therefore, that one should obey the laws of national and contemporary characteristics in a spectacle designed to divert, delight, and incidentally to instruct, rather than comply with certain precepts attributed to Aristotle or Horace. Those haters of novelty who insist on a complete accord with bygone standards appear to me like physicians who refuse to prescribe quinine for the sole reason that Hippocrates or Galen had not yet adopted it.[21]

My countrymen, I think, would never have been so severe with me but for the ill-balanced zeal of my partisans, on whom they reacted. Well-informed people merely condemned the fanaticism of those who set too high a value on my work. Meanwhile, disputes waxed ever warmer,[22] complaints and compliments coming thick and fast. To me the two opposing parties were a thorn in the flesh. Trying to content both, I submitted to the task of constructing improvised plays without ceasing to write character comedies. I had the inveterate mask actors do their work in one class, and employed the more capable and adaptable human material in the other. Thus each party had its innings, and in the course of time, with patience, I slowly led them into a common understanding. After a few years I enjoyed the satisfaction of seeing myself authorized to follow my own ideas, and they became the most generally accepted and the most popular in Italy.[23]

But before I was able to write comedies which could pass muster, I, too, constructed bad ones. I wrote some plays after the Spanish manner; that is to say, comedies of intrigue with considerable complexity in their plots. They met with unwonted success through a certain logical texture and regularity which distinguished them from the usual pieces of that sort, as well as through an undeniable naturalness and plausibility that made them worthy of note. I thought that if they succeeded so well when only the principal characters were provided with the proper directions and words, and the others were left to improvisation, with a resulting unevenness and precariousness in the performance, these plays would have turned out considerably better if all the roles had been

[21] Pasquali I, p. xiii.
[22] *Memoirs* I, p. 311.
[23] *Memoirs* II, p. 40.

written out. Thereby more variety could be introduced, all the characters could be smoothed on the lathe of Nature, national taste could be completely met. The success of *The Clever Woman, The Prudent Man, The Artful Widow, The Respectable Girl, The Cavalier and the Lady, The Antiquarian's Family,* and others belonging to my debut proved that I was right and that efforts to restore manners and decency to the stage of Italy were not likely to be in vain.[24]

I cannot boast that I developed to this degree of better sense through an assiduous and methodical study of the best ancient and modern writers and poets. Although I have not neglected reading them, thus receiving as from good teachers the best examples and precepts, I must confess that the two books upon which I have meditated most and which I shall never repent having used are the World and the Stage. It is a fact that no one becomes a master in playwriting who neglects the study of these books. The first of the two, the World, shows me so many characters, and depicts them to me so invitingly, that it seems to have been created expressly to provide me with plots for pleasing and instructive comedies. It presents to me the depth, the power, the effect of every human passion; and calling my attention to curious happenings, it informs me concerning current customs; furnishing me with knowledge of the foibles and defects common in our century and nation, it indicates to me, through the medium of some excellent person, how virtue resists corruption. Hence I draw upon this book as upon a bank, returning again and again, and meditating upon whatever I take from it under all the circumstances of life. My experience shows how indispensable it is to anyone who would exercise my profession.

The second, that is the book of the Stage, makes me see with what colors the characters, the passions, the action we read about in the book of the World should be bodied forth, how these must be painted and shaded to throw them in relief, and how varied to render them grateful to the discerning eye of the spectator. I learn from the stage what is most likely to impress the minds of men, what will awaken wonder and laughter, and what will cause that delightful sensation which people come to enjoy in the theatre. It teaches me that this is provoked mainly by filling comedy with natural images, and by tactfully placing before the vision of the audience

[24] Pasquali I, p. xiv.

those foibles and ridiculous delusions which can be seen in
what happens all the time.

The stage shows me through the fate of my comedies how
to estimate the character of the nation for which I write.
Some of my productions which I held in no esteem at all
have aroused great praise, while others, from which I expected
no ordinary applause, gained but a languid interest, if they
did not receive adverse criticism. Through this experience I
have learned that if I would make my plays more practically
useful, I must regulate my ideas in accordance with those
that prevail universally, without paying much attention to
the dicta of men who assume the right of prescribing rules of
taste for a whole people, nay, for the entire world and for
all centuries to come, and who do so upon a foundation of
mental arguments only. These do not reflect that in certain
nonintrinsic respects tastes and ideas change with impunity,
and that the public is the arbiter in this case, as it is in the
matter of clothes and language.[25]

This then is what I have learned from my two great books,
the World and the Stage. My comedies are in the main regulated upon the precepts found in them only, and I shrewdly
surmise that the first authors of comedy consulted no others.
"Whatever is represented on the stage ought to be a copy of
what occurs in the world," says Rapin. Comedy is what it
should be when we seem to be in a company of neighbors or
taking part in some familiar conversation, while in reality we
find ourselves in the theatre. Nothing must be shown that
has no counterpart in everyday life.[26]

I have read, it is true, all manner of treatises on Poetics,
on Tragedy and Comedy, but only after having formed my
own style, or during the process of developing it in the light
which the World and the Stage provided. Afterwards I perceived that I had unconsciously conformed very largely to
the most essential precepts of the art as recommended by
the great masters: like that physician who, having discovered
partly by chance, partly through experience, a wholesome
medicine, subsequently applies to it the accepted principles
of his art, regulating and systematizing it.[27]

Comedy was invented to expose foibles and ridicule dis-
agreeable habits. When the ancients wrote comedies on that

[25] Pasquali I, p. xv.
[26] Pasquali I, p. xvii.
[27] Pasquali I, p. xviii.

plan, the whole world liked them, for on seeing the facsimile of a character upon the boards, everybody saw the original in his neighbor or himself. When comedy became merely ridiculous, however, the most extravagant absurdities were gradually introduced under the pretext of causing laughter. Now that we are again fishing in the *mare magnum* of nature, men find themselves searching their hearts anew and identifying themselves with the persons presented, for they know how to discern whether or no a passion is well depicted, a character well developed and sustained: in short, they observe.[28]

My play of *The Punctilious Ladies* afforded me a striking illustration of this fact. I wrote this comedy in Mantua and had it performed on the local stage in order to try it out. It pleased greatly, but I ran the risk of drawing upon my head the wrath of one of the first ladies of the region. I learned later that she had not long before been in the situation of the countess in the play, who introduced Rosaura into society for a pecuniary consideration. Everybody stared in the direction of her box, but luckily for me, the lady was too broad-minded to lay herself open to the malice of the audience, applauding as she did every passage that might apply to her. Similar incidents occurred in Florence and Verona: in each of these cities it was thought that I had found my subject on the spot.[29]

Yet I always direct my criticism at social foibles in general, never at any sinner in particular; besides, it never becomes satire.[30] While writing a play I always strive to please the land of my fathers, to make it novel and yet keep it national, to win hearts through the attractiveness of virtue rather than by the sorry sight of vice. Indeed, a comedy which is truly an imitation of nature need not shun clean and pathetic sentiment, provided that it be not barren of those comic and witty features which are the fundamental basis of its existence.[31] I have had no other care than to please the average man, to induce people to frequent the theatre, and to procure profit for him who pays me for my work.[32]

[28] *Teatro comico,* Act II, Scene 1.

[29] *Memoirs* I, p. 329.

[30] *Teatro comico,* Act III, Scene 9.

[31] *Memoirs* I, p. 312.

[32] Lettera dell' Autore dell' opera intitolata *Nerone* scritta ad un suo amico che serve di prefazione all' opera stessa. Venice, December 28, 1748. See also *Memoirs* I, p. 455.

For you must know that during most of my career I have placed my muse and my pen at the disposal of the owners or directors of theatres. Such engagements may be thought peculiar. A man of letters, you will say, must be free, and should despise servitude and restraint.

If an author is well-to-do, like Voltaire, or cynical, as is Rousseau, I have nothing to reply; but if he be one of those who do not refuse a share in the receipts or in the benefits of publication, if he enjoy no emolument from a court, no pension or gifts, and yet is disposed to contribute products of his brain, he has no other resource in Italy.[33] After all, when one possesses a talent I do not see why one should make no practical use of it.[34]

My contracts with theatrical managers were generally quite satisfactory. My reputation once established, my work was accepted before being read, and paid for before the first performance.[35] And this is bound to be, for if the public applauds a play, it may be said without a doubt that the author has done a good piece of work. The box-office receipts show the manager whether a comedy has drawing power,[36] and while he will respect a poet as a man of education, he will not read his manuscript or listen to him through mere curiosity. What a manager looks for is a good new idea.[37] In the drama novelty is of prime importance.[38]

To make a play succeed, many things of beauty must be united. The least flaw may make it a failure.[39] Though lacking an interesting story, a comedy may have nevertheless many beautiful details; yet if there is no complication and suspense in the action, it cannot be other than a poor play.[40] The style, too, must be proper to comedy, that is to say simple and natural, not academic or elevated. The great art lies in adhering to nature in all things, never deviating from it. Sentiments must be true, not affected; expression within the comprehension of all. The commonest traits please more than

---

[33] *Memoirs* I, p. 290.
[34] *Memoirs* II, p. 213.
[35] *Memoirs* I, p. 291.
[36] *Teatro comico,* Act I, Scene 7.
[37] *Teatro comico,* Act I, Scene 6.
[38] *Teatro comico,* Act I, Scene 2.
[39] *Memoirs* II, p. 211.
[40] *Memoirs* I, p. 376.

delicate conceits.[41] Moreover, it is with national morals and customs, with our own foibles and absurdities, that Comedy should be concerned.[42]

My *Campiello*, for instance, gave great pleasure. Everything in it was copied from the lower classes, to be sure, but the whole action was of a truth which all recognized, the great and the small being interested in the story, for I had substituted simplicity for tinsel, and nature for the phantasmagoria of a diseased imagination. My *Buona Famiglia*, on the other hand, may be one of those plays of mine which, if taken to heart, might benefit society morally. It was enjoyed by well-bred folk, by virtuous households, wise fathers, and prudent mothers; but as these do not belong exactly to the sort of people who make managers rich, it had but few performances. Though revived occasionally by amateurs, it died a speedy death on the public stage,[43] for when the groundwork is not felicitous, there is no remedy that avails, the structure being unable to rise with vigor.[44]

Indeed, writing comedies is a difficult business, and I do not flatter myself with the illusion that I shall ever learn just in what comic perfection consists.[45] But this I know, that in order to create wholesome laughter, one must first laugh oneself.[46] When things are said and done with grace, they get a double value. The shorter, therefore, and the more unexpected comic scenes are, the more they please. The principal comedian should act copiously and speak sparingly. When he speaks, he should deliver his thrust pungently and at the right time, not cynically, as if under stress. He may be allowed to mutilate expressions naturally, as in dialect, but he must not twist and murder words. Especially should he beware of that cheap innuendo in which so many would-be comedies abound. In order to succeed, you must create something of your own, and to create you must study.[47]

I have also learned not to seek my subject in the associations of crime, but rather to choose it among the merely

[41] Pasquali I, p. xviii.
[42] *Memoirs* II, p. 42.
[43] *Memoirs* II, p. 89.
[44] Pasquali I, p. iv.
[45] *Teatro comico*, Act III, Scene 11.
[46] *Teatro comico*, Act I, Scene 8.
[47] *Teatro comico*, Act III, Scene 11.

ridiculous,[48] and to know that while improbability will kill a play,[49] an artistic mixture of the pathetic and the comical is ever an element of surprise.[50] The catastrophe, too, must be in accordance with human nature.[51] Although one may ridicule changes in fashion, headdress, or summer life in the country, in order to make woman a fit subject for comic attack the ridicule must be supplied by the vagaries of her mind, not by the whimsies of her heart. Even so, though the presentation of a female character may thus be comic in its own right, it has to be propped up by interesting and pleasing situations, else it may easily bore.

Rosaura in *The Fickle Woman* is such a comic character. She falls in love at one moment, and in the next falls out again; now she utters with apparent conviction certain principles and maxims, then flies, with lightheaded calculation, after passions which contradict them quite. The situation at the end of the play fits the ridiculous but not vicious folly under attack. Rosaura has finally made up her mind to marry, but all now avoid her; no man wants her for a wife.[52]

To the benefit of the public, and through the influence of my example, the evil stage manners that once were customary have at last been banished, and scandálous scenes have been abolished. No longer does one hear obscene expressions, filthy ambiguities, or depraved talk.[53] Yet I had to spend many years in dramatic labor before I was allowed to do things worth while. I did not become a comic author suddenly, but succeeded little by little, after long and arduous practice and a continuous, untiring study of reality.[54] Let no one think, however, that I have the temerity to believe that my plays are devoid of defects. Far from that presumption,[55] I am always a-tremble when a new comedy of mine goes on the boards,[56] and I take daily pains to improve my methods of writing.[57]

[48] *Memoirs* I, p. 235.
[49] *Memoirs* I, p. 278.
[50] *Memoirs* I, p. 279.
[51] *Memoirs* I, p. 337.
[52] *Memoirs* I, p. 354.
[53] *Teatro comico,* Act III, Scene 3.
[54] *Teatro comico,* Act III, Scene 2.
[55] Pasquali I, p. xviii.
[56] *Teatro comico,* Act III, Scene 11.
[57] Pasquali I, p. xviii.

It may, indeed, interest some readers how I progressed in that respect. My rules cannot be safe to follow, however, for in mental work the result frequently depends on the state of mind in which one happens to be, rather than upon established and proved ability. Hence it is that among the works of any author the first are often better than the last, and sometimes the last better than the first; while again and again one may notice that variety of good and bad which is the despair of Olympus.

Perhaps more than anyone I have fallen into inequalities of manner, style, and verve, because of the quantity of plays I have produced in a short space of time or the haste with which I have many times been forced to write, and because of the consequent disinclination I have often felt for creative work. Revision for purposes of publication may have imparted a little more evenness, producing better results in language and expression, but the shrewd reader will nevertheless be able to say: "This was a stroke of genius, that was written when the author was apathetic." [58]

Indeed, how many comedies have I not dashed off in six or seven days! How often, when pressed for time, have I not sent away a first act for rehearsal and, without seeing it again, written the second, the third being done with the same celerity! In the course of time, however, I would notice the effect which my plays made upon the public. I heard the criticism and the censure, and when some of them were about to go to press, I would reconstruct them, better them, and sometimes change them completely.[59] Yet I am bound to say that experience and habit by degrees so familiarized me with the art of playwriting that, when the subject was once thought out and the characters determined upon, the rest finally became mere routine. I knew I possessed a good deal of aptitude, and I knew I could work with greater ardor when under pressure.[60]

To illustrate this point, the time when I had promised the Venetian public sixteen comedies may be cited. Only one play remained to be written to fill my engagement. We had

---

[58] Pasquali I, p. iv.

[59] Lettera dell' avvocato C. G. ad un suo amico in Venetia. Florence, April 28, 1753. In *Lettere di C. Goldoni,* ed. by G. M. Urbani de Ghelthof, Venice, 1880, p. 65. See also *Fogli Sparsi,* ed. by A. G. Spinelli, Milan, 1855, p. 25.

[60] *Memoirs* II, p. 119.

reached the last Sunday but one of the Carnival, and I had
not done a single line of the last one of the series. I had
nothing in mind for it yet. I left my house for a walk about
St. Mark's Square, seeking distraction. I looked about to see
if any of the masks or jugglers might furnish me with the
subject of a comedy or farce for Shrovetide. I met, under
the arcade of the clock, a man with whom I was instantly
struck, and who provided me with the subject of which I was
in quest. This was an old Armenian, ill dressed, very dirty,
and with a long beard, who went about the streets of Venice
selling the dried fruits of his country, which he called
Abagigi. This man, who was to be seen everywhere, and
whom I had myself frequently met, was so well known and
so much despised that when any one wished to tease a girl
seeking a husband, he proposed to her Abagigi.

Nothing more was needed to send me home satisfied. I
entered my house, shut myself up in my closet, and began a
popular comedy, which I called *I Pettegolezzi delle donne,* or
Women's Tittle-tattle. I could not get it performed until
Shrove Tuesday, and it closed the Carnival season. The
crowd was so great that day that the price of boxes tripled
and quadrupled, and the applause so tumultuous that the
passers-by did not know whether it was an effect of satisfaction or a general riot. I sat quietly in my box, surrounded by
friends who wept for joy. Then a crowd came for me, bade
me come out, and carried me in spite of myself to the Ridotto, where, dragging me from room to room, they forced
me to accept a series of compliments which I would gladly
have avoided.

I was too tired to bear the ceremony; besides, not knowing whence came the enthusiasm of the moment, I was vexed
that this play should have been placed above so many others
which I liked better. Little by little, however, I unraveled the
motive of this general acclaim: it was the triumph of having
fulfilled what I had contracted to do.[61]

At another time, after the success of *Pamela,* my friends
insisted that, in order to save myself the trouble of inventing
a plot, I should again write a play based on some novel. Tired
of their importunings, I finally said that I should prefer to
construct a comedy from which a novel might be made.
Some began to laugh, while others took me at my word.
These said: "Then write us a novel in action, a piece as

[61] *Memoirs* I, p. 355.

complicated as a novel." "I'll make you one," I replied.
"Will you?" "I will." "On your word?" "On my word." So
I went home and, excited by my wager, I began the play
—and the novel at the same time, without having a plot for
either.

I need, so I said to myself, a lot of action, surprise, bewilderment, and an interesting situation, with comical and
pathetic elements besides. A heroine would interest more
than a hero. Where shall I look for her? We shall see. In
the meantime, let us take an unknown lady for protagonist.
So I wrote on the paper: *The Unknown*, a Comedy, Act One,
Scene the First. This woman must have a name; yes, let us
call her Rosaura. But will she enter alone to announce the
argument of the piece? No, that's just where Comedy used to
fail. Let her enter with— Yes, with Florindo. Rosaura and
Florindo.

This is how I began *The Unknown*, and how I continued
writing it, thus building a large structure without knowing
whether I was building a temple or a barn. Each scene led
to another, one incident produced the next, and the next.
At the end of the first act the plot was outlined; I merely
had to fill it in. I was astonished at the quantity and the
novelty of the events with which my imagination provided
me. At the end of the second act I bethought myself of a
catastrophe, and from then on all my skill was exerted to
make it unexpected and surprising, yet so that it would not
fall from the clouds, as it were. The play pleased my friends
and the public, and everybody averred that it could supply
the material for a novel of four volumes in octavo.[62]

It was not always success and friendship, however, which
spurred me on to bursts of speed. I had thought that *The
Whimsical Old Man,* for instance, would have had at least
the success of *The Man of the World,* but I was horribly
mistaken. Rubini had never played without a mask and was
so uncomfortable and so embarrassed that he lost all his
grace, as well as his wits and his common sense. The play
fell flat, most humiliatingly for himself and for me. It came
to an end under difficulties, and when the curtain fell, hisses
arose on every side.

I escaped quickly in order to avoid backhanded compliments, and went to the Ridotto. Concealed beneath my mask,
I mingled with the crowd which collects there after the

[62] *Memoirs* I, p. 351.

theatre, and had the time and the opportunity to listen to the eulogies lavished upon me and my piece.

Passing through the gaming rooms, I saw groups everywhere in earnest discussion, and they were all talking about me. "Goldoni is through," some said, "Goldoni has emptied his bag." I recognized the voice of a mask who spoke through his nose, and who said in a loud voice that my portfolio was exhausted. He was asked to what portfolio he referred. "It is the collection of manuscripts," he answered, "that has furnished Goldoni with everything he has done till this day." In spite of the wish of all to make fun of me, everybody began to laugh at the nasal voice. I was looking for criticism, and found only ignorance and animosity.

I went home, passed the night somehow, and searched the while for a way to avenge myself upon the mockers. I found one at last, and at sunrise began a comedy in five acts and in verse, entitled *The Ball*.

Act by act I sent it to the copyist. The actors learned their roles as they came forth; on the fourth day the play was announced on a poster, and it was performed on the fifteenth day. It was, indeed, a case of *facit indignatio versus*. The gist of the piece was again a phase of *cicisbeatura*, a husband forcing his wife to give a ball for his *cicisbea*. I arranged for a gathering of tired dancers in a drawing room adjacent to the ballroom. There I caused the conversation to fall on *The Whimsical Old Man*. I had all the ridiculous talk which I heard at the Ridotto repeated; I made all the characters argue for and against the piece, and my defense was approved by the applause of the public. It was evident that Goldoni was not through, that his bag was not empty, that his portfolio was not exhausted. Listen, my fellow authors, there is no other way for us to take revenge on the public than to force it to applaud us.[63]

I used to go through four processes before taking up the construction and final polishing of a play. The first step was the making of the outline with its division into the three principal parts: the exposition, the arch of the plot, and the catastrophe. The second step consisted in the apportioning of the action among acts and scenes; the third in the dialoguing of the most interesting incidents, the fourth in the general dialoguing of the whole.

It often happened that, when the last process was reached,

[63] *Memoirs* II, p. 34.

I had by that time changed everything I had done in the second and third, for ideas succeed one another, one scene produces the next, a word found by chance suggests a new thought. After a time, therefore, I came to combine the four operations into one. With the plot and the three divisions constantly in mind, I now begin at once: Act One, Scene One; so I proceed to the end, ever remembering that the lines must converge toward a single point, determined beforehand; that is to say, toward the climax of the action, which is the principal part of the play, and for which it appears that all the machinery of planning and constructing has been set in motion.

In my climaxes I have rarely been mistaken. I can say this with assurance, for the whole world has told me so. Besides, the problem does not seem difficult to me. It is, on the contrary, quite easy to find a satisfying solution when you provide for it at the beginning of the play and do not lose sight of it in the course of the work.[64] Tastes, however, keep on changing from day to day, and my comedies, which are now triumphant, will surely become mere rubbish in the course of time.

Indeed, all comedy becomes old-fashioned in the long run, however well it may have been written, or revamped and revived. But the manner of writing it, I hope, always has room in which to improve. True and recognizable characters never grow stale, and although their number is not infinite in kind, it is infinite in species, since every virtue, every vice, every custom, every defect assumes its hue from the continuously varying circumstances which surround it.[65]

[64] *Memoirs* II, p. 119.
[65] *Teatro comico,* Act III, Scene 9.

Molière and Shakespeare

by

CONSTANT COQUELIN

Translated by Florence Hallett Matthews
With an Introduction by Brander Matthews

Introduction

When Coquelin's illuminating lecture on "Art and the Actor" was issued in 1915 as a volume in the second series of the Publications of the Dramatic Museum of Columbia University, Henry James kindly revised his brilliant essay on the many-sided accomplishment of the unrivaled French comedian to serve as an introduction to this stimulating discussion of the principles and the processes of the art of acting. James's acute analysis of Coquelin's histrionic prowess relieves me from any obligation to dwell on his powers as a performer, on his vigor, on his variety, on his versatility, on his rich endowment for his profession, on his acquired skill, or on his certainty of execution. At the Conservatory Coquelin was the pupil of Régnier, but, as he once confided to me, he profited almost as much by his assiduous observation of Samson as by the direct instruction of Régnier.

Coquelin absorbed from these predecessors, the two chief comedians of the Comédie-Française, the traditions of the House of Molière; and it was from them that he may have derived his ambition not only to practice his art but to theorize about it. They were both actors first of all, but they were also, to a certain extent, men of letters. Samson in his youth had composed two or three little plays; and after he had retired from the stage, he distilled his experience in the rimed couplets of his *Art Théâtrale,* a most penetrating study of the histrionic craft, abounding in apt anecdotes and in pregnant maxims. Régnier in his turn had been a playwright, having anonymously aided Jules Sandeau to dramatize *Mademoiselle de la Seiglière.* He also published an edition of *Tartuffe* in which he indicated the best readings and recorded

224

the appropriate business whereby this masterpiece of Molière's has been made effective on the stage of the Théâtre Français; and Coquelin long hoped to find time to follow Régnier's example and to put down in black and white the traditions which enrich the performance of certain others of Molière's comedies.

It has been pointed out more than once that actors if they can write at all are likely to write well. The practice of their profession has taught them the necessity for construction, for clarity, for logic, and for concision; it has also supplied their memories with an ample vocabulary. We can perceive the benefit of these professional advantages in the *Apology* of Colley Cibber and in the *Autobiography* of Joseph Jefferson, as well as in the didactic poem of Samson and the erudite disquisition of Régnier. So Coquelin in his turn was truly a man of letters, even as were Cibber and Jefferson, Samson and Régnier. Perhaps he surpassed these eminent predecessors in the wider range of his criticism, as all four of them, and one after another, confined themselves to the discussion of acting and to the portrayal of distinguished actors and actresses, whereas Coquelin, while writing most frequently about his own art, was wont now and again to stray into the fold of purely literary criticism.

He was the friend of many writers, poets, and playwrights, as he was also the intimate of many painters and of many politicians (notably Gambetta and Waldeck-Rousseau). He was helpful to a host of young poets and especially to those young poets who were ambitious to become playwrights. When Théodore de Banville brought him the manuscript of *Gringoire* Coquelin suggested certain changes in the plot which strengthened the dramatic interest and the theatrical effectiveness of that lovely little play. I believe he did a like service to François Coppée, who wrote the pathetic *Luthier de Crémone* specially for Coquelin's acting. Yet, a few years later when the poet and the player fell out, Coppée in his next novel elaborated a malicious caricature of the actor who had befriended him.

With Edmond Rostand Coquelin's association was intimate and prolonged. *Cyrano de Bergerac* was put together to order to utilize Coquelin's infinite variety and to enable him to reveal in one play the versatility he had displayed in a score of earlier pieces—to be in turn comic and pathetic, to be heroic and grotesque, to be swashbuckling and tear-compelling. It was on a hint of Coquelin's that Rostand began *L'Aiglon,* although the actor did not play Flambeau, the part intended for him, until he came to America; and he did not survive to impersonate the feathered hero of *Chantecler,* also closely adjusted to his personality and even suggested by Coquelin's habit of signing his notes "Coq."

His excursions into literary criticism are cast in the form of lectures. Even though they were ultimately published, they were devised for oral delivery, which permitted the lecturer to make plain by his own incomparable skill in recitation the charm of the poetry he was praising. One of these lectures was on a philosophic poet, Sully-Prudhomme; another was on a poet of the hearth, Eugène Manuel; and a third, which I am glad to have had the pleasure of hearing, was on Béranger. "Art and the Actor" was a lecture; and so was "Molière and Shakespeare." These literary and dramatic criticisms are all the better because of the limitations of the lecture form, which compel a rigorous restriction of duration, an orderly and progressive arrangement of the subject matter, and an obligation to arouse and retain the attention of the listeners.

Of the half score of Coquelin's lectures this on Molière and Shakespeare seems to me to be the most interesting and the most important. It is a comparative criticism by an actor whose special knowledge of his own art and whose enforced apprehension of the kindred art of playmaking aid him to understand and to appreciate the qualities and the methods of the two great modern dramatists, who were themselves players intimately acquainted with the theatre long before they began to write plays. In succession to Samson and to Régnier, Coquelin had inherited the parts which Molière had composed for his own acting. He had impersonated nearly all these characters, one after another; and, as Sarcey said in his eulogistic study of Coquelin (in the illuminating series entitled *Comédiens et Comédiennes*), "there is no part in our classic drama in which he is not excellent; in some Coquelin has shown himself exquisite; one may say that he has lent them a renewed charm for us, that he has, so to speak, revealed them to us."

For the interpretation of Shakespeare's plays the French actor's equipment was less adequate, since it had been confined to *The Taming of the Shrew,* which, thanks to Coquelin's exertion, established itself in the repertory of the Comédie-Française. It was his own experience in the comedies of Molière and his own study of similar qualities in the plays of Shakespeare that led Coquelin to the opinion he once expressed to me: that these two dramatic poets stand alone in the skill with which they "take care of their actors." They knew what the actor could do and what he could not do; and they never imposed on him any needless difficulty of execution. Their parts are easy to perform—if only the actor is one who is capable of performing them. Both poets provide their performers with lines that fall trippingly off the tongue; and these lines are always suggestive of the appropriate action. The actual dialogue of a play by Molière or by Shakespeare is the best commentary on the text. If a speech is found to be difficult of utterance, then the fault is in the actor, who has failed to master its meaning.

This lecture on Molière and Shakespeare had been preceded by three others on single plays of Molière, one on *The Misanthrope,* another on *Tartuffe,* and a third on *The School for Wives.* He may have intended to prepare a fourth on the only play of Shakespeare in which he had had the pleasure of acting, *The Taming of the Shrew;* but if he had ever had the wish to do this he failed to carry it out. Yet the lecture for which these few paragraphs must serve as an introduction discloses an energetic study of Shakespeare's plays, a piercing insight into Shakespeare's dramatic methods, testifying to persistency almost as obvious as that which the actor-lecturer had given to Molière.

BRANDER MATTHEWS

Molière and Shakespeare

Everything has been said about Molière, and in France he has been the object of the most extravagant theories. There is only one suggestion that no one has ventured: this is to deny that he is the author of his works. In England there is a school which declares that Shakespeare was but a man of straw, and that the true poet of *Hamlet* and of *The Tempest* was the lord chancellor Bacon. We have not yet a school like this. Is an hypothesis of this sort impossible? Could we not, with equal likelihood, attribute the paternity of *The School for Wives* and *Don Juan* to the great Condé, for instance, to whom tradition already imputes at least one line of Tartuffe—

Il est de faux dévots ainsi que de faux braves,—

and who was the avowed protector of Molière? He prided himself, as we know, on his wit and on his freedom of thought, and he was fond of the stage. Why may he not have had a hand in these plays? That would explain why this same *Tartuffe* was acted at his house in full long before it was revised; why it was at his house again that the revised version was first seen; and also why Molière left no manuscripts behind him.

It would not be difficult, I think, if some imaginative scholar would but undertake it, to establish this hypothesis as solidly as the famous Baconian theory; and it could be proved that Molière and Shakespeare are but masks, just as it has been proved that Napoleon and Mr. Gladstone have never existed and that the first of these is a sun myth and the second an old Breton deity—no doubt, the deity of eloquence!

But I have no intention of fighting the Baconian revelation, or of building up any theory of that kind; I wish only to throw on paper a few notes inspired by the study and the comparison of the two masters of the stage.

If Molière seems like a belated twin of Shakespeare, it is not only because of an admirable equality of genius, it is also because of the many likenesses shown in their lives and in their habits. First actors, then authors, then managers, they entered the profession very young and pretty poor; and both made money by the theatre and died rich, one at fifty-two and the other at fifty-one; leaving almost the same number of works, as to which they seem to have been negligent, since these were printed in full only after their deaths, and by the care of their comrades. Born in the burgher class, they had princes for friends and knew the royal favor; and Louis XIV asked Molière for *The Magnificent Lovers,* as Queen Elizabeth had asked Shakespeare for *The Merry Wives of Windsor.* Thus one and the other, turn by turn, amused the court and the city, the people of quality and the rabble. Their free genius brought them out safely.

Wherefore the classic Ben Jonson cried out against his comrade Shakespeare; wherefore also the rigorous Boileau condemned judicially the author of *The Misanthrope,* thrust into the sack of Scapin. Nevertheless, they went on, taking their property where they found it, borrowing everywhere the matter which their alchemic genius turned to gold, bearing in mind no rules but to be true and to please; pleasing indeed, and always pleasing, the foolish as well as the wise, the ignorant as well as the refined.

Not only did they skirmish with pedants, but they also quarreled with the envious, a viler tribe: Shakespeare had Greene, Molière had Visé; they were hunted even into their private life, and infamous vices were imputed to them. They were, however, excellent comrades, liking a large life, good fare, and frank friendships; they gladly had wit-combats at the Syren or at the Cross of Lorraine; and they kept open house. If we believe the legend, it was because Shakespeare entertained too liberally his old friend Ben Jonson and his compatriot Drayton that he took to his bed and died. It is thus that our Regnard died; but it is not thus that Molière

died. His heart-rending death is familiar; and God, who does
not disdain an antithesis, crowned these careers so alike with
the most opposite ends, making a comedy of the death of the
great tragedian and of the death of the great comedian a
tragedy.

In yet another point the end of Shakespeare differed from
that of Molière. He had retired. He was living in his dear
Stratford as a rich country gentleman, taking very good care
of his property; even careless of his glory, and not having
written, when he died, perhaps one verse in four years. His
will does not mention his works, nor do the four lines inscribed over his tomb. Aeschylus also, in the epitaph he wrote
for himself, forgot his hundred tragedies, but he had fought
at Marathon, and this he recalled proudly; and it is conceivable that he should claim this glory in preference to the
other. But the tomb of Shakespeare makes no similar claim:
it begs that it be left alone, and this is not for the sake of
Hamlet or of *Lear* or of so many masterpieces, but for
Jesus' sake.

Molière never retired; scarcely even did he take a vaca-
tion: he worked while ill and he worked when dying; and he
died almost on the stage. One of the reasons for this difference—not enough noticed, I think—is that Molière was a
much better actor than Shakespeare.

Shakespeare the actor has left no trace. It is vaguely
known that he played the old Adam in *As You Like It* and
the Ghost in *Hamlet*. But it was not he, but Burbage, who
"created" his great parts. It seems probable that, becoming
an actor by accident, he was such without passion, and that
he ceased to play as soon as possible.

Not so Molière. There is no doubt that his vocation as an
actor was his master passion. He did not leave the paternal
roof for the purpose of writing plays—but for the purpose of
acting them. And we know that these were not comedies—
the Illustrious Theatre had in stock at first nothing but
tragedies. When he wrote *L'Étourdi,* his first work, Molière
had been an actor for nine years, and for fifteen when he
wrote the *Précieuses Ridicules.* Never could his great success
as an author tempt him to leave the boards. He not only continued to act in his own plays, but he acted in the plays of
others and did not consider this as lost time. He acted, as
we have said, although coughing and spitting blood; and to
Boileau, who advised him to leave the stage, he replied, "It

is for my honor that I remain"—so much did he love his profession, which was killing him. But then he excelled in it. His contemporaries are unanimous on this point. He was extraordinary—"Better actor even than author," one of them goes so far as to say. We can imagine what joy it must have been to see him in his great parts—Sganarelle, Orgon, Alceste, Harpagon.

He had come to this degree of excellence only by dint of hard work, for his appearance was not pleasing and his voice difficult to manage. It was his voice, above all, that gave him trouble; but, notwithstanding the hiccough that remained, he made it so rich in varied inflections that it seemed as though he had many voices. He was particular about the articulation: it is to him that we owe the right way of pronouncing certain words; for example, the infinitives in *er*. He left nothing to chance, and insisted that an actor should have counted all his steps and decided upon every glance before he stepped upon the stage. We have in the *Impromptu* a theatrical criticism of his that we can compare to the theatrical criticism of Shakespeare in *Hamlet*. At bottom they agree: they have the same passion for nature, the same aversion from overemphasis—but Molière had the advantage in that he practiced what he preached.

It will be objected that he was not good in tragic characters. That is possible; it is so human to err! But perhaps we have been too quick to believe his enemies on this point. The manner of acting tragedy in those days was very different from his theories. He may have disconcerted the public by abstaining from bombastic delivery and by bringing down the heroes to a more natural level. Notice, however, that he played Corneille up to the very last. It seems likely that if the pit had disapproved of him so strongly in these parts, he would not have been so insistent; then it would have affected the receipts—and Molière was a manager. Finally, it was he who trained Baron; and Baron in tragedy, as in comedy, was incomparable. This passion of Molière's for his profession as actor was eminently advantageous. It increased his power of observation. The gaze he fixed on man was in some sort a double mirror; he studied first to know, and afterwards to reproduce. What might have escaped him had he only written the play came to him when he acted it. Then—forgive me the metaphor—the ink becames blood. Therefore it is, I think, because Molière was a greater actor than Shakespeare that he was a more sure and more complete observer, although in a narrower sphere.

And to this quality of actor, which was accompanied in both by the gift of stage management, they each owed the dramatic force that today animates their works. We feel that these were not written coldly in the silence of the closet, but thrown alive upon the stage. And it is this too—I think the remark is Sainte-Beuve's—that explains the indifference of Shakespeare and Molière to the printing of their works. They did not recognize these on paper. *Tartuffe* and *Hamlet* existed for them only before the footlights. It was only there that they felt their plays bone of their bone and flesh of their flesh.

It has been possible, after much erudition, to establish the chronological sequence of the works of Shakespeare; and through this study has been evolved the history of his thought. It is at first a period of experiment; Shakespeare begins, he feels the need of living, he is the Jack-at-all-trades at the Globe; he makes over old pieces and writes new ones in imitation of Plautus or the Italians: no originality as yet, and, oddly enough, no dramatic genius; he was, above all, the poet of *Venus and Adonis,* in whom it was difficult to foresee the writer of *Hamlet.* But the time of groping ceased: he wrote *Richard III,* and in that he discovered character; he wrote *Romeo and Juliet,* and in that he discovered drama. Still, the second part of his career is almost entirely devoted to comedy. If he attempts drama, it is through the national history; which gives him the chance of creating Falstaff, perhaps his best-rounded comic type. This was the time when he began his fortune and his glory. He is full of hope and gaiety; he takes delight in those adorable compositions *A Midsummer Night's Dream, The Merchant of Venice, Much Ado about Nothing.* Fancy is his queen, and if Melancholy seizes him, it is to draw him to that marvelous forest of Arden, where so many songs are sung that the wickedest become good and the things that seem the most difficult to arrange end there—as you like it.

To this period of youth succeeds the prime of life. Shakespeare is rich and seems happy; but his thoughts are more somber. He doubts, he despairs, "Man pleases him not," and if he forgives Woman it is to make her fall under the injustice of destiny. From 1601 to 1607 were written these dramas: *Julius Caesar, Hamlet, Measure for Measure, Othello,*

Lear, Macbeth, Antony and Cleopatra, Timon of Athens—
masterpieces, all of them, and all disconsolate; it is the
triumph of evil; the more Hamlet thinks the more he is discouraged; and it finishes with the anathema of Timon giving
society at large over to destruction.

But now what happens? Because he has so often shown
Man as the miserable plaything of heredity and chance,
Shakespeare takes pity on him; and pity engenders serenity.
Then the last period opens, the period of *A Winter's Tale*,
of *Cymbeline*, of *The Tempest*, of the fragments of *Pericles*.
Always life and its troubles; but a dream mingles strangely
with action, and it is Providence that settles the end. The
drama loses in concentration; but, on the other hand, the
poetry becomes wonderful: it attains to the ineffable in *The
Tempest*, the most divine poem ever dreamed by man.

Is it now possible to discover in the work of Molière, as in
that of his rival, a history of his private thought? And does
the chronological sequence of his comedies reveal to us something of his views on man and of the secret leanings of his
genius?

I think so; but only on one condition: the date of *Tartuffe*
must be that of its composition, and not that of its first representation, as is generally taken. Then we find in the work
of Molière, as in that of Shakespeare, four distinct periods.

The period of groping, first: Molière is likewise the Jack-
at-all-trades of his company; he acts in tragedy, tinkers old
plays with the help of Madeleine Béjart, and writes farces,
most of them imitated from the Italian, many of them derived from our old stock of fabliaux. Then, as success comes,
he attempts better things—writes *L'Étourdi* and *The Lovers'
Quarrel*. We have there only his gaiety unfailing and full of
go; his observation betrays itself only in comic touches, and
does not rise as high as character drawing; but what an admirable choice of words—lively, alert, and full of savor!
And he not only finds words but scenes, such as the delicious
quarrel in the *Dépit.*

At last he is in Paris; and as though he became conscious
of his genius upon touching his native soil, he throws the
Précieuses at the society of the day. No imitation of the
ancients this time, no more Italian comedy; he paints the
times, but he paints only its absurdities.

It is a great step forward. No matter. The work is brave
and alive; it begins the second period; but strange to relate,

although the *Précieuses* was a success, Molière did not follow it up; he returned to bolder farce with *Sganarelle,* to tragi-comedy with *Don Garcia de Navarre*; and it is from the ancients, from Terence, that he borrows *The School for Husbands.* But these were still but gropings: the last was at all events a real work, and Molière became more confident. A lucky chance brings him to the notice of the king, for whom he prepares the *Fâcheux,* a sparkling improvisation; and then he is in favor, sure of himself, sure of the princes; and he writes *The School for Wives.*

It is the first of the great masterpieces, it is the beginning of the third period; Molière has discovered himself. He has the vocabulary, he has the daring and the invention; he creates; Arnolphe, Agnes are immortal. But there is still more, and this it is that to my mind characterizes this third manner: *The School for Wives* is a social comedy. I beg pardon for the word, which is modern, but I could replace it only by a long periphrase. What I mean is that *The School for Wives* shows society itself; Arnolphe has his own ideas on these eternally serious points, woman's education and marriage, and he calls religion to the aid of his ideas.

Molière is there on delicate ground, but it is by his own wish; and it is very valiantly that he takes part against Arnolphe's theories and turns them into ridicule. This causes a tempest; the bigots discover an enemy. Molière is censured, cast forth, vilified. He does not care. Ever since the *Critique of the School for Wives* one feels that he will not recede. In that play he attacks the marquises, and more than one anecdote shows that this needed courage. But what is this skirmish compared with the battle of *Tartuffe*! Here evidently is comedy as it was dreamed of by the master in full possession of his strength; it turns towards satire of society; it makes itself a power, and shows on the stage the secrets of social organization. What will he respect, this Molière? He touches the Church! And it is in the name of nature that he scoffs at the theories of the mystics. But what happens? This time he is beaten. *Tartuffe* is forbidden. Well! Molière does not give in. Such is then his ardor for the fray that, after having attacked false piety, he combats what next is most dangerous— false science. He begins his war on the physicians. But this is a mere episode: he meditates a revenge; he creates *Don Juan.* This is his most extraordinary work; we are stupefied by what he has dared to say in the scene with the Poor Man, and in that with Don Louis, and in the whole of the fifth act. After the Church, it is autocracy which he shakes. He was never so free, or, as they said in those days, so libertine.

Unfortunately—others perhaps will say fortunately—*Don Juan* was not enough of a success, and the piece met much dangerous hostility in high quarters; at the same time the flood of insults increases. Molière, ill, perhaps discouraged, and feeling, doubtless, that he could not go farther on this road, that the people of his century would not follow him there—Molière reasons with himself. A contest arises within him: Molière the indignant protests, wants to combat, and would let loose "the vigorous hatreds"; Molière the philosopher puts reason first, which wishes that we be wise with sobriety, and which counsels man, being incorrigible, to accept fate without cursing him, and to observe him as one observes the "evil apes" and the "mad wolves."

This profound mental debate gave birth to *The Misanthrope,* another masterpiece, that belongs to the third manner by Alceste and to the last by Philinte. For it is Philinte who gets the best of it. Certainly Molière does not renounce the correction of men, but he gives up calling to judgment the powers of society. With more sharpness than ever he studies character, but individual character, not the social character. He avoids the soldier; he leaves the speculator to Le Sage; while the judge will await Beaumarthaes.

He no longer fights—he contemplates. Even after *Tartuffe* was authorized he persisted in not giving a companion piece to *Tartuffe.* He will come back to Plautus—*Amphitryon, The Miser;* he will come back to Italian comedy—*The Tricks of Scapin;* he will come back to the satire of the provincials— *Pourceaugnac, Georges Dandin;* and in each of these returns he will create masterpieces, for he is absolute master of his art, and not for one instant does his genius pale. But he never returns to *Don Juan.* Twice he approaches the forbidden ground; but *The Would-be Gentleman* is not the whole of the burgher class; and if you would see how much the new Molière differs from the old, compare the youth, the fierceness, the set purpose of *The School for Wives* with the serene maturity, impartial and profound, of *The Learned Ladies.*

We must say at once that Molière's self-denial cost his vivacity nothing; this dazzles us to the last moment, and it is with one of his gayest farces that he ends. It is true that this farce is, upon reflection, one of his strongest comedies.

He is, I repeat, in this last period absolute master of his art; I would add that he is much more careful of form; to such an extent that not having time to give to his verses that degree of perfection which he desired, he wrote no more except in prose. From *The Physician in Spite of Himself* to *The Imaginary Invalid* there are ten plays in prose, three in verse, in with which must be counted *Psyche*, although *Psyche*, it is well known, was principally by Corneille. But the other two are the most finished works of Molière in point of style. We may regret sometimes the Rabelaisian freedom of the earlier manner, the large and oily brush marks of *Tartuffe*; but we must render homage to the adorable workmanship of *Amphitryon* as well as to the judicial and sustained grandeur of style of *The Learned Ladies*.

After all, if he from preference used prose, it was not that he might be negligent, for now he cadences it and fills it with blank verse, and now, as in *The Would-be Gentleman*, he gives it such a variety of shading that the author disappears, leaving only his characters to be heard, each one speaking his own language, like the good Madame Jourdain, according to the frankness of their nature.

I will not enter upon the comparisons that these historical portraits of the minds of the two masters might suggest. I would insist on but one point. It does not appear that, at any moment of his career, Shakespeare thought it possible to reform society by the stage. Neither in his fantastic, optimistic comedy nor in the merciless, pitiless drama of the somber period, nor in the providential drama of the last period, did he appear to occupy himself with correcting men of their vices. He makes works of art—that is all. If there be in them a lesson, it is, in a way, unmeant by him, and as there might be one in the spectacle of human affairs. Molière, on the contrary, has taken seriously his duty as a comic author. He has, just like old Corneille, frankly wished to put into practice Aristotle's principle of purging mankind of its faults. He has accepted comedy as a social power. And, even after he was forced to renounce *Tartuffe*, he renounced neither correcting nor instructing; and almost all his plays, if not all, have an aim and a moral. This difference is accounted for, I think, by another, which is to a certain extent primary: Molière was a Latin, Shakespeare was not. Shakespeare very probably received a much better education than Ben Jonson leads us to believe. He loved and read the ancients much; many Latin-

isms have been found in his style. In his youth he imitated
the *Menæchmi* of Plautus; and in his maturity he took from
Plutarch not only the plots of dramas, but phrases, even
whole discourses, to which he gave only the rhythm of verse,
but which are absolutely opposed in tone to his poetry. Notwithstanding all this he remains free, original, and modern.
It is with deliberation that he rejects the classic rules promulgated and put in use by the Ben Jonsons.

What connection is there between the spirit of antiquity
and that of *Venus and Adonis,* his sensual poem, all sparkling
with *concetti* of the Italian type? Has he not gone as far
as to parody the *Iliad* in *Troilus and Cressida?* Finally, in
his great Roman drama, are they real Romans that he shows
us? The place, the costume, the speech, and the soil—all are
contemporary with Shakespeare. Romans, no; but men
surely! And that is enough. And as for the people, whom he
loved to paint—though not to flatter—it is the populace that
he has known and mingled with, the mob and not the plebeians, to such an extent that one might say that *Coriolanus*
was one of the most English of Shakespeare's plays.

In short, the spirit of the Renaissance breathed upon
Shakespeare, but did not transform him. Shakespeare was,
in his country, the definite and supreme end of the Middle
Ages. In France, on the contrary, the Middle Ages did not
end. In the sixteenth century the Latin spirit seized the people once more, and instead of finding, with Shakespeare, their
inspiration in the miracle plays, in the Gesta, in the Round
Table, in the fabliaux, our authors turned back to Rome.
Thus did Molière. It was not that he despised our immense
repertory of farces and moralities; he was too fond of Rabelais for that, and he borrowed from the fabliaux for his little
pieces, now almost all lost; but for his great comedies it is
Plautus, it is Terence, who are his models and his inspiration.
He imitated them, one may say, up to his last hour. To this
he was predisposed not only by race, but by education; we
know what vigorous training he had received, and that one of
his pastimes—if he ever had any pastimes—was translating
Lucretius in verse.

It is the alliance of the Latin and the French genius that
has given to our comedy its character and its superiority.
The Frenchman has inherited from the Celt, at the same time
with the love of combat and the love of speechmaking, an
admirable promptness in seizing the ridiculous and in imitat-

ing it. He has found in his Latin heritage the taste for generalizations, the sentiment of measure, and the cult of reason. French comedy has been born of all these. It is gay on its Celtic side, and on its Latin side realistic and practical. In its most dizzy flights you would never see it, like the comedy of Shakespeare, beat its wings and fly into pure fantasy and the dream of a midsummer's night; it would not leave the earth, it would observe, it would keep one shred of truth, it would wish to be of use, to serve, to *prove* something.

Castigat ridendo mores. It has a mission; later, we might call it a function. I have said that it is a power, and Beaumarchais is there to show it. It has not been lost. What is Augier? What is Dumas? They are reformers! What is Labiche? A moralist! Sterne has said and shown in his way that the French people is the most serious of peoples; for he who loved so much to laugh does not care to laugh for nothing. He wishes that something should stay in the mind after even the lightest of farces, and that after having laughed one should think. Musset went further: he wished us to weep. That is too much. And I ask myself if there be not a grain of exaggeration in our contempt for the useless laugh. To laugh is good in itself. What is left after a laugh? the philosophers ask. Ah! what remains of a beautiful day after it has passed? And yet happiness is made up of beautiful days. But, to be definite, it is this taste for truth, this respect for reason, even this pretension of lifting up human nature, that makes the force of our comedy, and this is why it would be unjust to compare the comedies of Shakespeare with those of Molière.

Shakespeare's comedies are mostly youthful works. We find in them humors rather than characters, and no comedy of situation. They are imaginings, often charming; equivoques; disguises; forest surprises, as in *As You Like It*, where everyone becomes good; islands, as in *The Tempest*, enchanted with invisible music, where life is painted like a soap bubble —iridescent and empty. What likeness can there be between these exquisite fairy tales, made of dreams, and the comedy of Molière, all kneaded with reality?

There are exceptions, however. There is one of Shakespeare's comedies that approaches the French manner: it is *The Taming of the Shrew.* This has a logical action and a moral. Petruchio tames his devilish wife by showing himself more of a devil than she. But they are both eccentrics rather than true characters; and the play is a farce, where caricature

injures the truth. No matter, it is one of the gayest, and—
see the power of the French form—it has remained one of
the most popular.

He was less successful, to my mind, in *The Merry Wives
of Windsor,* another exception in his works, for it is a contemporaneous satire, notwithstanding the date, and a portrait
of middle-class manners. It has excellent scenes. Ford recalls
our Arnolphe. Like Arnolphe he is jealous, like Arnolphe he
is kept informed of all that is being prepared against him (at
least he thinks so), and like Arnolphe he succeeds only in
getting himself laughed at. But how feeble and brutal he is!
What unreason in all his actions! In short, he is any husband,
while Arnolphe, in representing the old sect which insists on
the subjection of woman, is one of those faces in which the
humanity of all times recognizes itself laughing at the recognition. Even in the Falstaff of *The Merry Wives* one can pick
flaws. Is this the Falstaff of *Henry IV,* who was always brimming over with audacity and humor? Alas! how he is faded!
What a fall! No, no; this dupe is not Falstaff! Shakespeare
was no more at ease in working on an idea of Elizabeth's
than was Molière when he composed *The Magnificent Lovers*
on an outline of Louis XIV's.

A few words must be added on the *wit* of Shakespeare, the
sparkling of which fills the first plays. It is with double mean-
ings, with puns, that he makes the laughter break out; coun-
terfeit coin, doubtless, but so prettily struck off, so brilliant,
so resonant! Recall the battles of wit between Beatrice and
Benedict, and the loving chatter of Rosalind and the elegant
babble of Mercutio. But all this has sadly cooled in three
centuries.

Molière has no mere wit. Puns, points, the collocation of
droll sounds, words taken one for another—all these are
absent from his work. At most he permits himself, in his
farces, some Gallic equivoques. He wishes to bring a laugh
only by touches of nature. It is not from him as author that
his witticisms come: it is from his characters, and they come
naturally and by the force of things. He himself explains this
in his criticism. "The author has not put this in as a clever
saying of his own, but only as a thing that characterizes the
man." So with him there is nothing unnecessary. Each touch
brings out the character in the living reality.

Can we here say that from this point of view Molière has
the better of his rival? But it would be easy to reply that

Shakespeare in his mighty maturity renounced witticisms to seek effects only from nature. And it is by their masterpieces that these great men must be compared. Thus we admire in them the same creative fecundity, the same intensity of life, the same dramatic vigor. This latter is so great in Molière that it was able to lead astray his fervent admirer the great Goethe, who attributed to him tragic genius. This seems an error; but nothing shows better than this error the force of the situations in *The Misanthrope,* in *Tartuffe,* and elsewhere. They have suggested to Molière, as to Shakespeare, those phrases that suddenly shed light into the very depths of the soul. Pathetic in Shakespeare, comic in Molière, they are sublime in both. Sublime, you say? Can the comic be sublime? Why not? After all, the sublime is but a stroke of truth, so brilliant, so deep, that it calls for no explanation or reasoning, leaves nothing to be said, and sometimes—like the "Let him die!" of the old Horace—attains a pure and simple absurdity.

Even in Shakespeare there are strokes of this kind of comedy; such is the famous acclamation of the "Brutus! Hail Brutus! Let Brutus be Cæsar." And another saying, in *Coriolanus,* "Let us kill Marcius, and we'll have corn at our own price." As for the pathetic cries, it is unnecessary for me to recall the apostrophe of Lear to the storm, "Nor rain, wind, thunder, fire, are my daughters!" Or the saying of Macduff, "He has no children!" Nor all those that spring from the troubled conscience of Hamlet. But is not the Poor Man in *Tartuffe* of the same caliber? Does not Alceste's "Morbleu! Faut-il que je vous aime?" spring from the same depths? And the innocent question of Arnolphe, "Why not love me, Madam Impudence?" But Molière has whole scenes written in this tone. Recall the scene before the last in the third act of *Tartuffe* between Orgon, Tartuffe, and Damis. There is not a line that does not carry. If it were not so funny it would be terrible. Never has human credulity been so truly painted, neither has the faculty which Tartuffes have of dishumanizing the best of us. If one forgets to laugh, the scene leaves an impression of stupefaction; and this I think is the duty of the sublime.

In Shakespeare Othello is less deeply duped by Iago. For from the moment that he has made the germ of jealousy tremble that had been sleeping in his breast, from the moment that this frightful passion is wakened, it is this that acts and governs; it is this that makes the unhappy creature believe what it will; it is this that, in one word, cheats him and makes him breathe blood and death.

Passion—this is the true domain of Shakespeare. It is the domain of the drama. (Shakespeare has the heart, Molière the head.) Shakespeare's personages are the *changing* and *differing* men, frequently made or unmade by the torrent of blood and of life. Those of Molière are man built all of a piece, born what he is, and dying as he was born. Could anything modify Tartuffe? Could Alceste have been different from what we see him? And was not Harpagon from his mother's womb a petty usurer? Did Arnolphe need to develop to become the pedant and the brute that he is? Scarcely has study added to the natural bent. And it is certainly not by philosophizing on a school bench that Don Juan came to the denying of all things. He came into the world unbelieving, and never admitted the existence of any other God but his own good pleasure. Molière shows us these unchanging characters in the most diverse situations; they remain there true to themselves and make their own fate.

Shakespeare likes to take an irreproachable man; he shows him coming straight from nature's hands, full of the milk of human kindness and seeking nobly all that he most ardently craves. But there is in him a germ, sometimes imperceptible; this germ circumstances, chance, the perfidy of an *Iago,* the meeting of the three old women on the heath, a dream, even less—a doubt—may cause suddenly to ferment; it rises up, swells, and becomes a devouring and irresistible passion; the end is fatal, it is crime, despair, death. Nothing can help it; the will of the man is the sport of chance and the heat of his blood. Even in the last works—in which the ending is happy—the man has had nothing to do with it; it is again chance which this time ends everything well; but Posthumus and Leontes are as miserably the prey of their imaginations as Othello or Lear.

Thus Molière's personages *are;* Shakespeare's *become.* I leave it to the philosophers to decide which are the more true. But we must not exaggerate; one finds likewise in Shakespeare innate characters. Iago, Lady Macbeth are certainly born what they are. Likewise it is a great wrong to Molière to reproach him with not knowing the contradictions of the human heart; his works are filled with it. See Alceste in love with Célimène, see Tartuffe at the same time so arrogant and so humble; see Argon, most tender of fathers and most humane of men, led by his bigotry to sacrifice his daughter and his whole house to the egotistic needs of his own salvation! These contradictions are marvelously natural; they do not indicate a single modification of man, they only reveal his complexity, and Molière knows how to render the comic side of this with his usual superiority.

This difference between the characters of drama and those of comedy has still another reason. To laugh one must be impersonal. He who sees that it is he himself who is on the stage and made fun of does not laugh willingly. Other people —that is all right; one can laugh at others without scruple. And this is why Molière shows us from the first his people well characterized, well possessed by their proper individuality, in a way resembling us as little as possible. After this, quite at our ease, sure of being neither Harpagon, nor M. Jourdain, nor Sganarelle, we can follow the master in laughing at them and at the same time at the Harpagons and the M. Jourdains and the Sganarelles that we know in real life and that we are delighted to find before us here.

The drama needs a contrary sentiment. To make us shudder or weep it must show us in its personages, if not the man that we are, at least the man that we flatter ourselves on being—good, valiant, and wise. Then we are interested in what happens to these men who are like us. It seems as though we were following our own possible history. And this is why Othello or Macbeth is at first neither ambitious nor jealous; they only become so after we have contracted a fellow feeling for them.

Hamlet has been compared to Alceste, but what ground can they offer for comparison? The one delicate, scant of breath, an obstinate dreamer, whom destiny makes a dispenser of justice in spite of himself; and the other robust, bristling, scolding, misanthropic—not as Hamlet is, in consequence of a melancholy that makes him see everything through a black veil, but from the effect of a vigorous nature full of itself and not understanding that all the world does not resemble him, and irritated by the differences as by so many personal injuries.

It would be easier to compare Alceste and Timon of Athens. They have common hatreds, and both end with the desert. But Alceste is born a misanthrope: Timon, on the contrary, begins with the love of man, as immeasured in this liberal tenderness as later he will be in his execrations. With all his faults Alceste is better balanced; he is a character. Timon is ill. (Note in passing, as a matter of curiosity, that the repast of hot water offered by Timon to his lukewarm friends is found again in *Le Misanthrope et L'Auvergnat* of Labiche.)

It is remarkable that in *Timon* Shakespeare, who intended a drama, should have deprived himself of that powerful element, Woman, and that it should be the comic author who had that idea of genius, profoundly dramatic, of making his misanthrope in love with a coquette. Shakespeare had put his Célimènes elsewhere: as a young girl she is in Cressida; mature and sovereign, she is in Cleopatra. It would be pleasant to compare with each other these attractive and perverse figures, but let me note only this characteristic point: it is that Célimène is cold, and that Cressida and Cleopatra are sensual. Cressida, a maiden yet, has instinctively all the trickery of an accomplished coquette, but she is sensual and she succumbs. And as she belonged to Troilus, so she will belong to Diomede; she has wit, perfidy, and weakness; she is a courtesan.

As for Cleopatra, she is the enchantress, but the irresistible grace that emanates from her is sustained by a deep art, which experience has developed. Then, too, how she leads him on, her Antony! But she is sensual; she loves him. Célimène is cold: she neither loves nor is capable of loving; her heart is in her head. She is a flower special to society, selfish, despotic, charming, deceiving everybody to nobody's profit, for the pleasure of it.

In general Shakespeare's women are admired; and yet what diversity in this curious series—the young girls, Ophelia, Cordelia, sister Isabella, Juliet, Perdita, Rosalind, and Celia; Beatrice; and the wives, Portia, Desdemona, Hermione, Imogen, Catherine of Arragon. I pass over some, and not the least celebrated. But among these delicious types, either profound or sublime, it is strange that you meet neither an Agnes nor an Armande. In Shakespeare the most chaste maid is not without knowledge. Ignorance, so dear to Arnolphe, seems impossible to our poet. Juliet is fourteen years old and she is a woman. And Miranda, brought up in a desert island between her father and Caliban, and so like Agnes in so many ways—Miranda has not the innocence of Agnes. She feels for Frederick the same admiration that Agnes feels for Horace;

when Prospero threatens the young prince and inflicts upon him a slave's duties, she gives the same cry that Agnes does when Arnolphe orders Horace to throw a stone from the window if the young man calls, "But he is such a fine fellow!" Finally, like Arnolphe's ward, she gives herself secretly to him whom she loves; but she reserves her chastity, as Agnes does not, not knowing enough.

I said there is no Armande in Shakespeare either. In truth, there is not a trace of that fine contempt of the flesh which the young philosopher boasts. Even sister Isabella, so rigid, has only a horror for the sin, and not aversion for the matter. The severe young girl recognized the sanctity of marriage, which Armande will not have mentioned; and in the end she marries the Duke. Armande, you will say, would have the same sort of yielding for Clitandre. I agree, but none the less does she feel the sentiment that she expresses; and it is rather strange that Shakespeare, although nearer than Molière to the mysticism of the Middle Ages, seems not to have known it. All his plays are of flesh and blood! Besides, Molière, who is the apostle of nature, laughs at the philosophical disgust of the beautiful Armande, and is careful not to give it to Henriette. Although his young girls are often quite adventurous, they have neither the ardent love of a Juliet nor the romantic intrepidity of a Rosalind. They are sweet and sentimental, like the adorable Marianne in *Tartuffe*; exquisitely sensible, like Henriette; very likely later to become sincere Eliantes, or wise and keen Elmires. As for those whom reading has spoiled, like Cathos and Madelon, it is not for the love of love that they would lose themselves, but for love of wit.

Other physiognomies might be compared. Harpagon and Shylock, for example—two misers. But it seems precisely as though in these two characters Shakespeare and Molière had two absolutely contrary aims; that Shakespeare, with a generosity not common in his day, wished to show the man in the Jew, and in the insulted man surviving the insult and bent on vengeance, the sacred feelings of a father and a husband; while Molière showed in Harpagon these same feelings and all the human sentiments, smothered by the encroaching vice. I fear that it is Molière who is right. But there is much to say in favor of Shylock, in whom avarice—being a fault of his race—has not the dominant and special character that it takes with Harpagon. Do we find a Tartuffe in Shakespeare? Iago has been cited: but Iago only seeks the satisfaction of a personal hate; Tartuffe, in the name of the Church, seeks complete dominion. Honest Iago knows what he wants and does not hide from himself the fact that he is a rascal. Tartuffe goes so far as to deceive himself; he believes in the goodness of his actions; they are only for the glory of Heaven. Iago is but a passing scamp, an individual. As for Tartuffe, he is legion; Tartuffe is eternal, perhaps indestructible.

There is more of Tartuffe in Richard III, I think. Richard has no illusions about himself, but he plays his part with a perfection worthy of Molière's character. We can even discover rather frequent resemblances between the scene of Richard with Anne (Act I) and those of Tartuffe with Elmire. Each proposes to seduce a woman who holds him in horror—Tartuffe, the wife of his host, whom he ruins and betrays; Richard, the wife of his king, whom he murders. Both plead marvelously, with the same catlike softness, the same captious theories, the same subtleties. In both scenes the husband is present: he is under the table with Molière, in his coffin with Shakespeare. The difference is not so great as might be supposed, since the corpse denounces the presence of its murderer by the bleeding of its wounds. But where the two scenes differ is in their ending. For Richard III succeeds, Tartuffe fails. Has, then, Tartuffe less wit than Richard? No, but he has to do with a stronger woman. Anne is the feminine character, feeble, vain, inconstant; Elmire is the lady, fashioned by society, who knows and guesses, a woman of taste and reason, who uses the advantages of her sex, but who watches herself and does not lose her head. As she has no vanity, no sensuality, Tartuffe has no hold on her.

Molière and Shakespeare both worked fast. Molière, however, retouched none of his plays, except *Tartuffe*. Shakespeare, on the contrary, rehandled, sometimes considerably, a number of his. *Hamlet,* for instance, was probably to him what *Faust* was to Goethe—the preoccupation of his whole artistic life. He did not ripen his plans, and in the rapidity of his work he was too easily contented with helping himself (from the novels or the histories from which he took his plays) to the scenes in the order in which he found them, adding, it is true, the characters and the poetry. From this comes a lack of simplicity, incoherencies, contradictions, that revision does not always efface and sometimes even augments

Molière has more art and more method; he graduates his effects better.

Volumnia and the Roman matrons arrive at the camp of Coriolanus. The fierce refugee is seized with respect; he bends the knee at once. But Volumnia wishes only to be the suppliant; she, in her turn, kneels and makes all those who have followed her kneel, and with them the wife and sons of Coriolanus. Here is surely a powerful dramatic effect, but it is not led up to—it ends in nothing. Coriolanus gets up, then Volumnia, and then long discourses are pronounced that Shakespeare takes almost word for word from Plutarch. The emotion evaporates, the impression disappears. Compare to this the double kneeling of Tartuffe and Orgon in the scene before the last of Act III. How well it all goes, how all is developed from it later, and how the effect is prepared and sustained up to the fall of the curtain! It is a marvel of skill, as well as a marvel of truth.

It must, however, be said that Molière, more careful of his plots, neglected his endings; whereas Shakespeare worked over his with a kind of predilection that has given us some of an unnecessary length. He stuffs them with emotions, makes royal personages appear and pronounce great words. Everything is cleared up, even what the public knows best. No matter, the emotion is immense. See the catastrophe of *Lear*. The soul of the spectator is plunged into a kind of desolate annihilation with the unfortunate old man. In a different style, reread the endings of *Pericles* and of *A Winter's Tale*. The sweetest tears that earth can know will flow of themselves from your eyes. And again, that close of *The Merchant of Venice*, which one does not dare call an ending—for the play was finished in Act IV—and which is a tailing off of a comedy after a comedy. What ravishing poetry and what malicious grace!

Shakespeare delights in complexity. He has often two, sometimes three, plots in his plays. He likes to vary the place of action, which changes without one's knowing why. In *Antony and Cleopatra* the scene is the world. The poet leads us almost to the Parthians to present to us Ventidius, of whom afterward we shall hear no more, and who is of not the least importance to the play. He needs these vast distances. Yet he did not despise the power of concentration (see the last acts of *Othello* and *Macbeth*). But he then falls into the excess that our tragedians are reproached with. He hurries the events, makes them take place in too short a time. If we may trust the text, the duration of *Macbeth* is hardly eight days. Who will ever believe that this somber and terrible history developed itself in so short a time, and that the Lady Macbeth of the sleepwalking night was but one week more advanced in life than the Lady Macbeth of the night of the crime? Molière, on the contrary, fancies the greatest simplicity in his plots and expedients.

There is some resemblance between *The School for Wives* and *Romeo and Juliet*. A perfume of youth is exhaled from these two masterpieces, both of them love stories. It is impossible to listen to them without profound interest. But, to keep up this interest, how many incidents did not Shakespeare need? Duels, a secret marriage, a potion, poison, a final killing, where the County Paris takes part most unnecessarily! Molière does not ask so much. Hardly anything happens in his play: Horace loves Agnes, Agnes loves Horace; they let each other know it, notwithstanding Arnolphe; and by the help of some innocent ruses that Horace's manly experience suggests and that Arnolphe's jealousy cannot detect, they get married in the end, to our great content. The story has happened a thousand times. It has happened to us—or something like it. And this is why it touches us, and why we laugh with such good will at that jealous wretch, taken in by an innocent girl.

For the rest, poetry is not wanting in *The School for Wives*. The whole part of Agnes is as poetically naive as the words of children. And the part of Arnolphe is comic poetry, rich in color, and rising into humor. But on these two points, poetry and humor, the advantage is with Shakespeare.

Molière contents himself with humanity; he does not know nature. Shakespeare does not separate one from the other. There is in him no deed that has not an echo in things; no phenomenon of nature that is not prolonged in the soul. For him creation is one; the earth feels what man does, and shares his emotions. Is she not full of unknown forces? Are there not more things in heaven and earth than are dreamed of in all philosophy? From this union of the world and man, of the world of things and the world of mind or of forces, Shakespeare draws forth the most strange, the most mighty, the most bewildering poetry. I will not try to describe its thousand sides; it would be beyond my powers. Music has been called the art of expressing the inexpressible; it can be said too of Shakespeare's poetry. In fact, there is visibly too much of it in his last plays, as there was too much wit in the first ones. *Cymbeline, A Winter's Tale* are lengthened with episodes and descriptions admirable but parasitical, and almost all the characters in them are lyrical. The supernatural is introduced in the action; the gods it is who proclaim the innocence of Hermione, the gods bring about the climax (interminable besides) of *Cymbeline.* As for *The Tempest,* of which I have already said a word, we are there in full fairyland. There the exquisite and visionary poetry is in its true place.

Shakespeare likewise has humor, little known to Molière, although Molière was a grandson of Rabelais. It is to the humor of Shakespeare that we owe the incomparable Falstaff. Yet Shakespeare is not, strictly speaking, a humorist, like Swift or Sterne. As it seems to me, humor is more literary than dramatic, with its hints, its ironies, and its intentional incoherencies. It is not always clear; and it is clearness that the playgoer demands.

Many definitions of humor have been attempted. It seems as though the true one were still to be found. It is, I think, that they attempt to make a quality of the mind out of what is rather a state of the spirit. There is the humorous state, just as there is the poetic state. He who is subject to it sees things in a special manner, out of proportion, out of place, upside down; then he discovers in them unexpected resemblances, and he expresses his sensations in appropriate language; that is to say, in affecting the tone contrary to that which he would have used were he in the ordinary state. This manner of seeing things does not absolutely disfigure them; it gives them a new aspect, striking and singular, comic because it is crazy, useful because by exaggerating the proportion it can bring to light certain points of truth that were not before suspected. You know the story of the husband who did not love his wife; he had no knowledge that she was pretty. Chance let him one day see her on the stage masquerading as a man, and he fell desperately in love with her. Humor sometimes renders this same service and ideas; by clothing them in what seems to be the least suitable it makes them most pleasing.

But this turning of things upside down, as the humorist does, to see what is in them, this dislocating of the thought and sentiment, is greatly against the spirit of reason; this is why we care but little for it. Yet, as it is a very Celtic taste, it comes back to us now and again. Witness Rabelais, whom I cited just now, and who is the universal father of humorists; witness also Voltaire's tales.

Molière knows not humor except on the extreme and extravagant side. It is certain that in this kind the ceremony in *The Would-be Gentleman,* and above all that of *The Imaginary Invalid* are masterpieces of humor in the Rabelaisian taste, full of vengeful irony and irresistible comedy. But, to be precise, Molière did not seek humor any more than he sought wit; one and both were for him too easy. "There is nothing common," said the great Goethe, "that does not appear humorous if you express it in a grotesque way." As for poetry, that of Shakespeare, it will be conceded, would be little in place in the comedy of Molière. But if the force and the delicacy of expression are elements of it, if the freshness or vivacity of the language, if the beautiful marriage of words, if this living breath of truth is poetic, then Molière is a poet. He has the "vigorous hates," "the well-placed soul," "the clearness of everything." He knows where is the "tenderness of the soul," and dictates to Agnes a delicious letter. He is, in more than one scene, as eloquent as Corneille, and he handles the popular proverb with the same vigor. There is as much lightness and grace in Acaste as in Mercutio. And the verses of Eliante are as charming as those of Rosalind, and truer. What is not in this poetry—what could not be in it—is the dreaming. It is the loyal reflection of the true depth of humanity.

Molière and Shakespeare had an entirely different conception of life. Shakespeare saw it moving, troubled, changing, uncircumscribed in its development by human will, subject to "the winds and the rain and all the breezes that blow." He says in one of those passages of *The Two Noble Kinsmen* that were evidently written by him:

This world's a city full of straying streets,
And death's the market-place where each one meets.

It is in these straying streets that Shakespeare moves, the obscure labyrinth where man goes blindly, meeting here an ambush, there a precipice, and where he changes fortune from a chance meeting. There is nothing certain, not one of his characters who could swear to what he will do an hour later. They do not belong to themselves. They are so much the plaything of a higher force that they do not even feel sure of their conscience. "I believe myself passably virtuous," says Hamlet.

But who shall explain Hamlet? Hamlet is an enigma. How far was he mad? When is he completely mad? But no one in these plays is quite sane. Lear is out of his senses long before he is demented; Macbeth has hallucinations; Othello sees blood at the first word; Brutus talks to a ghost; that terrible skeptic Richard III sees visions. Events themselves sometimes seem half crazy. What I have said of *Macbeth* might be said of *Romeo and Juliet,* where in five days Juliet sees, loves, marries, dies, resuscitates, and dies once more. All is falsehood, deceit, bewilderment. This cavalier, it is Rosalind; this page, Imogen; this judge, Portia; this statue, Hermione. One scene in *King Lear* makes Lear (who goes mad from sorrow) and an exile (who pretends to madness) and a fool (who is mad by profession) all talk together amid the thunder and lightning. We ask ourselves, Where are we? Who are we? Prospero tells us:

> We are such stuff
> As dreams are made on; and our little life
> Is rounded with a sleep.

Shakespeare saw life as in a dream, and thus he has shown it. Molière saw things in their reality. He went down to the immutable. As for life, in his plays he sees it simple. Only those events happen which happen to all of us. We love, we marry, we have children, we consult the doctor, we die. The other incidents that may occur spring from the shock of character; they can be deduced logically one from another, and would remain in the control of man if he would but listen to reason.

And this is the great moral that can be drawn from Molière: Keep your head, and all will go well. His work is as clear as day; hatred of vice shows itself, and the love of truth —no platonic love, but an active love, armed and fighting to the last hour. For Molière is in the thick of the crowd; Shakespeare dwells in the Temples of Serenity; he observes,

somber at first, peaceful later on; and he gives to our medita-
tion and reflection the immense and painful spectacle of the
world, but draws from it no rule, for what rule can be found
used in a dream? Perhaps, to finish, it might be said that
Shakespeare teaches us to think, but that Molière teaches us
to live.

Eugène Scribe

by

ERNEST LEGOUVÉ

Translated by Albert D. Vandam

Eugène Scribe

The theory of environment is very much the fashion just now. It appears to me to contain a good deal of truth. The spot in which we happen to be born, the circumstances amid which we grow up, exercise a powerful influence on our lives. Scribe is a striking instance.

He came into the world on June 11, 1791, in the Rue Saint-Denis, in a silk warehouse kept by his mother, at the sign of the "Black Cat," a stone's throw from the (then) central market; consequently in the midst of a business quarter inhabited by a frugal, hard-working middle-class, far removed from the aristocracy and almost in contact with the people, not to say the populace. His talent bears the stamp of his origin.

A second point worthy of notice is the fact that his guardian was a celebrated barrister to whom he went every Sunday. To this connection he probably owed the understanding of business matters with which he has often been reproached, but which, after all, frequently proved advantageous to his plays. There is a third important circumstance that we should not overlook: he was educated at Sainte-Barbe. And his sojourn there gave him cronies eminently fitted to stir within his heart the love for companions of aforetime. Two of these were Germain and Casimir Delavigne. The three were called "the inseparables." Casimir and Germain went to their parents on the days when they had leave, and Germain, through his connection with the manager of a small theatre, had tickets for the play. He went to it every Sunday—went, as it were, for the whole three.

On the Monday, at "play time," there were endless discus-

sions between him, his brother, and Scribe on the play itself
—the acting of it, the effect play and acting had produced
on the public; the whole interspersed, of course, with num-
berless projects for comedies or farces and aspirations to see
their names together on playbills. Their beginnings were not
brilliant. "Do you know," said Scribe one day to Janin and
Rolle when all three were dining with me, "do you know
how I did begin? I began with fourteen failures. Yes, fourteen. But it served me right. My dear friends, you have no
idea how flat and heavy those pieces were. Nevertheless," he
added with engaging modesty, "there is one I would fain
rescue from the ignominy inflicted on it. It was hissed more
than it deserved, for it was not as bad as any of the others.
Really and truly, the verdict was unjust." We could not
help laughing. "Yes, you laugh, and I laugh myself, but it
was no laughing matter to me in those days. After every
failure Germain and I tramped the whole length of the Bou-
levards, desperate, furious, I saying over and over: "What
a beastly trade! But this is the end. I give up. *After the four
or five plots* we have in our desks, I write no more."

After the four or five plots—what a pretty touch of nature!
It is the rallying cry of every human passion under the sun.
"I'll have four or five throws more," says the gambler; "after
that I'll play no more." "One last farewell," says the love-
sick wight, "and then I'll leave her for ever." And the gambler keeps on gambling, and the love-sick wight does not
leave the damsel. And the dramatist, being both a love-sick
wight and a gambler, tries over and over again.

That was what Scribe did, and it was doing wisely. But,
Scribe or no, a playwright at the outset of his career is
bound to stumble. He is ignorant of his own particular ap-
titudes, and he needs someone to point them out to him. For
Scribe the someone was one of the oddest characters I ever
knew. Nominally among the French dramatic authors, he had
scarcely any talent; he had not even what is called sparkle
or wit. But the piercing eyes that flashed from behind his
glasses, the bushy mobile eyebrows, the sarcastic mouth, the
long and inquisitive looking nose, all these stamped him as
an observer, an inquirer, a kind of sleuthhound. He constantly admonished Scribe: "You are going to be all right.
You want only two things, perseverance in your work and
solitude. I am going to take you away. I have got some
friends a few miles distant from Paris. They have a very

nice house in the country, and that's where I am going to take you."

"You are going to take me, you are going to take me! What's the good of telling me you are going to take me? Your friends do not know me, I do not know them."

"I know them, and that's enough. We'll take up our quarters for four months with them, and in the autumn you'll come back to Paris with five or six fetching pieces."

In another week our friends were comfortably settled in two adjoining rooms, Scribe under the careful surveillance of his gaoler, who only allowed him to go down to his hosts after he had finished his day's work, when he was sure to find excellent fare and a cordial welcome. One thing, though made Scribe feel uncomfortable: his friend's occasional rudeness to his host. When the meat happened to be done too much or the vegetables too salt, the friend simply exclaimed: "This is horrible stuff; take it away, take it away!" Scribe leaned forward over his plate, kicked his friend under the table, and after dinner remonstrated with him in the liveliest terms. "That's not the way to speak to one's hosts," he said.

"Don't trouble yourself about that; they like it."

"They like it? Why, you are behaving as if you were at an inn."

The fact was that they *were* at an inn, or at any rate in a boarding-house—one in which the friend paid for Scribe, whom he housed, fed, and generally provided for in order to compel him to work and to force his genius to sprout. It would be difficult to find a more curious instance of idolatry of talent. Only, for the sake of complete accuracy, I ought to add that the friend was not wholly prompted by pure love of art. For, if he had as much as suggested the title of the piece, indicated its starting point, or inspired a song, he assumed the rôle of *collaborateur,* claimed acknowledgment, and shared the author's fees and glory. He undoubtedly worshipped Scribe, but Scribe balanced the budget of that worship.

I often went to see him in the morning. One day I found him in a state of great excitement.

"You are the very man I want," he said, "you are going to give me a bit of advice. I have had an offer that both tempts and frightens me. The director of the Comédie-Française wants me to write a part for Mlle. Rachel."

"Well, who is to stop you?"

"Corneille and Racine. How can I possibly put my humble prose in that mouth accustomed to recite the verse of *Andromaque* and *Horace?*"

"What's that to you?"

"You would not be frightened?"

"Not in the least."

"You would dare to write a prose part for the portrayer of Phèdre and Camille?" *

"Certainly. Well, find a subject and we'll write the piece together."

Three days after that I enter Scribe's room with the classical "Eureka" on my lips. I tell him my idea.

"Your idea is not a good one. It is devoid of interest."

"Devoid of interest!" I exclaim, and begin to defend it.

"Let us try," he says; "if your idea has anything in it, *we'll find out in half-an-hour or so.*" And he starts to turn my idea upside down and inside out, pull it to pieces, and examine every shred of it. "Not a thing in it, as I told you; you must find something else," he winds up.

On that occasion I had the first practical demonstration of Scribe's marvellous facility in finding out at a glance whether an idea was dramatic or not. A few days later I call again, this time with the subject of *Adrienne Lecouvreur.* The words have scarcely passed my lips when he jumps from his chair, rushes to me, and flings his arms round my neck, shouting at the top of his voice: "A hundred nights, with six thousand francs receipts each night."

"Do you think so?" I say.

"I don't think; I feel certain. It is an admirable find. You have hit upon the only means of making Rachel talk prose. Come to-morrow morning, and we'll set to work immediately."

At ten o'clock next morning I was with him. He was being operated on by his barber, who held him by the nose. The moment he caught sight of me, he said quickly, in the peculiar voice of a man being shaved: "My dear boy, I have found what we want." "Take care, Monsieur Scribe, you'll make me cut you," interposed the barber. "All right, but be quick." And while the razor was gliding over his face, his fingers were twitching excitedly; he kept looking and smiling at me. No sooner is the man's back turned than there comes an avalanche of ideas, of more and less definite situations,

* In Corneille's *Horace.*

of outlined characters that had sprung up in his mind during the last four-and-twenty hours and were being rapidly sketched by him while he was dipping his face into the water, brushing his hair and putting on his shirt, changing his trousers and tying his cravat, getting into his waistcoat and jacket and fastening his watch chain (for he liked to sit down to his work dressed and ready to go out at a moment's notice). As a matter of course, I told him the result of my meditations, and then he seated himself on a small chair at his writing-table, saying: "And now to work, to work."

There is no need to enter into the details of that collaboration. I will only mention two or three facts that show Scribe as man, author, and *collaborateur*.

In our theatrical slang there is a very significant word: *numérotage*. It means planning the sequence of scenes. That sequential ordering is not only a kind of classification: it also comprises the development, the accumulating interest of the play. That numbering is the itinerary of the *dramatis personæ*, with the points of interest as land-marks. Each scene must not only be the logical outcome of the scene that preceded it and be integral with the one that follows it, but it must also transmit its own momentum to the next scene, so as to push the piece forward without interruption and in that way to reach, stage by stage, the final goal, the *dénouement*. Scribe had not only a talent for *numérotage*, he had sheer genius for it. No sooner had the plan of a piece been sketched than the complete materials for the work came to him as if by magic and bestowed themselves in their logical position. During one of our first conversations on *Adrienne Lecouvreur*, when the situations were still in a very sketchy state, he suddenly got up, then sat down again at his writing-table.

"What are you doing?" I asked.

"Writing out the sequence of scenes in the first act," was the answer.

"But we have not decided what we are going to put in the first act."

"Never mind, never mind. Don't break the thread." And forthwith he wrote:

Scene I.—The Princesse de Bouillon, the Abbé.

Scene II.—The Same, the Duchesse d'Aumont.

Scene III.—The Same, the Prince de Bouillon.

"But, my dear Scribe," I remarked, interrupting him,

"before we bring the Prince de Bouillon on the stage, we ought at least to know—"

"Never mind," was the answer, "the Prince de Bouillon is to appear twice in that act, and if I do not bring him on at that particular moment, I shall not know what to do with him"—saying which, he went on writing. A few days later, when all the incidents and scenic movement of that first act were finally decided upon, the characters almost automatically took up their positions at the points assigned them, like guests at a dinner where the hostess has used place cards. I was bowled over. I have rarely met with a more instructive occurrence.

In the midst of our work, Scribe was compelled to interrupt it. I wrote the first two acts myself and read them to him. During the whole first act, he kept rubbing his hand, and when it was finished, he said: "It won't do at all. Let's hear the second act."

At the fourth page, he begins to talk to himself in a low voice. "Bravo, excellent." And he sets to laughing and crying and clapping his hands, adding: "As for that act, I'll answer for its effect. Upon my word, I don't often get *collaborateurs* of your mettle. There is only one thing I object to in that second act: Adrienne's story that she enters with."

"You have hit the wrong thing," I said laughing. "That story is absolutely true. I took it almost word for word from the *Mémoirs* of Mlle. Clairon."

"That's just it; it hangs fire because it is true. I do not wish you to misconstrue my meaning. Truth is absolutely necessary on the stage, but it has to be focussed to conform to the optical conditions of the stage. I am not at all surprised that the story in Mlle. Clairon's *Mémoirs* struck you. It was sure to produce a great effect there. Why? Because it places before you an individual of flesh and blood, a consummated achievement; because the actress imparts, as it were, her own life to the story. Becoming interested in *her*, you become interested in what she says. But on the stage we are in the domain of absolute fiction; and fiction has its own laws. We are speaking, not to one reader, but to fifteen hundred individuals. The number of spectators and the very size of the house change the moral conditions of the effect, just as the laws of optics and acoustics modify the material conditions of the effect. For that true narrative I am going to substitute an absolutely fictitious one, invented for Adrienne, suited to Adrienne, and it will produce the most startling effect upon the audience."

A careful review of Scribe's career as a playwright must necessarily deal with every branch of dramatic art, because he himself dealt with every one of them, and in each he left us a model or two which, if they are not absolutely worthy of imitation, are at any rate deserving of study.

Among the foremost gifts of the dramatist, those of invention and imagination rank the highest. We must be careful not to confound those two faculties. They are closely connected, they support one another, but each has its special character and its distinct domain. Invention creates, imagination puts the creation to work. To the one belongs the primary idea, the finding of the subject; to the other, the practical application. Both are not always to be met with in the same man, and they are rarely in equal proportions. A man may have more imagination than invention, or more invention than imagination. Our own times afford us two striking instances. Balzac is a mighty inventor. He devises wonderful characters, splendid "starting points," but his execution, for lack of imagination, is often heavy; he falls short of that fertility of incidents, that liveliness of dialogue, that make a powerful work also amusing. The winged goddess did not pass that way. Look, on the other hand, at Alexandre Dumas. The starting points of his subjects belong as often as not to someone else. Sometimes he takes them from history, at others he has them given to him by his *collaborateurs*, then again he simply borrows them from other works. He himself, in his charming and unaffectedly good-natured *Mémoirs*, admits that *Antony* was inspired by the first performance of *Marion Delorme*. In order to stir his faculty of creation he often wanted that nudge that some philosopher or other said he had to have to set the world wagging.* But no sooner was that impulse given than Alexandre Dumas set the machine revolving, and with a vengeance. No carriage drawn by the most spirited team ever went down-hill at such a rattling gallop, with greater contempt for everything in its way or more unerringly than a drama or novel by Alexandre Dumas

---

* Probably a confused echo of Pascal's *mot* about Descartes, to the effect that he would have liked to make his entire philosophy get along without God, but that he could not forbear giving the Almighty a nudge now and then to get Him to set the cosmos in motion.—Tʀ.

proceeded to its *dénouement*. Even when the horses are not his he makes them his own by the way he handles the ribbons. Nay, they may give him cab horses, but he makes them step out like thoroughbreds.

In Scribe the powers of invention and imagination were of equal virtue, and of immense value. He has often been contemptuously classified among the mere adaptors. In reality, no literature in the world has produced so powerful a dramatic inventor. A single fact will suffice to prove his powers. For a score of years he held sway over the four principal theatres in Paris: namely, the Opéra, the Opéra-Comique, the Gymnase, and finally the Comédie-Française. Each of the four he endowed with fresh life and enhanced its intellectual as well as material wealth by writing for it. Before him, the repertory of the Opéra was composed, with the glorious exception of *La Vestale*, of classical tragedies, merely transformed into so many libretti; Iphigenias, Alcestes, Armitas, Œdipuses, or kindred subjects—always the same ones, which, taken up in succession by different composers, left the librettists scope for nothing save elegant versification. What did Scribe bring to it? Poems. *Le Prophète, Les Huguenots, La Juive, Robert le Diable, Guido et Ginevra, Gustave, ou le Bal Masque*—these are works the like of which were absolutely unknown before Scribe, and they make him one of our greatest lyric poets, if we take the word "poet" in the antique sense, ποιητής, creator.

One of Scribe's least favourably disposed critics has ranked *Le Prophète* among Shakespearean conceptions. Whence sprang that conception? From the simple perusal of an illustrated edition of the Bible. Reading the description of the marriage in Cana, he came upon the words, "Woman, what have I to do with thee?" He read no further, for his imagination had been struck and had already begun to transform the image of Christ. "A man gradually impelled to divest himself of all his natural sentiments in order to fulfil what he regards as his mission, a man sacrificing his duty as a son to assume the part of God: it would be a magnificent character to portray," he said to himself. "And what a splendid part for Talma!" Unfortunately Talma was dead; but fortunately Meyerbeer was alive, and Scribe composed the libretto of *Le Prophète*.

What was the Opéra-Comique before him? A charming but very mild kind of playhouse. But *Le Domino Noir, La Dame*

Blanche, La Sirène, La Neige, Fra Diavolo, L'Ambassadrice, La Part du Diable opened a new road to music by endowing lyrical comedy with a new form. Scribe contributed his share to Auber's glory; for Auber would not have been, without Scribe, the Auber he was.

"Do you know to whom I owe the aria *'Amour sacré de la patrie'*?" said the composer of *La Muette de Portici (Masaniello)* one day to me. "To Scribe. One day while we were out walking he brought out the rhythm of the lines so irresistibly that the melody forthwith imposed itself upon the words. He had spoken my duet to me." Scribe, therefore, is entitled not only to one patent as an inventor for the Opéra-Comique, but to two.

Before Scribe, a *vaudeville* was based upon a slight story, made palatable with rhymes; Scribe raised it to the level of the comedy of character.

And finally, at the Comédie-Française itself—not to speak of the freshness that *La Camaraderie, La Calomnie,* and *Le Verre d'Eau* brought to Molière's stage—what is *Bertrand and Raton?* Merely the one fine political comedy in the repertory.

Such was Scribe the inventor. As to his imagination, it was almost inexhaustible in devising startling incidents, in overcoming apparently insuperable obstacles. I need give only one instance. *La Révolte au Sérail,* a ballet by an author whose name I do not remember,* was being rehearsed at the Opéra. Mlle. Taglioni was to enact the principal part. Two days before the first performance, which was already advertised with the quasi-sacred and binding word "Irrevocably" over it, the Director of the Opéra (Dr. Véron) rushed into Scribe's study at nine in the morning. "I am simply going frantic, ruin is staring me in the face, you alone can avert it," he said.

"What is the matter?" asked Scribe.

"The performance of my ballet is impossible."

"Why?"

"Success depends on the situation of the second act, and that situation is this: Mlle. Taglioni, who is shut up and besieged by the revolutionaries in the palace, enlists all the women of the harem, provides them with arms, drills them, and converts them into soldiers, command of whom she assumes. She repels the attack."

* He was Mlle. Taglioni's father.—TR.

"That's a very original idea," replies Scribe.

"That may be," says the director, "but we discovered yesterday that it is perfectly absurd."

"Why?"

"Because in the first act a talisman has been given her by a magician. Hence, she would have only to show that talisman, and all the eunuchs would take to their heels."

"That's true," remarks Scribe, "and it makes the matter very serious."

"That's what I say, and in the circumstances my only hope lies with you."

"Very well, I'll be with you at rehearsal to-day and try to find something afterwards."

"That won't do at all. It's no good afterwards; I want you to find something now, this very minute. It's of no use your coming to dress rehearsal; there will be no more dress rehearsals. Between now and tonight, this very day, you must find some means of enabling me to give the ballet without changing anything, and without delay, for every day's delay means ten thousand francs."

"Very well," replies Scribe, "leave me to myself for an hour, and I'll try to think it out."

The director slowly descends the score of stairs leading to the ground floor. But before he can ask the concierge to let him out, he hears a voice shouting after him: "Véron, come back, I have what you want." As a matter of course, Véron comes up much quicker than he went down. "You have found what I want?" he gasps, panting for breath.

"Yes. What was Mlle. Taglioni's talisman?"

"A ring."

"Very well, we'll change it to a rose. Who was her lover?"

"A young attendant at the seraglio."

"We'll transform him into a young shepherd. What was the *divertissement* in the first act?"

"A dance before the Sultan in the garden of the palace."

"Good enough. After the dance we'll make Mlle. Taglioni sit down on a grassy knoll, where she'll fall asleep. The little shepherd will steal softly towards her and take the rose away, and when, in the second act, she wants to take the talisman from her bosom, it will not be there. It is as easy as that!"

"I felt sure you would be able to do it," exclaims Dr. Véron, rushing towards the stairs, which he descends even faster than he climbed them a few minutes before. A quarter-of-an-hour later an envelope is brought to Scribe which contains two notes of 1000 francs each, accompanied by the words: "This is not a fee, merely a grateful acknowledgment."

"That was the only time," said Scribe, telling the story, "I earned two thousand francs in two minutes."

Here is a fact illustrating still more forcibly his stupendous gift for transforming things. One of his friends came to consult him on a very harrowing and sombre five-act drama intended for the Ambigu.

"Well, my dear friend and master, what's your opinion?" says the author after the first act.

"Go on," remarks Scribe, seemingly absorbed in thought. "Let us have the second act."

The author goes on reading, the drama getting more sombre as he proceeds, and Scribe's face lighting up as the drama gets more sombre. Somewhat surprised at a kind of success that he had certainly not foreseen, the poor author begins to stammer and feel very confused, until Scribe, unable to hold out any longer, suddenly exclaims: "Upon my word, it's absolutely side-splitting."

"I'll trouble you no longer, we have had enough of this," says the author, somewhat nettled. "I perceive that my piece is very bad."

"What do you mean by bad? Say rather excellent, positively delightful. It contains some overwhelmingly comic effects. Ferville will be as amusing as Arnal."

At the name of Arnal, the tragic author, indignant beyond measure, leaps from his chair. He had the impression that Scribe had not heard a syllable of his play. But he was utterly mistaken. Not only had Scribe heard it all: he had reconstructed it. As each lugubrious scene dragged its weary length along, he transformed it into a comedy-scene. When the reading was over the huge, heavy, commonplace five-act melodrama had become the delightful, sparkling one-act comedy known as *La Chanoinesse*.

Next in importance to the invention of the subject stands the planning of a play. Nowadays planning is widely scoffed at. The author who happens to plan his piece carefully is given all sorts of nicknames—"bone-setter," "osteologist," "anatomist," "dissector," "skeleton-maker," and so on. To all of which sobriquets I have but one reply. During the last thirty years a goodly number of old pieces have been re-

vived; the only successful ones are those founded on a good
plan. A plan is to a play what it is to a house: the first condition of its beauty and stability. You may overload a building with the most magnificent decoration, you may use the
most solid materials: if it be not erected in accordance with
the laws of equilibrium and due proportion, that building will
neither please nor last. The same holds good of a dramatic
story. It must first of all be clear; and without a plan there
can be no clarity. It must proceed without a stop to a defined
goal; without a plan such a progression is impossible. The
dramatic story must assign to each character his proper position; each action must be placed at an exact point; without
a plan there can be no due regard to proportion. The plan
includes not only the *order* of events, but also what Alexandre Dumas the elder called the first article of the playwright's creed, the art of preparing situations; in other words,
of logically and naturally leading up to them. The public as
a collective entity is a very odd creature, very exacting, and
most often very illogical. It insists that everything be led
up to, be hinted at; at the same time, it wants to be startled
by the quasi-unforeseen. If, to use the popular expression, a
thing drops upon them from the skies, they are shocked. If
a fact is too plainly announced beforehand, they are bored.
In order to please them, then, the playwright has to treat
them as both confidant and dupe: that is, he must casually
drop at some point a word that shall pass almost unperceived
and yet give them an inkling of what is going to happen; a
word that goes in at one ear and out at the other, and that,
when the "situation" bursts upon them, shall elicit an excla-
mation of content, that *Ah!* which signifies: "True, he warned
us; how stupid we were not to have guessed as much!"

Finally, the crucial point in a well-constructed plan is the
dénouement. The art of *dénouement* in comedy is in some
respects almost a new art. The public has become much more
difficult to please, and authors much more expert. I do no
slight to the memory of Molière when I say that in general
he does not unravel his plays, but simply finishes them. The
moment he has finished portraying his characters, and developing their passions, he brings upon the stage, one knows
not whence, a father who finds the long-looked-for son, one
knows not how; everybody embraces everybody else and the
curtain goes down. That fashion of ending a piece, by hook
or by crook, would not be tolerated nowadays; one would

have to be a Molière to dare do such a thing. Nowadays one of the first laws of the dramatist's art it to make the *dénouement* the logical and enforced consequence of the characters or the events of the play. The last scene of a play is often written before the first, because till that last scene has been found there is virtually no play, and as soon as the author has got hold of his *dénouement* he must not lose sight of it for a moment; he must subordinate everything else to it. The novelist may at a pinch begin without knowing exactly whither he is going. He may, like the hare of the fable, stop every now and then to browse the grass, to listen from which quarter the wind blows. But the dramatic author is bound to take the tortoise as his model (though he must move at a somewhat quicker pace): he must start at the right moment and not loiter by the way. While advancing, he must never lose sight of his goal.

Scribe was fully alive to the importance of the *dénouement* and succeeded in applying the severest laws to it. Nay, he applied these laws to the works of others also and most often to the works he admired most. One day I heard him, in the heart of a conversation on the art of writing comedy, reconstruct two *dénouements* of Molière, that of *Les Femmes Savantes* and that of *Tartuffe*.

"What a pity," he said, "that Molière ends that beautiful comedy of character like a genre-comedy, by the trivial artifice of a false piece of news, a fictitious ruin! He had such a capital *dénouement* ready to hand; the conclusion sprang so naturally from the very core of the subject. I should have finished my piece with the admirable scene between Vadius and Trissotin. The picture of those two prigs, abusing and unmasking one another, destroying their own and their dupes' illusions, would have rounded off a masterly work in a masterly way. As for *Tartuffe*, that is altogether different. As a rule people cavil at the *dénouement;* personally I think it admirable. First of all, without it we should probably not have had the piece at all; there is very little doubt that Molière got the play sanctioned only by making the king one of the actors in it. Secondly, that *dénouement* is unquestionably a striking picture of the times. Here we have an honest, upright man who has valiantly fought for his country and who, having become the victim of the most obvious and odious of machinations, finds not a single weapon for self-defense either in society or in the law. In order to save him, the sovereign

himself has to intervene like a *deus ex machina*. Where could
we find a more terrible indictment of Louis' reign than in
this immense tribute to the king?

"That's why I admire that *dénouement* so much," said
Scribe, "and that's why I would change it if I had to write
the piece to-day. To-day, in fact, the only sovereign is the
law itself. The word of the sovereign simply means the articles of the Code. The code, therefore, should be entrusted
with the rôle of Louis XIV; it is to the code that I would look
for my *dénouement*. I would change Cléante into a magis-
trate, and when Tartuffe says, 'The house belongs to me, and
I'll show you that it does,' Cléante should exclaim: 'No, it
does not belong to you, for you owe it to the generosity of a
benefactor, to an absolutely free gift, and the law has provided for wretches of your stamp by these two avenging
lines: "Every donation may be revoked on the proof of the
ingratitude of the recipient." I dare you to come and claim
this house before the law. If you do, you will find me there
also with the patent proofs of your abominable ingratitude.
You had better come then, but remember, I'll be waiting for
you.' "

Next to the plan of a comedy comes, as a matter of course,
its style and the portrayal of its characters; before ventur-
ing to discuss these two subjects, I would dwell for a moment
on a fundamental point of our art which, moreover, occupies
a considerable place in Scribe's work and which partly con-
stitutes its originality.

Scribe's original place in the literature of the Restoration
is that he was the living and natural antithesis to romanti-
cism. While *Antony* dragged us with him, bewildered and
intoxicated like himself, into the maëlstrom of adulterous
passion, while *Hernani* made us frantic with enthusiasm for
a band of brigands, while *Marion Delorme* endeavoured to
force upon us the dogma of the redemption of the fallen
woman by pure love, Scribe sang the praises of conjugal
happiness, and selected for his heroines girls who had not
been subject to such temptations. One has but to take up
the various works that compose Scribe's repertory, such as
*Le Mariage de Raison, Une Chaîne, Les Premières Amours,
Le Mariage d'Argent,* and at no matter which page we open
them we shall find the defence of paternal authority, sense
getting the better of passion. Scribe's muse is the feet-on-the-
fender muse, the bread-and-butter-cutting muse, if you like;

it is the muse of the home. The story goes that after seeing *Le Mariage d'Inclination*, a young girl flung herself into her mother's arms, confessing her plan to elope; after a play by Alexandre Dumas she would have flung herself into the arms of her lover, saying, "Run off with me."

And now let us look for a moment at some of the characters of Scribe's plays and at his style. I may frankly confess that these show the two weak points in Scribe's works. He failed to look at humanity in any other light than that of the "float." He had a profound knowledge of men and women, but he invariably saw them like so many theatrical characters; hence the curious fact that, though he has created a great number of very attractive parts, he has produced very few general and deeply pondered types. Not that life and truth are wanting in the characters he brings on the stage. His subtle observation expertly unmasks and boldly accentuates their foibles, their passions, their aims. They talk as they should talk; they behave as they should behave in the situation in which they are placed. But they are only the men and women of that situation. They fill it adequately but never go beyond it. On the other hand, and to take only one instance, when one reads Shakespeare, his characters seem to be endowed with such vitality, they are stamped with such individuality, that you see not only what they are in the momentary situation, but also what they would be in any imaginable situation. They are not only stage parts, they are men and women, and what is more, men and women equipped for the whole battle of life.

We look in vain for something similar in Scribe. He rarely seems to have the power to create strongly marked characters, and except for *Bertrand and Raton* and the admirable last scene of *L'Ambitieux*, one is compelled to admit that his comedies are stage pictures rather than real pictures of the human heart.

His style is open to similar objections. The language of comedy should be at the same time a spoken and a written language. To perceive this at once we have but to read *L'Avare*, *Le Festin de Pierre*, and *Georges Dandin*. No doubt, it is Harpagon and Don Juan who speak, but we also feel that it is Molière who makes them speak. Scribe has only half of those gifts. His style has all the requisites of conversation. The conversation is natural, bright, it trips along and sparkles, but one regretfully notices the want of that

richness of colouring and that sureness of outline which alone
constitute the great writer. He falls short in one other respect. A comic writer putting on the stage the characters of
his own time is bound to give them the speech of his own
time. Unfortunately there is a great deal of jargon in that
speech, and consequently there are a great many ephemeral elements. Strangely, the most indestructible feeling expresses
itself in the most transient idiom. That part of a stage play
which grows obsolete soonest is the love episode. Even such
love letters as have been written to yourself, should you
take them up after a lapse of years, will make you die laughing. Their comic effect is in direct proportion to their tenderness. The art of the great dramatist is to sift out the perish-
able element from the current idiom, that he may borrow
from it only what is strictly necessary to give his dialogue
the tone and the flavour of the moment.

Molière writes both in the language of his time and in the
language of all time; Scribe, in virtue of his very scenic
instinct, makes too much use of the vocabulary of the Restoration. Finally the impetuosity, the despotism of his dramatic temperament led him to make everything subservient
to the action of the play—absolutely everything, even to
grammar; not from ignorance, for he knew his own language
very well, but knowingly, and with premeditation. I happened
to be present one day at a rehearsal of one of his pieces,
when all at once one of his characters delivered himself of
a slightly incorrect phrase. I suggested a more correct one.
"No, no, my dear boy," says Scribe, "your sentence is too
long; there is no time for it. My sentence is probably not
very orthodox, but the action is proceeding apace, and the
sentence must follow suit; that's what I call the economical
style."

The staging of plays, too, especially of comedies, is a
wholly modern art. No doubt, in former days, the author
wrote on his manuscript: "The stage represents a drawing-
room," but there was nothing to show that the action did
take place in a drawing-room. First of all, the *dramatis personæ* kept on their legs. We all recollect the actors at the
Comédie-Française stepping to the footlights, side by side,
and delivering their speeches before the prompter's box. A
clever writer who since then has become an official personage
wanted to introduce on the stage of the Comédie-Française
what he called "seated comedy." Unfortunately, his piece

turned out a failure and what he called "seated comedy" became prostrate comedy. Scribe was one of the first to introduce on the stage the animation and bustle of real life. The very nature of his talent compelled him, as it were, to do so. His bustling, sparkling comedies, full of incidents and apparently spontaneous situations, did not lend themselves easily to the sobriety of movement of the traditional stage. In reality, a manuscript of Scribe contains only part of his work—the part which is spoken. The rest must be enacted. The gestures must complete the meaning of the words. The intervals of silence are part of the dialogue, and the small dots finish the sentence.

Those who never saw Scribe conjure up a dramatic work from what, for want of a better term, I may call the limbo of the manuscript, those who never saw Scribe put a piece on the stage and remain with it until it could stand alone know only half the real Scribe. I happened to come in at the very moment when Scribe was arranging the grand revolt in the third act of *Le Prophète*. I cannot do better than ask the reader to picture to himself a general on the battlefield. He was here, there, and everywhere at the same time. He was enacting every part. At one moment he was the crowd, the next the Prophet, the next the woman, then striding at the head of the insurgents with a fierce air, his spectacles pushed up to his forehead; after that, and with his spectacles still on his forehead, rushing to the opposite side of the stage, and enacting the part of Berthe, pointing out to everyone his or her place, marking with a piece of chalk the exact spot where this or that actor had to stop; in short, co-ordinating so skilfully the evolution of his diverse characters as to impose an order on their most animated movements and invest that order throughout with grace.

No sooner was the third act finished than we rushed away to the Comédie-Française to attend another rehearsal, that of the second act of *Les Contes de la Reine de Navarre*, an act altogether different from the other, played by four characters only and completely intimate in effect.

In accordance with the theme, Scribe becomes all of a sudden a different man. The energy displayed but half-an-hour previously in handling large masses and in making them convey by their gestures and grouping some of the effects of popular passions, that energy had made room for a subtle, critical interpretation of the most refined and delicately shaded feelings. Before his arrival the actors themselves had become aware that the act wanted life, that it was dragging. No sooner does he set foot on the stage than, without adding a word, he sows the dialogue with gestures so telling, postures so effective, pauses so ingenious, he makes such adroit use of the chairs and tables, as if they were natural obstacles, that the situation is heightened, the interest brought out, the characters made vivid, the action given briskness and life. A magician had touched it with his wand.

Nor is that all. The art of "staging" became a kind of revelation to him. By the light of that small, dim lamp that stood on the rickety little table during rehearsals his manuscript revealed to him things he did not suspect of being there. He has often told me what happened to him with a very interesting drama, entitled *Philippe*, written in collaboration with Bayard, which turned on the mystery of an illegitimate birth.

The piece opened with the disclosure of that secret. Scribe, who was to attend the rehearsals, makes his appearance at the very moment the actor is revealing the secret to the public. "It is too soon," he exclaims, "we must put off that revelation till the second scene." Next morning the revelation is introduced into the second scene. "Too soon," he exclaims once more, "it must be put off till the third scene." The revelation was put off accordingly, but Scribe still considered it premature. He kept on deferring it until finally the original exposition became the *dénouement* of the piece.

Nevertheless, I feel bound to qualify my praise. If Scribe was the founder of the modern art of staging, it is but fair to admit that two important branches of that art were utterly beyond his ken. He had no knowledge of either scenery or costumes. Odd to relate, it would be difficult to find an imagination going farther afield than Scribe's and remaining so thoroughly within the limits of home. His imagination wandered through every country of the world, while at the same time it always remained in Paris. At the beginning of his comic operas and operas he put: "The scene of the piece is laid at St. Petersburg," "The scene of the piece is laid in Madrid," "The scene of the piece is laid in Pekin," notwithstanding that the scene of the piece was virtually in Paris. When he wrote the words "an inn," "a kitchen," "a palace," his mind's eye always perceived the selfsame inn, kitchen, or palace. As for his characters, he mentally decked them out in all kinds of finery, not to say rags, which had not the slightest connection with the country in which those characters were supposed to live and act. He made them speak and bestir themselves, but as for housing and clothing them, he did not trouble about it. This defect, apparently altogether on the outside, was due to the deficiency in his intellect to which I have already drawn attention. He lacked the gift of individualising. Fortunately he met with a marvellous *collaborateur* in M. E. Perrin, who had not only an instinctive taste for scenery and costume, but a practical knowledge of them. He has often told me of Scribe's amazement at the sight of the transformation of his interiors and characters by a consummate stage manager.

The following story will give a striking portrait of him. Scribe generally spent the autumn months with his friends in the country. In the evening they amused themselves with reading English novels, and the reader was a poor governess who, in an interval between two chapters, said with a sigh, "Ah, if I could only realise my dream."

"And what may your dream happen to be, mademoiselle?" asked Scribe.

"To have one day, not now, but many years hence, an income of twelve hundred francs a year, which would insure my peace and quietness and independence."

A few weeks later, one evening, after she had come to the end of some insignificant novel, Scribe all of a sudden said to her, "Do you know, mademoiselle, that there is a subject for a capital one-act comedy in that story? If you like, we'll write it together, seeing that you gave me the subject."

As a matter of course the girl was but too glad to accept. Three days after, Scribe comes down to the drawing-room with his comedy finished, and three months after that the papers announce its first performance. On the morning of the advertised *première*, Scribe repairs to his dramatic agents. "To-night there is a *première* of a piece of mine, which has been written in collaboration with a lady," he says. "I have not the faintest idea what the result will be; this much I do know, that piece will have to yield twelve hundred francs a year for life to the joint-authoress. You may arrange the matter just as you please, provided it looks genuine."

Rather a delicate proceeding, this, on the part of Scribe, who has been so often accused of plagiarism, but who in this instance did not borrow his plot from any one, and who, I fancy, has in that not had many imitators. But the best of the story has to be told. The governess, who relished her success, kept constantly suggesting to Scribe new plots for comedies, drawn from English novels, which Scribe as constantly declined with a smile. After that, the governess, whenever they praised Scribe to her, protested in a soft, cooing tone. "Yes, yes, there is no doubt about it, he is a charming young fellow. But I am afraid gratitude is not one of his pet virtues. We wrote a very pretty piece together. Seeing that it brings us each twelve hundred francs per annum, why does he refuse to write another?"

Scribe never dispelled her illusion.

Assuredly a man who is not only superior to most men but a good fellow to boot is a delightful phenomenon, not to mention the imagination which not only concocts a pretty piece out of an indifferent novel, but also makes it the basis of a kindly action.

The last years of Scribe's life were years of happiness. And by his sudden death, which struck us all like a thunderclap, he was spared the sadness almost inseparable from moral and physical decline. Twenty-six years have gone by since that sorrowful March day in 1861, and at present when I look back upon him down the years he is to me what I feel convinced he will remain to posterity—the most complete representative of French theatrical art in the nineteenth century. Some of his contemporaries did, no doubt, surpass him in many phases of that art, but not one has possessed in the same degree the two fundamental qualities of our national art: invention and the faculty of composition. No one created so many subjects for dramatic presentations as he. No one proved himself master of so many different *genres* as he. No one knew so well as he how to lay down the basis of a plot, to conduct it through its various windings, to tie and untie its knots. Here is a final and conclusive proof of his talent: In two *genres* he was without a rival during his own lifetime and has had no successor since he died. Who since that death has written a beautiful libretto for an opera or a masterpiece in the way of a comic opera? I will not venture to call Scribe a man of genius, but he certainly had a remarkable genius

for the drama, and withal one so original that no literature has produced, I will not say his equal, but an author
analogous to him. Scribe deserves to have applied to him the
line of Michelet on Alexandre Dumas: "He is a force of
Nature."

NOTES ON LOPE DE VEGA

1. The opening passage of Lope's poem is thus rendered into English verse by Lord Holland:

Bright flow'rs of Spain, whose young academy
Ere long shall that by Tully nam'd outvie;
And match'd the Athenian porch where Plato taught,
Whose sacred shades such throngs of sages sought,—
You bid me tell the art of writing plays
Such as the crowd might please, and you might praise,
The work seems easy—easy it might be
To you who write not much, but not to me.
For how should I the rules of art explain,
I, whom nor art nor rule should e'er restrain?
Not but I studied all the antient rules:
Yes, God be praised, long since in grammar schools,
Scarce ten years old, with all the patience due,
The books that subject treat I waded through:
My case was simple,—in these latter days,
The truant authors of our Spanish plays
So wide had wander'd from the narrow road
Which the strict fathers of the drama trod,
I found the stage with barbarous pieces stor'd:—
The critics censur'd; but the crowd ador'd.
Nay more; these sad corrupters of the stage
So blended taste, and so debauch'd the age,
Who writes by rule must please himself alone,
Be damn'd without remorse, and die unknown.
Such force has habit—for the untaught fools,
Trusting their own, despise the antient rules,
Yet, true it is, I too have written plays,
The wiser few, who judge with skill, might praise:
But when I see how shew and nonsense, draws
The crowd's, and, more than all, the fair's applause,

275

Who still are forward with indulgent rage
To sanction every monster of the stage.
I, doom'd to write, the public taste to hit,
Resume the barbarous dress 'twas vain to quit;
I lock up every rule before I write,
Plautus and Terence drive from out my sight,
Lest rage should teach these injur'd wits to join,
And their dumb books cry shame on works like mine.
To vulgar standards then I square my play,
Writing at ease; for, since the public pay,
'Tis just, methinks, I by their compass steer,
And write the nonsense that they love to hear.

The two lines in which Lope declares that he locks up Plautus and Terence with six keys were quoted by Victor Hugo in the proclamation of his theories of dramatic art prefixed to his unactable *Cromwell* (1827). But Souriau in his annotated edition of the "Préface de Cromwell" thinks it possible that Hugo may have borrowed the quotation second-hand from a pamphlet by Scudéry, *La Preuve des Passages,* put forth during the quarrel over Corneille's *Cid.* It is amusing to note that M. Emile Faguet, quoting these lines in his *Drame Ancien, Drame Moderne* (p. 122), inadvertently credits them to Cervantes.

Fitzgerald, in the preface to his translations from Calderón, asserts that certain of the defects discoverable in these pieces do not represent "Calderón's own better self, but concession to private haste or public taste by one who so often relied upon some striking dramatic crisis for success with a not very accurate audience." It may be objected that this plea is dangerous in that it is based on the unwarrantable assumption that Calderón's private taste was different from that of the public to which he appealed; but it can be urged in behalf of Lope as potently as in behalf of Calderón. Lope's own plea that he must give the public what it wants is more effectively put by Molière, in the preface to the *Précieuses Ridicules:* "I should needlessly offend all Paris, if I accused it of having applauded a piece of stupidity; as the public is the absolute judge of works of this sort, it would be impertinent in me to contradict it; and even if I had the worst possible opinion of my *Précieuses* before the performance, I ought now to believe that it has some value, since so many persons together have spoken well of it."

6. Morel-Fatio points out that this paragraph is practically a literal translation from Robortello's *Paraphrases in libram Horatii De Comedia.* It is mainly from Robortello that Lope derives all his parade of erudition.

8. In this paragraph, as Morel-Fatio informs us, Lope is again relying on Robortello and also on Donatus.

9. At the end of this paragraph Lope, following Donatus

blindly, attributes to Terence the loftiness of style to which Plautus occasionally attained. As Damas-Hinard noted in his French translation of certain of Lope's plays, the Spanish poet is here sinning against light, since he had a first-hand knowledge of the comedies of both the Latin dramatists.

15. Professor Rennert (p. 180) points out that this distinction between tragedy and comedy is arbitrary and un-Aristotelian, although it was "the one that obtained throughout the Renascence and down to the end of the period of Classicism." It was the doctrine of Robortello and of the later Italian theorists that it was "the rank of the characters, and this only, which distinguished a tragedy from a comedy." This is the distinction which Sir Philip Sidney maintains in his *Apologie for Poesie*.

Here is Lord Holland's metrical version of the concluding lines of this passage:

> Once to behold a monarch on the stage,
> England, 'tis said, our prudent Philip's rage;
> Or that he deem'd such characters unfit
> For lively sallies and for comic wit;
> Or crowns debas'd, if actors were allow'd
> To bring the state of kings before a low-born crowd.

In his *Hamburg Dramaturgy* (pp. 394-95 of the English version in Bohn's series) Lessing translates a score of these lines, ending with Lope's assertion that nature has set us the example of commingling the ludicrous with the serious; and then he asks: "Is it true that nature sets us an example of the common and the sublime, the farcical and the serious, the merry and the sad? It seems so. But if this is true, Lope has done more than he intended; he has not only glossed over the faults of his stage, he has really proved that these are no faults, for nothing can be a fault that is an imitation of nature." But Mezières in the introduction he prefixed to the French translation of Lessing's dramatic criticism quotes a passage from Diderot on the danger of uniting tragedy and burlesque: "Tragicomedy is never more than a bad species, because in it are confounded two disparate species, separated by a natural barrier." Here Lessing, who had derived so much from Diderot, reveals himself as in advance of and on firmer ground than his French contemporary. It is amusing to note that Diderot, so often hailed as a forerunner of the Romanticists, is here a belated echo of so strict a classicist as Sir Philip Sidney, who asserted that the plays he saw on the English stage were "neither right tragedies, nor right comedies, mingling Kings and Clowns, not because the matter so carrieth it, but thrust in Clowns by head and shoulders, to play a part in magestical matters, with neither decency nor discretion: So as neither the admiration and commiseration, nor the right sportfulness is by their mongrel Tragicomedy attained."

16. Morel-Fatio notes that this passage also is derived directly from Robortello.

17. These lines Lord Holland turns into English couplets:

> The tragic with the comic muse combin'd,
> Grave Seneca with sprightly Terence join'd,
> May seem, I grant, Pasiphaë's monstrous birth,
> Where one half moves our sorrow, one our mirth.
> But sweet variety must still delight,
> And, spite of rules, dame Nature says we're right,
> Thru' all her works she this example gives,
> And from variety her charms derives.

With this statement of Lope's may be compared the theory set forth by Victor Hugo in the preface to *Cromwell*.

19. Here once more, as Morel-Fatio has shown, Lope is leaning upon Robortello. Three and a half lines of this passage Lord Holland translates freely in this triplet:

> Who seated once, disdain to go away,
> Unless in two short hours they see the play
> Brought down from Genesis to judgment day.

This popular liking for the whole story without selection or omission is a survival from the Middle Ages when the mystery play began with Genesis and ended, if not with Judgment Day, at least with the casting of the wicked into Hell-Mouth. To the Classicists this prolongation of the action was always most offensive. Lord Holland turned into English the four lines in which Boileau denounces the custom:

> The Spanish bard, who no nice censure fears,
> In one short day includes a lapse of years.
> In those rude acts the hero lives so fast,
> Child in the first, he's greybeard in the last.

And Sir Philip Sidney had earlier expressed his disgust for this license, blaming the English playwrights for their liberal allowance of time, "for ordinary it is that two young Princes fall in love. After many traverses, she is got with child, delivered of a fair boy; he is lost, groweth up a man, falls in love, and is ready to get another child; and all this in two hours' space: which how absurd it is in sense even sense may imagine, and Art hath taught, and all ancient examples justified." With this may be compared Corneille's opinions in his "Discourse on the Three Unities" and in his discussion of his own *Mélite*.

Lope's limitation of the duration of performance is exactly equivalent to Shakespeare's "two hours traffic of the stage." But Shack, and after him Morel-Fatio, adduce evidence that the customary stay of the spectators in the Spanish theatres was two hours and a half.

20. Lope's advice, that a play should first be written in prose to be turned later into verse, Menéndez y Pelayo believes to be borrowed from a passage in Vida's Latin poem on the poetic art—a passage thus rendered in English in Pitt's translation:

> At first without the least restraint compose
> And mould the future poem with prose,
> A full and proper series to maintain
> And draw the just connection in a chain.
> By stated bounds your progress to control,
> To join the parts and regulate the whole.

Morel-Fatio thinks this very likely, since Lope was familiar with Vida's work. Oddly enough, the principle Lope here lays down was not in accord with his own practice, since the state of the existing manuscripts seems to show that he composed originally in verse, although on occasion he drew up a preliminary scenario in prose. It may be noted that the method here recommended by Lope was that actually adopted by Molière, who (in his haste to meet the wishes of Louis XIV) had to call on Corneille to versify more than half of the *Psyche,* which he had completely constructed in prose and which he had not been able wholly to turn into verse within the limits of time set by the king.

Lord Holland thus renders certain lines of this paragraph into English couplets:

> Plays of three acts we owe to Virues' pen,
> Which ne'er had crawled but on all fours till then;
> An action suited to that helpless age,
> The infancy of wit, the childhood of the stage.
> Such plays not twelve years old did I complete,
> Four sheets to every play, an act on every sheet.

And Ticknor also employs the rimed couplet for his transla tion of a longer passage:

> The Captain Verues, a famous wit,
> Cast dramas in three acts, by happy hit;
> For, till his time, upon all fours they crept,
> Like helpless babes that never yet had stept.
> Such plays I wrote, eleven and twelve years old;
> Four acts—each measured to a sheet's just fold—
> Filled out four sheets; while still, between,
> Three *entremeses* short filled up the scene.

But Camille de Senne and Guillot de Saxe in the preface of their study of *The Star of Seville* (Paris, 1913, p. 44, note) assert that the three-act form had established itself in the Spanish theatre half a century anterior to Verues. And Lessing in his *Hamburg Dramaturgy* (December 4, 1767) had pointed out the discrepancy between Lope's assigning the credit of this change to Verues and Calderón's claim (in the preface to his comedies) that he was the first to make this reduction.

If Lope had been familiar with Aristotle he might have justified the three-act form as simply the carrying out the Greek critic's principle that a play must have an action with a beginning, a middle, and an end.

As Attic tragedies were acted without any intermission, they had only a single prolonged act—although a trilogy was a story shown in three acts. Yet the traditional five-act form of the seventeenth and eighteenth centuries is indirectly derived from the Athenian drama, wherein the number of choral passages came in time to be limited to four, separating five passages in dialogue, which, when the lyric interludes were omitted, stood forth as five separate acts. Horace, probably following the precepts of the Alexandrian critics, prescribes five acts (see Weil's *Etudes sur le Drame Antique,* p. 325). The manuscripts of Latin comedy show no division into acts (see Fairclough's edition of Terence's *Andria,* pp. lii, liii). It may be noted that as soon as the five-act form was disestablished the tendency of the leading modern dramatists has been to adopt the logical three-act form. Most of Ibsen's social dramas are in three acts, just as Lope's are.

Commenting on Lope's strange prescription of the number of pages a comedy should have, Professor Rennert (p. 163, note) tells us that "this rule, as to the length of the *comedia,* which Lope here lays down, was carefully followed by all the other dramatists of the time, and deviations from it are rare. Four sheets—sixteen leaves for each act, that is forty-eight leaves to a *comedia.* An examination of Lope's autograph plays shows how strictly he adhered to this rule. Where slight variations are found they are due to the difference in the size of the leaves—the *comedia* always consisting of about three thousand lines. . . . On the other hand, the comedies of Miguel Sanchez, a predecessor of Lope, contain about four thousand lines."

Lope, like his fellow dramatists Calderón and Corneille, Molière, Voltaire, and Goldoni, had been a pupil of the Jesuits; and it was doubtless when he was a youthful student of the Jesuit school in Madrid that he became acquainted with the critical theories of the Italian commentators of Horace and Aristotle.

21. The rule forbidding the dramatist ever to leave the stage empty Morel-Fatio traces to a passage in Donatus dealing with the omission of the chorus from the New Comedy of the Greeks. Although Corneille does not expressly discuss this rule, he obeyed it; and it was generally obeyed by all the French dramatists who accepted the Classicist theory, possibly because the leaving of the stage empty became the conventional signal of the end of the act. Even today at the Théâtre Français the curtain does not always fall on the termination of an act; the stage is left unoccupied

for a moment and then the three raps of the wooden hammer are heard, whereupon the characters enter who are to begin the next act. On the English-speaking stage this rule has never established itself; and our dramatic poets have now and again achieved an effect of expectancy by leaving the stage bare and letting the spectators wonder who is next to appear.

23. A part of this paragraph is turned into English couplets by Lord Holland:

> In ten line staves should wailing grief be shown;
> The sonnet suits a man who speaks alone;
> Let plain narration flow in ballad lines;
> Though much a tale in copious *octaves* shines;
> Grand weighty thoughts the triplet should contain
> But *redondillas* suit the lover's strain.

In the introduction to his *Select Plays of Calderón* Norman Maccoll gives a clear explanation of the various sorts of verse that Lope mentions here: *Romances* are "octosyllabic trochaics—the customary measure of the Spanish ballads. As in the ballads, these trochaics are sometimes rimed and sometimes assonant. *Redondillas* are arranged in strophes of four lines each. Strong endings and weak endings are both employed. The first and fourth lines rime together, and so do the second and third. This is the simplest of the riming measures in common use. . . . *Quintillas* are arranged in strophes of five lines each. The only rule observed in the riming is that the same rime must not occur in more than two successive lines. . . . The *Decima* is a combination of two *quintillas* in one strophe of ten lines. The arrangement of rimes is as follows: the first five are disposed . . . a, b, b, a, a, and the second five are arranged c, c, d, d, e. . . . Three other forms of iambic verse are borrowed from the Italians, the *Terceto* (the *terza rima* of the Italians), the *Octava* (or *òttava rima*) and the Sonnet." Maccoll in his turn renders several of Lope's lines into English rimes:

> In *décimas* finds voice the mourner's wail;
> The sonnet's fitted for the action's stay;
> *Romances* serve to tell the player's tale.
> Yet octaves well can stirring news convey;
> While deed of high import in *terzas* shines,
> And *redondillas* are the lover's lines.

The incessant employment of these various lyric measures is evidence, were any needed, of the prevailing lyrical quality of the dialogue of the Spanish drama when Lope and Calderón were its chiefs. It may be noted that in *Prunella, a Fantasy in Three Acts*, by Laurence Housman and Granville Barker, the authors emphasize the lyrical element in their rococo story by scattering riming stanzas at irregular intervals throughout the dialogue.

That the sonnet with its artificial and arbitrary scheme of intricately interlaced rimes should be intercalated into dramatic dialogue may seem to modern readers a strange suggestion. Yet Lope was here only recommending a practice inherited from the medieval mysteries, wherein various fixed forms of verse were frequently employed. Their stanzaic rigidity did not prevent the deviser of a French passion play from utilizing the triolet, the ballade, and even the long-sustained and stately chant-royal; and the playwright availed himself of their aid not only in passages of lyrical emotion but also in the swift give and take of the intenser dramatic moments of the action. This tradition of the religious pieces was taken over by the founders of the secular drama in most of the modern languages—in English as well as in French and in Spanish. Corneille's first play, *Mélite,* was composed especially to bring in a sonnet; and even as late as *The Cid* Corneille cast his lyrical monologues into stanzas, for which he was censured by the Abbé d' Aubignac and by Voltaire; and Brunetière (in his annotated edition of Corneille's more important plays) likens the lyrical soliloquy of Rodrigue at the end of the first act to the bravura solo of a tenor coming down to the footlights with his hand on his heart (p. 69). Shakespeare used the looser Elizabethan sonnet for the prologue to *Romeo and Juliet,* spoken by Chorus; and Ben Jonson employs it for the Prologue for the Court of his *Staple of News.* The incongruity of the fixed form is least obvious when the sonnet is thus kept outside the play itself and when it is utilized only in the address to the audience before the action begins. But Shakespeare did not hesitate to employ this fixed form inside the play; in *Love's Labour's Lost* (act iii, scene 2) and also in *All's Well that ends Well* (act iii, scene 4) he casts a letter into fourteen lines, with three riming quatrains and a terminal couplet. And again in *Romeo and Juliet,* where hero and heroine meet and fall in love at first sight, the lyrical significance of this meeting is suggested by the employment of the fourteener, Romeo speaking the first quatrain, Juliet the second, while the third quatrain and the final couplet are shared between them, each taking in turn a line or two. M. Rostand prefixes a sonnet to every act of his *Chantecler,* utilizing them for a poetical description of the successive sets in which the action of his lyrical play is supposed to take place.

The ballade is to be found in two nineteenth-century French plays, the *Gringoire* of Théodore de Banville and the *Cyrano de Bergerac* of Rostand; but in both these pieces it is frankly presented as what it is—a poem composed in the fixed form by the hero of the play. Maccoll suggests that sonnets were introduced by the Spanish playwright "to please the more cultivated part of the audience"; and he remarks that "from their nature [they] could be employed sparingly—not more than two or three sonnets were usually put into a play." He notes that in one of

Calderón's pieces, *Gustos y Disgustos,* a duenna who is in doubt as to her immediate duty begins her speech "by saying that she must either indulge in a soliloquy or pronounce a sonnet. She elects the former, and proceeds to soliloquize in *redondillas.*"

28. Lord Holland has turned these lines into English couplets:

None than myself more barbarous or more wrong,
Who hurried by the vulgar taste along,
Dare give my precepts in despite of rule.
When France and Italy pronounce me fool.
But what am I to do? who now of plays,
With one complete within these seven days,
Four hundred eighty-three in all have writ,
And all, save six, against the rules of wit.

It needs to be recorded that Lope's commentators have been sadly put to it in their endeavor to identify the half dozen of Lope's plays which he here claims to be in accord with the theories of the Classicists.

Attention has been called also to the similarity of attitude between Lope here and that taken by Webster in the preface to his *White Devil,* published in 1612, only three years after the Spanish poem had been delivered: "If it be objected that this is no true Dramatic Poem, I shall easily confess it; *non potes in nugas dicere plura meas Ipse ego quam dixi;* willingly, and not ignorantly, in this kind have I faulted; for should a man present to such an Auditory the most contentious Tragedy that ever was written, observing all the critical laws, as height of style and gravity of person, enrich it with the sententious chorus, and, as it were, life 'n Death in the passionate and weighty Nuntius, yet after all this divine rapture, *O dura messorum illa,* the breath that comes from the incapable multitude is able to poison it; and ere it be acted, let the author resolve to fix to every scene this of Horace,
Haec Porcis hodie comedenda relinques."

NOTES ON BRONSON HOWARD

This lecture was originally delivered in March 1886 in the Sanders Theatre, before the Shakspere Society of Harvard University; and it was repeated before the Nineteenth Century Club in New York in December 1889. On the latter occasion two other dramatic authors were requested to debate the points made by the speaker; and as a result he added a few supplementary remarks:

The Nineteenth Century Club looks for a discussion, I believe, on the subject brought forward in the paper of this evening. If the word "discussion" implies "argument," I fear there is nothing in the mere struggles of a dramatist in his workshop to justify that difference of opinion which is necessary to an argument. My American colleague, Mr. Brander Matthews, must feel like a man whose wife persists from day to day in saying nothing that he can object to, thereby making his home a desert and driving him to the club. As for the great Irish dramatist, this paper leaves him still wishing that someone would tread on the tail of his coat. But, with all true Irishmen, the second party in a quarrel is merely a convenience, not a necessity. Whenever Mr. Boucicault feels that a public discussion is desirable for any reason, he can always tread on the tail of his own coat, and make quite as good a fight of it all by himself as if someone was assisting him.

And he ended with this reference to the constructive skill of Ibsen:

Another thing strikes me in connection with this subject: the praise of Ibsen, the Scandinavian dramatist, is abroad in England; and again, as so often before, mine eyes have seen the glory of the coming of the Lord in the direction of Boston. But some of the loudest worshipers of this truly great man in both countries either willfully ignore, or else they know nothing about, his real greatness.

Ibsen holds in his hand the terrible power, in dealing with the evils of society, which dramatic construction gives to a genius like his; he has not laid this power aside and reduced his own stage to a mere lecture platform. A man armed with a sword who should lay it down in the heat of battle and take up a wisp of straw to fight with, would be a fool. Ibsen, like his great predecessors and contemporaries in France, deals his vigorous blows at social wrongs through dramatic effects and the true dramatic relations of his characters. I know of no writer for the stage, past or present, who depends for his moral power more continuously at all points on the art of dramatic construction than Ibsen does. He, himself, would be the first to smile at those who praise him as if he were a writer of moral dialogues or the self-appointed lecturer for one of those psychological panoramas which are unrolled in acts, at a theatre, or in monthly parts in a periodical.

In conclusion: to all who argue that careful construction is unnecessary in literary art, I will say only this: it is extremely easy not to construct.

It may be noted also that Bronson Howard returned to the

topic of his lecture in a contribution to the *Dramatic Mirror* in 1900; he called this

A MERE SUGGESTION

So much is written in critical notices of plays, about their "construction," that I should like to suggest a few of the considerations which that term involves. It is possible that some of the beginners, who are to become the future dramatists of America, will see the necessity of thinking twice before using the term at all. Some of the more general considerations to be kept in view, when a careful and properly educated critic feels justified in using the word "construction," may be jotted down as follows:

I. The actual strength of the main incident of a play.

II. Relative strength of the main incident, in reference to the importance of the subject; and also to the length of the play.

III. Adequacy of the story in relation to the importance and dignity of the main incident and of the subject.

IV. Adequacy of the original motives on which the rest of the play depends.

V. Logical sequence of events by which the main incident is reached.

VI. Logical results of the story after the main incident is passed.

VII. The choice of the characters by which the sequence of events is developed.

VIII. Logical, otherwise natural, use of motives in these particular characters, in leading from one incident to another.

IX. The use of such human emotions and passions as are universally recognized as true, without those special explanations which belong to general fiction and not to the stage.

X. The relation of the story and incidents to the sympathies of the audience as a collection of human beings.

XI. The relation of the story and incidents to the sympathies of the particular audience for which the play is written; to its knowledge and ignorance; its views of life; its social customs; and to its political institutions, so far as they may modify its social views, as in the case of a democracy or an aristocracy.

Minor matters—such as the use of comic relief, the relation of dialogue to action, the proper use of superfluous characters to prevent an appearance of artificiality in the treatment, and a thousand other details belonging to the constructive side of a play—must also be within the critic's view; but a list of them here would be too long for the space available. When the young critic has made a careful study of the standard English drama, with a special view to the proper considerations above indicated, his opinion on the "construction" of a play will be of more or less value to American dramatic literature.

There is, of course, no overt novelty in the theory advanced by Bronson Howard in his address. The same theory was held by Francisque Sarcey, who declared that all the principles of playmaking might be deduced from the fact that a piece is always intended for performance before an audience. And Marmontel, dramatist as well as dramatic theorist, asserted that the first rule the playwright must obey is "to move the spectators, and the second is to move them only in so far as they are willing to be moved. . . . This depends on the disposition and the manners of the people to whom appeal is made and on the degree of sensibility they bring to the theatre. . . . This is therefore a point in which tragedy is not invariable."

The same principle underlies George Meredith's statement in regard to Comedy: "There are plain reasons why the comic poet is not a frequent apparition; and why the great comic poet remains without a fellow. A society of cultivated men and women is required wherein ideas are current and the perception quick, that he may be supplied with matter and an audience."

BIBLIOGRAPHIC ADDENDA ON
ROBERT LOUIS STEVENSON

I

Deacon Brodie, or, The Double Life: A Melodrama, founded on Facts. In Four Acts and Ten Tableaux. By Robert Louis Stevenson and William Ernest Henley. MDCCCLXXX.

This issue was privately printed in Edinburgh by T. and A. Constable. In 1888 a revised edition, "in Five Acts and Eight Tableaux," with Henley's name preceding Stevenson's on the titlepage, was privately printed by the same press. The play was first separately *published* in 1897 by William Heinemann, London. It had previously been included in *Three Plays,* by W. E. Henley and R. L. Stevenson, 1892, and in *Four Plays,* 1896.

Deacon Brodie was first produced at Pullan's Theatre of Varieties, Bradford, on December 28, 1882. In March 1883 a performance of the play took place at Her Majesty's Theatre, Aberdeen; and on the afternoon of July 2, 1884 it was introduced to a London public at the Prince's Theatre. Nothing more than a *succès d'estime* was accorded to the play at any of these representations. The chief feature of the play was the performance of the Deacon by the late E. J. Henley, a brother of Stevenson's collaborator. In 1887 the piece was presented by E. J. Henley in several cities in America, the tour opening at Montreal on September 26.

II

ADMIRAL GUINEA. A Melodrama in Four Acts. By William Ernest Henley and Robert Louis Stevenson. Printed by R. & R. Clark, Edinburgh. For Private Circulation Only. 1884.

The play was first separately *published* in 1897 by William Heinemann, London. It had previously been included in *Three Plays*, 1892, and in *Four Plays*, 1896.

Admiral Guinea was produced at an afternoon performance at the Avenue Theatre, in London, on November 29, 1897. It was not well received.

III

BEAU AUSTIN: A Play in Four Acts. By William Ernest Henley and Robert Louis Stevenson. Printed by R. & R. Clark, Edinburgh. For Private Circulation Only. 1884.

The play was first separately *published* in 1897 by William Heinemann, London. It had previously been included in *Three Plays*, 1892, and in *Four Plays*, 1896.

Beau Austin was produced at the Haymarket Theatre, in London, on November 3, 1890. Mr. Beerbohm Tree [now Sir Herbert Tree] took the part of George Frederick Austin, and recited a prologue in verse which had been written for the occasion by W. E. Henley.

IV

MACAIRE. A Melodramatic Farce in Three Acts. By William Ernest Henley and Robert Louis Stevenson. Printed by R. & R. Clark, Edinburgh. For Private Circulation Only. 1885.

The first reprint of the play was made in America in 1892, when a very few copies were privately struck off by William Heinemann for purposes of copyright. The word "London," however, appeared on the titlepage of this American issue. The play was first *published* in England in the *New Review* for June 1895. It was afterward included in *Four Plays*, 1896, and was first separately published by William Heinemann, London, in 1897.

V

THE HANGING JUDGE.

At Bournemouth, early in the year 1887, Stevenson collaborated with his wife, Fanny Van de Grift Stevenson, on a play called *The Hanging Judge*. This piece was never printed, even privately, during his lifetime. After her husband's death Mrs. Stevenson printed a few copies and presented them to his intimate friends. I have seen a copy of this issue in the library of Mr. William Archer. In 1914 Mr. Edmund Gosse printed privately an edition of this play that was limited to thirty copies. The titlepage reads as follows: "The Hanging Judge, a Drama in 3 Acts and 6 Tableaux. With an introduction by Edmund Gosse. London,

1914." The manuscript of *The Hanging Judge* is in the possession of Mr. Gosse.

CLAYTON HAMILTON

[*For most of the data in this Bibliographical Appendix I am indebted to the invaluable* Bibliography of the Works of Robert Louis Stevenson, *by Colonel W. F. Prideaux, C. S. I., and to the admirable* Bibliographer's Handbook *of Mr. J. Herbert Slater. C. H.*]

NOTES ON AUGIER *ET AL.*

Abraham Dreyfus (1847—) was the author of half a dozen ingenious little plays, mostly confined to a single act. One of them, *Un Crane sans un Tempête,* adapted into English as *The Silent System,* was acted in New York by Coquelin and Agnes Booth. Dreyfus was also the author of two volumes of lively sketches lightly satirizing different aspects of the French stage— *Scènes de la vie de théâtre* (1880) and *L'Incendie des Folies-Plastiques* (1886).

In the spring of 1884 he delivered an address on the art of playmaking before the Cercle Artistique et Littéraire of Brussels. This lecture was entitled "Comment se fait une pièce de théâtre"; and it was printed privately in an edition limited to fifty copies (Paris: A. Quantin, 1884). In the course of this address he read letters received by him from ten or twelve of the most distinguished dramatists of France in response to his request for information as to their methods of composition. It was to these letters that the lecture owed its interest and its value. What M. Dreyfus contributed himself was little more than a running commentary on the correspondence that he had collected. This commentary was characteristically clever, brisk, bright, and amusing; but its interest was partly personal, partly local, and partly contemporary. The interest of the letters themselves is permanent; and this is the reason why it has seemed advisable to select the most significant of them and to present them here unencumbered by the less useful remarks of the lecturer.

Émile Augier (1820-89) disputes with Alexandre Dumas the foremost place among the French dramatists of the second half of the nineteenth century. The *Gendre de M. Poirier* (which he wrote in collaboration with Jules Sandeau) is the masterpiece of modern comedy, a worthy successor to the *Tartuffe* of Molière and *The Marriage of Figaro* of Beaumarchais.

Théodore de Banville (1823-91) was a poet rather than a playwright. Although he composed half a dozen little pieces in verse, the only one of his dramatic efforts which really succeeded in establishing itself on the stage was *Gringoire,* a one-act comedy in prose; and this met with a more fortunate fate than its more fantastic companions only because Banville revised and strengthened his plot in accordance with the skillful suggestions of Coquelin, who "created" the part of the starving poet.

Adolphe Dennery (1811-99) was the most adroit and fertile of melodramatists in the mid years of the nineteenth century. Perhaps his best play was *Don César de Bazan;* and perhaps his most popular play was *The Two Orphans.*

Alexandre Dumas *fils* (1824-95) was the son of the author of *The Three Guardsmen;* and he inherited from his father the native gift of playmaking, which he declared in this letter to be the indispensable qualification of the successful dramatist. His *Dame aux Camélias* has held the stage for more than sixty years and has been performed hundreds of times in every modern language.

Edmond Gondinet (1828-88) was the author of a host of pleasant pieces, mostly comedies in from one to three acts, and mostly written in collaboration. He believed that he preferred to write alone and that only his good nature kept tempting him into working with others. Probably to warn away those who wanted to bring him their manuscripts for expert revision, he asserted in this letter that he was "a detestable collaborator."

Ernest Legouvé (1807-1903) was the collaborator of Scribe in the composition of *Bataille de Dames* and *Adrienne Lecouvreur.* In his delightful recollections, *Soixante Ans de Souvenirs,* he has a chapter on Scribe in which he describes the methods of that master craftsman in dramatic construction; and in one of his *Conférences Parisiennes* he sets forth the successive steps by which another dramatist, Bouilly, was able to compound his pathetic piece, the *Abbé de l'Epée*—two papers which deserve careful study by all who wish to apprehend the principles of playmaking.

Eugène Labiche (1815-88) was the most prolific of the comic dramatists of France in the nineteenth century and the most richly endowed with comic force. Most of his pieces are frankly farcical, but not a few of them rise to the level of true comedy. The solid merit of his best work is cordially recognized in the luminous preface written by Augier for the complete collection of Labiche's comedies.

Edouard Pailleron (1834-99) was a comic dramatist of more aspiration than inspiration; and yet he succeeded in writing one of the most popular pieces of his time, the *Monde où l'on s'ennuie.*

Victorien Sardou (1831-1908) was probably the French playwright who was most widely known outside of France. In the course of fifty years he was successful in almost every kind of playwriting, from lively farce to historical drama. His first indisputable triumph was with *Pattes de Mouche,* known in English as *The Scrap of Paper* and as widely popular in our language as in the original.

Émile Zola (1840-1902) was a novelist who repeatedly sought for success as a dramatist, attaining it only in the adaptations of his stories made by professional playwrights. Yet one of his earlier pieces, *Thérèse Raquin,* is evidence that he might have mastered the art of the playwright if he had not allowed himself to be misled by his own unfortunate theory of the theatre as set forth in his severe studies of *Nos Auteurs Dramatiques* (1881).

In the *Année Psychologique* for 1894 the distinguished physiological psychologist, the late Alfred Binet—to whom we are indebted for the useful Binet tests—published a series of papers dealing with the psychology of the playwright, in the preparation of which he was aided by M. J. Passy. The two investigators had a series of interviews with Sardou, Dumas *fils,* Pailleron, Meilhac, Daudet, and Edmond de Goncourt. Although Daudet and Goncourt had written plays they were essentially novelists with no instinctive understanding of the drama as a specific art. Nor did either Pailleron or Meilhac make any contribution of importance. But Dumas and Sardou were both of them born playwrights of keen intelligence, having a definite understanding of the principles of playmaking; and what they said to M. Binet and his associate was interesting and significant.

Dumas declared that he made no notes for any of his plays and that he never composed a detailed scenario. He thought of only one piece at a time, brooding over it for long months sometimes, and then throwing it on paper almost at white heat, if it dealt with passion. If, on the other hand, it was a comedy of character, a study of social conditions, the actual composition was necessarily more leisurely and protracted. He had carried in mind for six or seven years the theme of *Monsieur Alphonse,* and he had actually put it on paper in seventeen days. He had written the *Princesse Georges* in three weeks and the *Etrangère* in a month; and the second act of the *Dame aux Camélias* had been penned in a single session of four hours. But he had toiled seven or eight hours a day for eleven months over the *Demi-Monde,* the second act alone costing him two months' labor. He rarely modified what he had written by minor corrections; but sometimes, when his play was completed, he discovered that it was weak in its structure or inadequate in its motivation, in which case he reconstructed one or more acts, or even the whole play, writing it all over again.

M. Dumas admitted that he took little interest in the setting of his plays or in the manifold details of stage management. He indicated summarily the kind of room that he desired; and he put down in his manuscript only the absolutely necessary movements of his characters. The rest he left to the manager and the stage manager.

Here—as indeed everywhere—Dumas revealed himself in the sharpest contrast with Sardou, who designed his sets himself and placed his furniture precisely where he needed it for the action of his play, sometimes finding that a given scene seemed to him to lose half its effect if it was acted on the left side of the stage instead of the right. He was a constant note taker, putting down suggestions for single scenes or for striking situations as these might occur to him; and as a result of this incessant cerebral activity he had always on hand more or less complete plots for at least fifty plays. When he had decided to write one of these pieces, he assembled his scattered notes, set them in order, amplified and strengthened them; and when at last he saw his way clear he made out an elaborate and detailed scenario, containing the whole story, with ample indication of all the changes of feeling which might take place in any of the characters in any scene.

Then when he felt himself in the right mood, he feverishly improvised the play, laughing over the jokes, weeping over the pathetic moments, and objurgating the evil deeds of the more despicable characters. But this was only a first draft of the play; and it had to be gone over three or four times, altered, condensed, sharpened, tightened in effect. The first version was always too long; and the successive revisions reduced it to scarcely more than a half of its original length. Sometimes he was able to compact into a single pregnant phrase the substance of a speech of many lines. And as the play slowly took on its final form Sardou not only heard every word which every character had to speak, he also saw every one of the movements which would animate the action. M. Binet reminded him that when Scribe and Legouvé were collaborating on *Adrienne Lecouvreur,* Scribe asserted that he visualized all that the actors would do, while Legouvé heard all that they would say; and Sardou then claimed that he was fortunate in possessing the double faculty of both seeing and hearing.

Of course, Sardou stage-managed his plays himself, teaching the performers carefully, and going upon the stage, if need be, to act the scene as he wanted it to be acted, indicating the expression, the intonation, and the gesture which he felt to be demanded by the situation.

He was equally meticulous in designing the scenery and the costumes; and he was inexorable in insisting on the carrying out of his wishes. He had a lively interest in painting, in sculpture, and in architecture; and, in fact, he confessed that if he had not been a playwright he would have liked to be an architect. This, it may be noted, is confirmation of the statement that there is a strong similarity between the art of architecture and the art of the drama, since both arts are under the necessity of providing a solid structure to sustain the fabric and to support the decoration.

NOTES ON W. S. GILBERT

William Schenck Gilbert was born in 1836, and he died in 1911. He was intended for the civil service, but after a brief experience in a government office he decided to study law, and he was called to the bar in 1864. It is possible to discover the influence of his legal experience in *Trial by Jury* and in the caricature of the Lord High Chancellor in *Iolanthe*. He did not succeed in establishing himself as a barrister; and like many another unsuccessful lawyer he turned to journalism as a less exclusive profession. Tom Hood, son of the writer of the "Song of the Shirt," had founded in 1861 a comic paper called *Fun;* and to this lively little weekly Gilbert became a regular and a prolific contributor, both in prose and in verse. He early won the favor of its readers by a series of clever humorous lyrics which revealed his comic fantasy and his command over rhythm and rime, and which he adorned with his own sketches signed "Bab." A collection of these *Bab Ballads* was published in 1869, and a second series appeared a few years later.

Gilbert also wrote theatrical notices for the *Illustrated Times;* and he supplied occasional articles to the *Era Almanack* and to the Christmas number which the editor of *Fun* called *Tom Hood's Comic Annual*. To these publications and to various magazines he contributed humorously fantastic tales, some of the themes of which he was to utilize in his later dramas—just as he found suggestions for some of the plots of his later librettos in the *Bab Ballads*.

At the end of the sixties and in the early seventies of the last century it was the custom in half a dozen London theatres to provide a pretty solid bill of fare, the program beginning with a farce, followed by a three-act comedy, which was succeeded by a burlesque. And in 1866 Gilbert improvised to order the earliest of a series of burlesques, the writing and producing of these dramatic trifles serving as a most useful apprenticeship for the later comic operas. He was also the librettist of several of the light musical pieces performed at the entertainment given by Mr. and Mrs. German Reed. In 1870 he ventured upon a higher flight in *The Palace of Truth,* a three-act comedy in blank verse. followed

the next year by the more ambitious *Pygmalion and Galatea*
(which was later very successfully revived by Miss Mary Anderson). In the following years he composed other pieces in blank
verse, *The Wicked World, Broken Hearts, The Princess,* and
Gretchen—a mild Victorian version of the Faust legend.

Of these efforts in verse only *Pygmalion and Galatea* could
fairly be called successful; and even that owed its vogue rather
to the opportunity it afforded to the actress who impersonated
Galatea than to its own poetical merit. The ordinary English play
of poetic pretension, so Professor Gilbert Murray has pointed out,
varies between rather slack and formless meter and ultrapoetical
diction. "The first enables the poet to slide into prose when asking
for his boots; the second, almost unassisted, has to keep up the
poetical quality of the atmosphere. It does so, of course, at the
expense of directness, and often with the ruinous result that
where you have Drama you have killed Poety, and where you have
Poetry you have killed Drama."

More valuable, because more individual and more spontaneous,
were Gilbert's comedies in prose. *Charity,* his most ambitious
attempt at serious drama, failed to establish itself in theatre; but
Engaged, originally produced in 1877, has been frequently revived and has had its influence upon later playwrights as divergent
as Oscar Wilde and Bernard Shaw. A pleasant and ingenious two-
act comedy, called *Sweethearts,* first seen in 1874, may have served
as the suggestion for Bronson Howard's *Old Love-Letters;* and the
artificial but theatrically effective *Comedy and Tragedy,* devised
to display the emotional range of Mary Anderson, has rarely been
performed since it was first acted in 1884. But these were all ambitious efforts to provide the English stage with plays of a more
vigorous veracity and of a solider substance than could be found
in the flimsy and insincere adaptations which then almost
monopolized the London theatres. In this Gilbert was a pioneer;
and he was a pioneer also in publishing his pieces to win a favorable verdict from the reader after they had been able to gain
the suffrage of the playgoer. In four successive volumes, issued
from time to time, under the title of *Original Plays,* Gilbert collected nearly two score of his pieces.

Of the thirty-eight plays contained in these volumes, seventeen
or nearly a half are librettos, most of them written to be set to
music by Arthur Sullivan. *Trial by Jury* was sung and acted in
1875; *The Sorcerer* in 1877, *H. M. S. Pinafore* in 1878, *The Pirates
of Penzance* in 1879, *Patience* in 1881, *The Mikado* in 1885. In
1881 Gilbert and Sullivan and their manager, D'Oyly Carte,
opened the Savoy Theatre, which they had built to provide a
permanent home for their comic operas. During a temporary dis-
agreement with Sullivan and after that composer's death, Gilbert
supplied librettos for other composers, but without meeting with
the success which had almost unfailingly attended the earlier col-

laboration. It is on the books written for Sullivan's scores that Gilbert's fame as a comic dramatist is firmly founded. He revived the tradition of earlier English ballad-opera, illuminated by Sheridan's sparkling *Duenna* and by Gay's audacious *Beggar's Opera*. He was stimulated also by the example of the more varied librettos prepared by Meilhac and Halévy for Offenbach and Lecoq, the *Belle Hélène*, the *Grande Duchesse*, and the *Petit Duc* —although he never sought the tender pathos which relieves the humor of the *Périchole*.

In Mr. Archer's introduction it is pointed out that "A Stage Play" was written in the earlier seventies; it appeared in *Tom Hood's Comic Annual* for 1873, which was published late in the fall of the preceding year. And Mr. Archer notes that when Gilbert takes it for granted that the merit of dialogue resides in the "good things" with which it is sprinkled he was "entirely under the dominion of that convention of 'wit' which played havoc with English comedy from the Restoration down to our own day." It might be urged that the convention is even earlier than the Restoration and that the prevalence of irrelevant witticisms is discoverable in Lyly and even in Shakespeare, especially in his earliest comedy, *Love's Labour's Lost*. This questing of so-called epigram is flagrant in Congreve and in Sheridan, although the latter satirized it himself in *The Critic*, making Mr. Puff declare that he is "not for making slavish distinctions and giving all the fine language to the upper sort of people." In his famous essay on the comic dramatists of the Restoration, Macaulay displayed his customary common sense in his assertion that "the sure sign of a general decline in an art is the frequent occurrence, not of deformity, but of misplaced beauty. In general, tragedy is corrupted by eloquence and comedy by wit."

If the frequent occurrence of misplaced wit is the sign of a general decline of comedy, the disappearance of the "epigram" which merely crackles for its own sake and which does not illumine either character or situation may be accepted as the sign of a general revival of the art. We may take it as a hopeful augury for the future of the drama that the comic playwrights of our language at the end of the nineteenth century and at the beginning of the twentieth eschewed this facile effect. Oscar Wilde is the only recent writer of comedy who descended to the sprinkling of his dialogue with "good things" copied from his note-book and as serviceable in one play as in another. And it is to be recorded that Gilbert, even if he accepted the convention in 1872, had released himself from it before he began the series of librettos, in which the dialogue is always pointed and pertinent and in which the wit is intimately related both to character and to situation.

There is a pleasant piquancy in the fact that the habit of writing plays to order to fit the special qualifications and the special desires of the members of a special company of actors, which Gilbert satirized in "A Stage Play," was a habit to which he himself conformed. His earlier more or less poetic plays, *Pygmalion and Galatea* for one, were carefully adjusted to the capacities and to the aspirations of the actors and actresses of the stock company at the Haymarket Theatre, then managed by Buckstone; and the later librettos, written for the Savoy Theatre, were devised with corresponding ingenuity to reveal and to contrast the talents of the group of singing comedians kept together year after year by D'Oyly Carte.

Many of Gilbert's elders and betters among the dramatists set him the example. The more closely we study the craftsmanship of Shakespeare and Molière the more clearly can we see that these masters of the art peopled their plots with characters composed for the members of the company to which the author himself belonged. It is equally obvious that Sheridan fitted every part in *The School for Scandal* to the several members of the incomparable company of comedians that he had inherited from Garrick when he took over the management of Drury Lane.

Now that the stock company, changing its membership very slowly, has ceased to be, the dramatists of today are released from the limitations under which Shakespeare and Molière had to work. Yet there always will be, as there always have been, commanding personalities among the performers; and the dramatist will always be tempted, as he always has been tempted, to profit by the exceptional histrionic endowment of these actors and actresses of assured popularity. Sophocles is said to have destined his tragedies for a protagonist whose name is now lost to us. Rostand tailor-made *Cyrano de Bergerac* to the myriad talents of Coquelin. Augier composed character after character for Got; and Sardou put together one showy part after another for Mme. Sarah Bernhardt. And in his instructive lecture on the author of the *Abbé de l'Epée*, Legouvé has told us how he and Scribe came to compose *Adrienne Lecouvreur* for Rachel.

NOTES ON FRANCISQUE SARCEY

Francisque Sarcey (1827-99) was a graduate of the Ecole Normale, having as classmates Taine, Edmond About, and Prévost-Paradol. In his *Souvenirs de Jeunesse* (1884), of which there is a translation in English, he has left an amusing account of his student years. Upon his graduation he was duly appointed as a professor of French literature in one of the smaller cities of

France. Those were the most dismal and depressing days of the Second Empire; and Sarcey's frankness in expressing his liberal opinions rendered it certain that he could not hope for promotion. In 1858 Edmond About persuaded him to drop teaching for journalism—just as Jules Lemaitre was to do a quarter of a century later.

At first Sarcey was a journalistic free lance, writing in all the periodicals, daily or weekly, which he could persuade to accept his articles and writing on all sorts of subjects, literary and linguistic, social and political. It was only after several years of this miscellaneous newspaper hack work that he began to specialize as a theatrical reviewer; and he attracted little attention until 1867, when he was appointed dramatic critic of the *Temps,* then as now the most reputable and the most dignified of Parisian dailies. Thereafter for forty-two years he contributed to the *Temps* every Sunday afternoon a dramatic criticism, which came speedily to possess an indisputable authority.

In 1878 he began a series of studies of the actors and actresses of the Comédie-Française and of the other important theatres of Paris—"Comédiens et Comédiennes." He continued to contribute to various newspapers articles on topics of contemporary interest, social and political. He became a frequent lecturer; and in his *Souvenirs d'Age Mur* (1892), also translated into English, he analyzed with his characteristic acuteness the principles of public speaking. He refused regretfully an invitation to become a member of the French Academy, fearing that he would not be free to express his opinions frankly and fully. He declined also the Cross of the Legion of Honor; and he declared that all he wanted upon his tombstone was the record that he had been both "Professor and Journalist."

At the beginning of the first volume of *Quarante Ans de Théâtre* the editor printed a selection from the many warmly appreciative articles which appeared in the French press immediately after Sarcey's death in 1899. Noteworthy among these were the tributes of Jules Claretie, Jules Lemaitre, and Emile Faguet. Jules Lemaitre had earlier published in the second volume of his *Contemporains* a characteristically clever study of Sarcey. The article by Henry James (to which reference is made in the Introduction) is entitled "The Théâtre Français," and it is included in his volume on *French Poets and Novelists* (1878).

The essential point of Sarcey's attempt to formulate a theory of the theatre is that all the laws of the drama are the result of the fact that every play is intended to be performed before an audience and that therefore the desires, the opinions, and the prejudices of the spectators must always be taken into account. No one has declared this undeniable truth so completely as Sarcey. Yet other French critics have set forth similar views. In his lectures on *The Epochs of the French Theatre* Ferdinand Brunetière pointed out that, although men of letters in France between 1550 and 1600 were trying to write plays, there were then no professional actors, no regular theatre, and therefore no public before which plays could be performed: "Now a play does not begin to exist as a play except before the footlights, by virtue of the collaboration and of the complicity of the public, without which a play never has been, and never can be, anything more than a mere literary exercise."

In Jules Lemaitre's *Corneille et la Poétique d'Aristote* there is an account of the vain struggles of Corneille against the rigors of the classicist code which the Italian critics had elaborated from their misreading of Aristotle; and Lemaitre quoted Corneille's plea for permission to employ a neutral ground, not specifically anywhere, in which all the characters of a tragedy might be supposed to meet. Corneille defined this as a "theatrical fiction," akin to the legal fictions accepted by lawyers; and Lemaitre commented that the theatrical fictions which Corneille asked the privilege of using are simply what we now know as the conventions of the drama:

"If the characters of tragedy speak in verse—that is a convention. If they meet every time they have something to say to one another—that is a convention. If they talk aloud when they are alone—that is a convention. If the poet develops under our eyes a single action, although there are none in real life not tangled up with a host of others—that is a convention. He who seeks to abolish conventions can only change them. The alleged Rules of the unity of Time and the unity of Place, had for their purpose, as Corneille admits, to suppress certain conventions, which were, however, easily acceptable; and then, to obey these Rules, Corneille invents conventions of his own, far less simple and far more difficult to accept" (pp. 67-68).

In the preface to his *Etrangère* the younger Dumas with his customary incisiveness lends his support to Sarcey, although without mentioning him: "In all the arts there is a share, larger or smaller but indispensable, which must be left to convention. Sculpture lacks color; painting lacks relief; and they are rarely, either the one or the other, of the dimensions of the object they represent. The more richly you bestow on a statue the colors of life, the more surely you inflict upon it the appearance of death, because in the definitive attitude to which it is condemned by its material, it must lack movement—and movement even more than color and form is the proof of life. . . . Nature is the basis, the means of art, it is not the aim of art. . . . Whether he wields the mallet, the pen or the brush, the artist really merits the name only when he can give a soul to the things of matter and a form to the things of the soul; when, in a word, he idealizes the real he sees and realizes the ideal he feels."

NOTES ON CONSTANT COQUELIN

Early in 1883 Courtlandt Palmer organized the Nineteenth Century Club on the model of a Boston organization, the Round Table Club, of which Thomas Wentworth Higginson was president. At first the Nineteenth Century Club met at the house of its founder, where it was addressed by not a few distinguished speakers, including Oliver Wendell Holmes and Charles William Eliot. After Palmer's death it held its meetings in public halls; and it was in the rooms of the American Art Association in the spring of 1889 that Coquelin delivered this lecture. For the first and last time all the speeches of the evening were in French, the two debaters being Horace Porter and Frederic R. Coudert, and the presiding officer the writer of these notes.

Coquelin's lecture was so warmly received by a brilliant audience crowded into the largest gallery that Richard Watson Gilder persuaded Coquelin to allow its publication in the *Century* for October 1889. The translation then made for the magazine is that here reprinted. Probably Coquelin had it published in the original French in one or another of the French reviews; but he never issued it in a little volume by itself as he had his earlier lecture on "Art and the Actor."

A comparison of the craftsmanship of Shakespeare and Molière is one that imposes itself upon students of dramatic technique. It is to be found here and there in Goethe's considerations of the theatre—more than once in his conversations with Eckermann and Soret. It is elaborated in a chapter of *Molière, his Life and his Works,* by the writer of these notes—a chapter that makes use of Coquelin's lecture and was inspired by it.

In another volume by the same author, *These Many Years; Recollections of a New Yorker,* can be found (page 428) a passage pertinent to Coquelin's appearance before the Nineteenth Century Club:

Coquelin's keen artistic susceptibility was illustrated by his possession of three distinct methods of delivery, adjusted to the three modes of self-expression in which he was incomparable— acting a character, reciting a monolog, and reading a lecture. When he acted a character he was completely and wholly the comedian, employing accent and look and gesture. When he recited a monolog he ceased to be an actor; he abjured gesticulation, he spoke quietly as became a gentleman in evening dress, and he relied mainly on the modulations of his voice. When he had a lecture to deliver he was simpler still; he sat in his chair; he put on his horn spectacles; and he did not raise his voice or attempt any dramatic variety of intonation. An auditor of one of his lectures would never have had occasion to suspect that the reader was also the most versatile and accomplished of comedians.

NOTES ON SCRIBE AND LEGOUVÉ

Eugène Scribe was born in 1791 and he died in 1861. Toward the end of his threescore years and ten he must have been aware that he had outlived his vogue. For forty years he had been the outstanding figure of the French stage; and his innumerable plays had been acted all over the civilized world. He was, as Legouvé has pointed out, essentially a man of the theatre, and he could scarcely win acceptance, even at the height of his career, as a man of letters. He had imparted his methods of playmaking to the host of collaborators who compassed him about; and these methods had been more or less modified by his immediate successors, Augier, the younger Dumas, and more especially Sardou. These successors were more emphatically men of letters, and they had a larger interest in life. They accepted Scribe's adroitly adjusted mechanism, but they simplified it and made it less obvious, because they needed more room for a morally vital presentation of character. Ibsen in his turn was greatly influenced by Augier and Dumas. He was as careful in construction as Scribe, but he was more adroit in concealing his framework and far bolder in his analysis of human motive. It is probably in the music drama that we can now see most clearly the effect of Scribe's invention and ingenuity. For example, the libretto of Wagner's early *Flying Dutchman* is quite in accord with Scribe's pattern.

Legouvé failed to mention that Scribe reorganized the Society of Dramatic Authors and Composers founded by Beaumarchais. It has been described as Scribe, but he was the most powerful trade-union now existing; and its existence—by giving playwrights their full share of the profits earned by their plays—was a potent factor in the prosperity of the French drama in the nineteenth century.

Ernest Legouvé was born in 1807 and he died in 1903. He was the most literary of Scribe's multitude of collaborators, and two of the plays they wrote in partnership, *Bataille de Dames* and *Adrienne Lecouvreur,* kept the stage well into the twentieth century. Legouvé had successfully produced a striking play, *Louise de Lignerolles,* before he joined forces with Scribe; and after their partnership had ceased he wrote for Rachel a *Medea* which she declined and which was later triumphantly performed by Ristori.

His tribute to Scribe was originally prepared as a lecture, and it appeared in his *Conférences Parisiennes* (1872). He amplified it a little when he revised it for inclusion in his delightful two-volume autobiography, *Souvenirs de Soixante Ans* (1887). An English translation, *Sixty Years of Recollections,* was made by Albert D. Vandam and published in London in 1893. In the present reprint the translation has been collated with the original, slightly modified, and also slightly abbreviated by the omission of a few paragraphs of relative unimportance to American readers.

An adverse but not unjust criticism of Scribe's *Verre d'Eau* can be found in Thackeray's *English History and Character on the French Stage,* reprinted from the *Foreign Quarterly Review* in the *New Sketch Book,* edited by Robert S. Garnett, London, 1906. A more penetrating criticism of Scribe can be found in the final chapter of Brunetière's *Époques du Théâtre Français.* Legouvé, in his *Fleurs d'Hiver,* recorded a remark Labiche once made to a 'prentice playwright: "If you want to learn your trade, do as I have done—take apart Scribe's plots." Scribe himself recognized that his own merit lay in the surpassing dexterity of his plot making; and Ludovic Halévy reported that Scribe once declared: "When my story is good, when my scenario is clear and complete, I might have my play written by my janitor! He would be sustained by the situations; and the play would succeed!" Every successful dramatist will recognize the fundamental truth of this willful exaggeration. It may be noted that both Menander and Racine, men of letters who were also men of the theatre, held the same opinion as to the predominant importance of invention and structure; both of them are represented as answering a query as to the work they had in hand by the assertion, "My play is done; I have now only to write it." And here their practice is in agreement with the precept of Aristotle.

PUBLICATIONS OF THE DRAMATIC MUSEUM
OF COLUMBIA UNIVERSITY
IN THE CITY OF NEW YORK

With a view to extending its usefulness beyond the circle of those who could actually visit its library and its model room, the committee in charge of the Dramatic Museum decided in 1914 to enter the field of publication and to issue in limited editions several series of documents dealing with the theory and the practice of the art of the theatre—reprints of inaccessible essays and addresses, translations from foreign tongues, selections from works not altogether dramatic in scope, and original papers. The committee believed that the interest and the value of these writings could be increased by introductions contributed by experts and by an annotation which should be at once succinct and suggestive. They decided that the several series should be uniform and that they should be strictly limited to 333 copies each, 33 being reserved for authors, translators, and editors and 300 being available for subscribers. It seemed best not to sell the volumes separately, and it was found possible to offer a series of four volumes for the subscription price of five dollars.

First Series, 1914. PAPERS ON PLAYMAKING

I. *The New Art of Writing Plays.* By Lope de Vega. Translated by William T. Brewster. With an Introduction and Notes by Brander Matthews.

II. *The Autobiography of a Play.* By Bronson Howard. With an Introduction by Augustus Thomas.

III. *The Law of the Drama.* By Ferdinand Brunetière. Translated by Philip M. Hayden. With an Introduction by Henry Arthur Jones.

IV. *Robert Louis Stevenson as a Dramatist.* By Arthur Wing Pinero. With an Introduction and Bibliographic Addenda by Clayton Hamilton.

Second Series, *1915*. PAPERS ON ACTING

I. *The Illusion of the First Time in Acting*. By William Gillette. With an Introduction by George Arliss.

II. *Art and the Actor*. By Constant Coquelin. Translated by Abby Langdon Alger. With an Introduction by Henry James.

III. *Mrs. Siddons as Lady Macbeth and Queen Katharine*. By H. C. Fleeming Jenkin. With an Introduction by Brander Matthews.

IV. *Reflections on Acting*. By Talma. With an Introduction by Sir Henry Irving; and a review by H. C. Fleeming Jenkin.

Third Series, *1916*. PAPERS ON PLAYMAKING

I. *How Shakespeare Came to Write "The Tempest."* By Rudyard Kipling. With an Introduction by Ashley H. Thorndike.

II. *How Plays Are Written*. Letters from Augier, Dumas, Sardou, Zola, and others. Translated by Dudley Miles. With an Introduction by William Gillette.

III. *A Stage Play*. By Sir William Schenck Gilbert. With an Introduction by William Archer.

IV. *A Theory of the Theatre*. By Francisque Sarcey. Translated by H. H. Hughes. With an Introduction and Notes by Brander Matthews.

V. (Extra volume) A catalogue of Models and of Stage-Sets in the Dramatic Museum of Columbia University.

Fourth Series, *1919*. DISCUSSION OF THE DRAMA

I. *Goethe on the Theatre*. Selections from the conversations with Eckermann; translated by John Oxenford. With an Introduction by William Witherle Lawrence.

II. *Goldoni on Playwriting*. Translated and compiled by F. C. L. van Steenderen. With an Introduction by H. C. Chatfield-Taylor.

III. *Prospero's Island*. By Edward Everett Hale. With an Introduction by Henry Cabot Lodge.

IV. *Letters of an Old Playgoer*. By Matthew Arnold. With an Introduction by Brander Matthews.

Fifth Series, *1926*. PAPERS ON ACTING

I. *The Art of Acting*. By Dion Boucicault. With an Introduction by Otis Skinner.

II. *Actors and Acting*. A discussion by Constant Coquelin, Henry Irving, and Dion Boucicault.

III. *On the Stage*. By Frances Anne Kemble. With an Introduction by George Arliss.

IV. *A Company of Actors.* By Francisque Sarcey. With an Introduction by Brander Matthews.

Manuscripts for the Sixth and Seventh Series as deposited in the Museum by Brander Matthews, July 29, 1926:

Sixth Series. DISCUSSION OF THE DRAMA

I. *The Pleasures of Playgoing.* By Emile Faguet. Translated by Philip M. Hayden. Introduction by Ferris Greenslet.

II. *Lope De Vega.* By George Henry Lewes. Introduction by James Fitzmaurice Kelly.

III. *Eugène Scribe.** By Ernest Legouvé. Translated by Albert D. Vandam.

IV. *Molière and Shakespeare.* By Constant Coquelin. Translated by Florence Hallett Matthews. Introduction by Brander Matthews.

Seventh Series. PAPERS ON ACTING

I. *The Paradox of Acting.* By Denis Diderot. Translated by Walter Herries Pollock. With an Introduction by Henry Irving.

II. *The Actor.*† By Robert Lloyd.

III. *Edmund Kean and Junius Brutus Booth.* By Edwin Booth. Introduction by Lawrence Barrett.

IV. *Poems About Players of the Nineteenth Century.* Chosen by Brander Matthews.

* Hatcher H. Hughes was to have written an introduction to the paper on Scribe.

† G. C. D. Odell was to have written an introduction to *The Actor.*

Index